Constitutional Theology

Allan J. Janssen

The Historical Series of the Reformed Church in America

No. 33

Constitutional Theology

Notes on the *Book of Church Order* of the Reformed Church in America

Allan J. Janssen

Wm. B. Eerdmans Publishing Co.
Grand Rapids, Michigan

© 2000 Wm. B. Eerdmans Publishing Co.
255 Jefferson Ave. S.E., Grand Rapids, MI 49503
All rights reserved

Printed in the United States of America

04 03 02 01 00   5 4 3 2 1

ISBN 0-8028-4882-6

To

Colleen

The Historical Series of the Reformed Church in America

This series has been inaugurated by the General Synod of the Reformed Church in America, acting through its Commission on History, for the purpose of encouraging historical research and providing a medium wherein this knowledge may be shared with the academic community and with the members of the denomination in order that a knowledge of the past may contribute to right action in the present.

General Editor

The Reverend Donald J. Bruggink, Ph.D.
Western Theological Seminary

Commission on History

Gerald F. De Jong, Ph.D., Orange City, Iowa
Sophie Mathonnet-Vander Well, M.Div., Pella, Iowa
Christopher Moore, New York, New York
Jennifer Reece, M.Div., Princeton, New Jersey
Jeffrey Tyler, Ph.D., Hope College, Holland, Michigan

Contents

Acknowledgments

A book is a collaborative task. The author is indebted to a number of persons in addition to those mentioned in the preface. Foremost are kind hosts at New Brunswick Theological Seminary and particularly at Gardner Sage Library who provided space and assistance during part of the writing of this book. Russell Gasero, archivist of the Reformed Church in America, not only saw this text through to print, but offered continuing encouragement.

The sixth chapter, on the disciplinary and judicial procedures, owes much to the fact that this author was a member of an ad hoc committee that prepared a major rewrite of that entire chapter of the *Book of Church Order* for the General Synod. I hereby acknowledge and thank those on that committee, whose understanding of such issues are much deeper than my own: John De Koster, Ronald Geschwendt, Wesley Kiel, Carol Myers, Andrea Van Beek, David Van Lant, and Susan Vogel-Vanderson.

A special thank you is due to Howard Hageman, who passed from our midst in 1992. Following his death his wife, Carol, allowed me a small book from his library, A. A. van Ruler's *Het Apostolaat der Kerk en het Ontwerp-Kerkorde*. This book was a small epiphany; church order is a theological reality. The order of the church can and indeed does disclose a particular ecclesiology.

I also must thank my wife, Colleen, who with my daughters, Sarah and Emily, and my son, Jonathan, offer encouragement and support, indeed who provide the delight in living which is the only context in which the laborious work of writing books is possible.

ix

Preface

For several generations, ministers in the Reformed Church in America had on their shelves a small, green book, William H.S. Demarest's *Notes on the Constitution of the Reformed Church in America*, published in 1928, cited simply and often as "Demarest." It guided ministers and assemblies through the often puzzling maze of the church order. It has been, and continues to be, a valuable resource.

Much has changed since 1928, of course. Most signally, as his title suggests, his was a commentary on what was called the *Constitution* (in full recognition that it in fact commented only on the government and on neither the *Liturgy* nor the *Standards.*). When in 1968, the Reformed Church revised its governing document into its current *Book of Church Order*, Demarest's notes, while still pertinent, no longer referred to a working document. Further changes in the past seventy years, not least of which was a major revision of the Disciplinary Procedures, called for an update of his work. Thus, in 1997, the Commission on Church Order of the General Synod requested of the Commission on History to consider a new volume to do for a new generation what Demarest did for his. That commission concurred and requested of this author that he prepare a volume for the Historical Series.

This commentary will likely be read in one of two ways. Most will use it as a reference to help them answer practical questions that arise in the ongoing governance of the church. They will profit by consulting the relevant section. Others will find within the commentary the broader principles, often with their historic foundations, of Reformed church order. The commentary intentionally does not first adumbrate such principles but instead uncovers them as they appear among the various prescriptions. The reader does best to read the entire commentary to grasp the church order as a whole within which the parts cohere.

I am grateful to those who have assisted in the production of this volume. Too many to mention are those who share interest in the arcane nooks and crannies of church order who either placed queries to me or responded to my own puzzlements. Of particular mention are Eugene Heideman and Marvin Hoff, who read and commented on early drafts. Their comments were most helpful, and to the extent that the commentary has improved, I thank them. They are not, of course, to be held responsible for the final interpretation to the extent that it is in error! I also am grateful to Laurie Baron, whose editing continues to make my prose read better than I had thought possible. And finally, I owe great thanks to Donald Bruggink, whose stellar work not only with this volume but with the entire series leaves the church greatly in his debt.

I must note that writing a commentary on the *BCO* over the period of several years was a bit like nailing the wind. The order changes quickly, at times, and this book as printed refers to the 1999 edition. Future revisions cannot, of course, be commented on in this space.

In its governance, the church participates in the kingly, or royal, work of the church. Thus it is with gratitude that we come to the completion of this volume as the ecclesiastical year concludes in 1999 with the celebration of Christ the King.

Allan Janssen
Christ the King, 1999

Introduction

"The Church is not simply an institution. She is a 'mode of existence,' a way of being."[1] So Orthodox theologian John Zizioulas opens his study, *Being as Communion*. It may seem odd to cite a thinker from a tradition so distinct from the one underlying this study of *Reformed* church order. But the theological claim that the church is more than institution, is fundamentally Reformed and expresses the presupposition that lies behind the construction of a Reformed church order.

It is important to state this at the outset thereby to circumvent two prevalent but mistaken notions of church order. The first emerges from the insistent individualism that informs much of American church life. This notion maintains that the church is built from the bottom up, so to speak. The primary interaction between God and the human happens with the individual.[2] The individual then gathers, voluntarily, with like-minded, or "like-souled" individuals

---

1 John D. Zizioulas, *Being as Communion: Studies in Personhood and the Church* (Crestwood, New York: St. Valdimir's Seminary Press, 1985), p 15. Emphasis in the original.
2 Here the term "individual" is intentionally used in contradistinction from the term "person" as two notions with distinctly different theological meanings.

1

in an institution we call church. The church may assist the individual as it provides a place where Scripture's story may be heard, where she may receive the benefits of the sacraments, and where she is united in solidarity with other believers, but the primary unit remains the individual.

A Reformed understanding of church moves in quite the other direction. The church is not a product of human activity or belief. *God* establishes and maintains the church. This is set most classically in the third article of the Apostles' Creed: "I believe in the Holy Spirit; the holy catholic church." The church is the product of the Spirit. From the more specifically Reformed side, we need only cite the Heidelberg Catechism: "I believe that from the beginning to the end of the world, and from among the whole human race, the Son of God, by his Spirit and his Word, gathers, protects, and preserves for himself, in the unity of the true faith, a congregation chosen for eternal life."[3] Here the church is the result of the activity of the second person of the Trinity. In any case, it is God who posits and maintains the church.

This fundamental distinction is illustrated in the history of the church from which the Reformed Church in America emerged, the Nederlands Hervormde Kerk. In response to an administrative church order imposed on that church in 1816, two major divisions occurred, the *Afscheiding* of 1834 and the *Doleantie* of 1886. The details of these events need not delay us here,[4] but the fundamental issue is important. The Dutch dissenters saw in the 1816 order a deformation of the church, and correctly so. However, those who split from the church did so under the principle that the church is formed from the bottom, from the gathering of believers. Many who remained within the church agreed with the dissenters on basic theological points. However, they took strong exception to the notion that the church was built on the foundation of the faith of

3 *The Heidelberg Catechism* (Cleveland: United Church Press, 1962), Answer 54.
4 See Gerrit J. tenZythoff, *Sources of Secession: The Netherlands Hervormde Kerk on the Eve of the Dutch Immigration to the Midwest*, for a fuller description in English of the *Afscheiding* of 1834.

the believer, even though a person's faith is itself a product of God's act. The church is God's work. And that needed to be expressed in the church order.

The second notion that distorts a proper understanding of Reformed church order holds that the order does little more than provide the institutional means by which the proper work of the church is conducted. The order provides a sort of external rule, an agreed upon means by which the business of church life, often little more than details for the arrangement of common life, gets done. Or the order becomes the most efficient means by which we get around to what is finally important, the "mission" of the church, however that is to be discovered and articulated.

I would add a gloss to the citation from our Orthodox friend and add that in its institutional form, the church expresses a way of being. From the outset the Reformed understood the believer's life to exist in covenantal communion. One finds expression of that crucial understanding in the Reformed sacraments of baptism and the Lord's Supper, the public proclamation of the Word, the administration of discipline, the care of the diaconate for the life of the community, the Reformed understanding of vocation, and concretely in church order. Indeed, what might be called the first Reformed order, Calvin's "Draft Ecclesiastical Ordinances of 1541," concern themselves with these very matters. The order of the church's life is shaped not by notions of efficiency and utility, but by Christ, who unites us together in one body with himself.

The church is, in fact, a theological reality that enjoys an integral place in a Reformed understanding of God's way with humans and with creation. That is so despite the relatively secondary place it has received in American Christianity, including that subset of churches that call themselves Reformed. One need only recall that Calvin dedicated the last book of his *Institutes of the Christian Religion* to the church. And one need but add that the Confession of Faith (commonly called the "Belgic Confession") devotes six articles to the church—nine if one counts the sacraments, as one must. That is more than the number of articles devoted to Scripture! It may be pointed out that this emphasis was necessitated by the historical need to claim that the Reformed were indeed a church in contradistinction to the (false) Roman church; however, that argument simply demonstrates that the *church* as a theological reality stood within the Reformers' understanding of a full confession of the faith.

Just so, Reformed order cannot be understood as an appendix to the "real action" in the church. It is part and parcel of the church's life. *How* it lives together, *how* it is governed, is to reflect the source of its life. Its institutional life does not of itself fully express the nature of the church; but its institutional life must express its fundamental commitment.

A peek at the earliest orders that inform the current *Book of Church Order* will uncover its sources. In 1568, the Dutch church gathered in synod outside the Netherlands in Wesel. The synod produced a church order that noted that the normative guidelines for church order were to be found in the Word of God, the use and example of the apostles, and the unbroken custom of the churches.[5] While we shall make continued references to these sources in the commentary proper, a few reflections are in order at the outset.

It is not incidental that the church as institution and communion plays such a central role in Reformed theology and life. Indeed, the Reformed claim that it is God who calls and organizes the church. Thus, the Word of God is given priority of place as the source of church order; the Word is the source of its very life. The Word, of course, is the living Word, God's address. The Reformed have seen that Word manifest in Scripture (see the Belgic Confession, Articles 2-7). That does not mean, of course, that the church order simply replicates an order that is found outlined in Scripture. The Scripture will function as the norm that "norms our norms." Nonetheless,

---

5   "Acts of the Synod of Wesel," chapter 1, paragraph 11, in *Kerklyk Handboekje* (Dordrecht: A. Blusse en Zoon, 1794), hereafter cited in the text as "Wesel" with chapter and paragraph. Any number of *handboekjes* containing early Dutch church orders are available.

the Reformed find in Scripture's story a basic foundation for its understanding of the offices and assemblies. While it cannot be claimed, and the Reformed have not claimed, that the four offices as described in the order exhaust the ordered ministry, the Reformed do discover outlines for the offices of elder, deacon, and minister of Word in Scripture. Likewise, the Reformed detect in Scripture a communal way of decision, the ur-form, of a synodical system, as for example in the Synod of Jerusalem (Acts 15). In any case, the construction of and alterations to a church order will appeal to Scripture as its fundamental norm.[6] The "custom of the churches" may sound foreign to readers educated in the notion that the Reformers rejected tradition as a source for its life. Such an idea is, of course, a half-truth; the Reformers did not completely jettison tradition. The Reformed churches made no claim to leap backward fifteen centuries to repristinate the first-century church. The fundamental truth in the claim that tradition no longer guides the church is that tradition must always be placed under the judgment of the Word of God.

Thus, we can grasp something of the import of the notion of the "custom of the churches" for the current shape of Reformed order by reminding ourselves that the church order is *confessional* at root. At its simplest that means that the Confession of Faith includes within its articles the outlines of how the church is to order itself. This is clearest in Article 30, as it confesses that the church will be governed by "servants or shepherds" who proclaim the Word and administer the sacraments and by "overseers and deacons" who together with the pastors function as the council of the church. The following articles outline the selection of officers, the equality of ministry, and the usefulness to the church that it "establish and maintain certain rules and regulations among themselves."

But the order is confessional in other ways as well. As we shall see in the commentary on the order, it centers around the celebration

---

6 See A. J. Bronkhorst, *Schrift en Kerkorde* (Den Haag: N.V. Zuid-Holl. Boek- en Handelsdrukkerij, 1947).

of the sacraments. And it provides the assurance that the life of the church will be shaped in conformity with the foundational truths of the gospel as articulated by the confessions.

In a more fundamental way, the order enables the church to live confessionally. As the Confession of Faith articulates the "marks" of the true church (Article 29)—that is, the pure proclamation of the Gospel, the pure administration of the sacraments, and the exercise of ecclesiastical discipline—it gives proper space for the church to respond confessionally to Christ's presence in its midst.

A final introductory word needs to be added concerning the history behind the Reformed church's *Book of Church Order*. As mentioned above, the earliest outlines of a Reformed order may be found in John Calvin's "Ecclesiastical Ordinances" of 1541. However, other strands came together to provide the historical backdrop of the current order. The exiled Dutch church in London, led by John a Lasco, produced a church order in 1554 which together with the Geneva order and the presbyterial system produced by the French Reformed formed the basis of the order written at Wesel in 1568. That order was further refined at Emden in 1571. The Dutch produced further orders at Dordrecht in 1574 (in provincial synod) and 1578, at Middelburg in 1581, and in the Hague in 1586. One reads in these orders a continuation of the line begun at Wesel. Finally, the great synod of Dordrecht in 1619 produced an order in its post-acta. It is that last order that shaped the order still present in the *Book of Church Order*, most significantly introduced into the RCA in the Explanatory Articles of 1792.[7]

It will be the burden of this book to show how the *Book of Church Order* gives expression to a fundamental way of being as the church. Church order is ecclesiology in action. As such it is practical theology in a foundational sense. But we will explore that way of being not only in broad outline, we will also attempt to show how

---

7   The full history of the RCA's constitutional structure is excellently described by Daniel J. Meeter, *Meeting Each Other: In Doctrine, Liturgy & Government* (Grand Rapids: Eerdmans, 1993).

the church shapes itself as it elects elders and deacons; as it practices discipline; as it outlines the responsibilities of its officers and assemblies; as it makes decisions on the color of the carpet as well as on matters of great confessional import. This book, then, is intended not simply as an educational primer, but as encouragement to the countless elders and deacons (and ministers too!) who minister year in and year out in innumerable consistories and classes and synods, often weary of the detail and worn with decisions that too often look like little more than institutional maintenance. To be gathered in the leadership of the church is not all the church is about; it is not even the most important business of the church. But it is crucial; indeed, it is to live in discipleship of the Lord who "gathers, protects, and preserves for himself, in the unity of the true faith, a congregation to eternal life." Such is high calling indeed.

1
Preamble

*[Par. 1] The purpose of the Reformed Church in America,
together with all other churches of Christ, is to minister to the
total life of all people by preaching, teaching, and proclaiming
the gospel of Jesus Christ, the Son of God, and by all
Christian good works. That purpose is achieved most
effectively when good order and proper discipline are
maintained by means of certain offices, governmental
agencies, and theological and liturgical standards. The Holy
Scriptures are the only rule of faith and practice in the
Reformed Church in America. Its* Constitution *consists of the
Doctrinal Standards (which are the Belgic Confession of
Faith, the Heidelberg Catechism with its Compendium, and
the Canons of the Synod of Dort), the* Liturgy *with the*
Directory for Worship, *the* Government of the Reformed
Church in America, *and the* Disciplinary Procedures.

The preamble is the most important section of the *Book of Church
Order* (BCO). It outlines clearly and constitutionally the foundation
of a particular church, the Reformed Church in America. It reminds
the church of the essence from which it lives and the principles by

which it is ordered. What is claimed in the first few pages of the document shapes both the *Government* and the *Discipline*. It is crucial, then, to give considerable space to these several pregnant paragraphs.

The preamble is a latecomer to the *Government*. While the Explanatory Articles included an important preface, later editions of the *Constitution* functioned without an extended introductory piece.[1] The preamble in its current form was introduced without comment in 1966.

The document begins with a statement of purpose. And the statement begins with a name. It is the "Reformed Church in America." The *Government* will delineate the shape of a church. That is, the Reformed church is not a collection or a fellowship of churches, although its various congregations are churches in the fullest theological sense of the term. But the collectivity of congregations, classes, and synods are together a church. As such they form an organic entity that can become the subject of a predicate.

One notes, too, that the statement of purpose makes no claim that the Reformed church is the *only* church, or the *true* church. It is true that in the heat of the Reformation, the Reformed would claim to be the true church in contradistinction from the Roman church; however they did so only because they understood that Christ's church was one. But the Reformed recognized other churches as true as well, albeit of a different nationality or even confession. In any case the Reformed Church in America states at the outset that it exists together with other churches, *and* that it participates with them in a common mission. It's in the verb, minister. The church exists not for its own sake nor for the perpetuation of its institutional life. It does not exist to draw persons within itself. Its focus is not inward, but outward in service, in common with a Reformed understanding of God's work in history.

---

1   Meeter, Daniel J., *Meeting Each Other: In Doctrine, Liturgy & Government* (Grand Rapids: Eerdmans, 1993), pp. 51-54.

The service the church extends is intended not only to benefit the religious life of either individuals or the society, but also to minister to the total life of persons and society. The Reformed had always held that God is sovereign of all of life and that Jesus is Lord in every aspect of life. The church will not limit its task solely to the care of souls or the conversion of individuals. The order will include provision, for example, for diaconal work, for witness to governmental authorities, and the like. Nor is the range of ministry limited to those whom it denotes as "members" and their families. The church exists within a society and among people who are not believers. Its task extends to all. By describing the church's ministry with such a wide scope, the statement of purpose instantiates the Reformed theological commitment that the church exists to further God's greater task of redemption of the entire world.

The church accomplishes this ministry primarily through the task entrusted to it, the task for which it was called into being: preaching, teaching, and proclaiming the gospel of Jesus Christ. At the outset the *Government* confesses that the church exists from its head and for its head, Jesus Christ. And it exists to announce gospel, to teach gospel, and to proclaim gospel.

It might be remarked odd that the preamble has little to say about the sacraments. This is especially to be noted as one discovers that historically the order focused as much around the sacraments as around the preached word. Membership, for example, was membership around the table; the new member was "admitted to the Lord's table." And discipline focused on the communal life gathered at the table. Do we detect here mid-twentieth century theological commitments, a theology of the Word that emerged from this century's dialectical theology? In any case, one needs at least to acknowledge that the task of proclamation includes the sacrament as enacted Word.

The first sentence appends a phrase, as almost an afterthought, when it adds "and by all Christian good works." While it can legitimately be argued that the church's central task is the announcement of gospel, its mission includes more. The church is an organic body. As such it not only speaks; it acts. How it acts is crucial. Its actions are part of its ministry, from tending soup kitchens to sending medical missionaries to providing shelter for the homeless. Even such "humble" activities as building churches and providing parsonages are acts, and they consequently express a way of being in the world.

The second sentence of the preamble puts order in its proper place. The church does not exist to serve its order; order is a skeleton that gives shape to the church's primary purpose. Additional details, from how a church calls a pastor to the responsibilities of a synod, are to be developed to further the purpose.

Nonetheless, one must be careful. For when we speak of "order," at least in a Reformed context, we do not mean simply the most convenient or efficient way of doing business. Reformed order makes no claim to finality. One can even read spirited debates—among Reformed folk!—over whether it derives its principles from Scripture. But order is not accidental either. It is a fully theological matter. It intends not only to give concrete form to a doctrine of church; it acknowledges that God works in and through concrete institutions. When one tinkers with order, one is tugging on a theological reality. In a real sense, we can say that order is a form of confession: this is the way God intends us to be in the world.

The preamble has mentioned order almost at the outset, as it should. The *Book of Church Order* that guides the church's common life is the business at hand. Yet, once order has come into view, Holy Scriptures immediately come into view. This is proper for two reasons. First, the order that follows will follow the guideline of Scripture. That is, Scripture precedes order. The *BCO* cannot carry the weight of Holy Writ! Second, Scripture is mentioned before one gets to the Doctrinal Standards and the *Liturgy*. Thus is signaled the order of priority, and authority, within the church.

This maintains the old Reformed commitment to Scripture as foundational for church order. The Synod of Wesel states clearly that some matters in the ordering of the church are to be *gegrondvast*, foundational. Those are first to be to be grounded in "God's Word." Interestingly, the synod added, "or in the use and example of the Apostles or in the established custom of the churches" (Wesel, I, 11).

The sentence, however, is odd. To claim Holy Scriptures as the "only rule of faith and practice" violates an older use of the term "rule of faith." In the early church, "rules of faith" were credal statements that delineated the believer from the pagan. A more accurate way of stating the claim might read: "Holy Scriptures are the *norm* of faith and practice."

The first paragraph ends by denoting the *Constitution*. Daniel J. Meeter has made the point well in *Meeting Together*: the *Government* is not to be understood as the *Constitution*. The Reformed church rests on what he describes as a three-legged stool: doctrine, liturgy and government. This is a crucial point as we work our way through the *Government*. To discover what is foundational for the Reformed when it comes to, say, the Lord's Supper, one must look not only in the *Government* (in which one will find little), but also in the *Liturgy* and the confessions. The system also works from the other direction. To understand ecclesiastical office, to take a very pregnant case, one must read not only their definitions and functions as outlined in the *BCO*, but also the standards and the *Liturgy*. It is crucial to read all three sets of documents together for a proper understanding of the constitutional nature of the church. A minister can be disciplined for failure to attend to promises made at her ordination, for example. This book is not a commentary on the *Constitution*. One can find other books on the Standards, other reflections on the *Liturgy*. However, there will be places where it will be helpful and even necessary to observe the connections between the *BCO* and the other "legs of the stool" upon which the church rests.

Until the early twentieth century, the Reformed church's constitutions contained a section, "Customs and Usages," that included directions on such matters as the celebration of the sacraments, the provision of what could be sung in public worship, visitation by elders and deacons, the nature of funeral sermons, provision for days of fasting and prayer, and marriage. The Dort order even included the following: "No person professing the Christian religion shall undertake to publish, or cause to be published, any book or writing on a religious subject, composed, or translated by himself, or another, without the previous inspection and *approbation* of the Ministers of his Classis, or of the Particular Synod, or of the Professors of Theology in that province, with the consent of the Classis."[2] Some of these matters would become the province of the *Liturgy*, while others were incorporated within the *Government* itself.

The four basic governmental units in the Reformed Church in America are the consistory, the classis, the regional synod, and the General Synod. The consistory is divided further into a board of elders and a board of deacons. The board of elders, the classis, the regional synod, and the General Synod exercise judicial as well as legislative powers. A governmental unit exercising its judicial powers is called a judicatory, and at all other times the governmental unit is known as an assembly. Deacons exercise a legislative function only in the circle of the whole consistory. Three offices are employed in the governmental functions of the Reformed church, namely, the minister of Word and sacrament (hereinafter referred to as "minister"), the elder, and the deacon. A fourth office, that of the General Synod professor of theology (hereinafter referred to as "professor of theology"), is employed in the seminaries of the church for the training of students for the ministry.

The second paragraph of the preamble outlines the basic structure of Reformed church order:

> *[Par. 2] The four basic or focal governmental units in the Reformed Church in America are the consistory, the classis,*

2 Articles of Dort, 1619, Article 55, in *A Digest of Constitutional and Synodical Legislation,* Edward Tanjore Corwin (New York: The Board of Publication of the Reformed Church in America, 1906), hereinafter cited in the text as "Dort, 1619" with article.

the regional synod, and the General Synod. The consistory is divided further into a board of elders and a board of deacons. The board of elders, the classis, the regional synod, and the General Synod exercise judicial as well as legislative powers. A governmental unit exercising its judicial powers is called a judicatory, and at all other times the governmental unit is known as an assembly. Deacons exercise a legislative function only in the circle of the whole consistory. Three offices are employed in the governmental functions of the Reformed Church, namely, the minister of Word and sacrament (hereinafter referred to as "minister"), the elder, and the deacon. A fourth office, that of the General Synod professor of theology (hereinafter referred to as "professor of theology"), is employed in the seminaries of the church for the training of students for the ministry.

Answer 54 of the Heidelberg Catechism describes the church in the following way: "I believe that, from the beginning to the end of the world, and from among the whole human race, the Son of God, by his Spirit and his Word, gathers, protects, and preserves for himself, in the unity of the true faith, a congregation chosen for eternal life."

The Son of God is the subject that brings forth the church. How does the Son, by his Spirit and his Word, "gather, protect, and preserve...a congregation"? The Reformed answered that Christ does this through the instrument of certain offices which gather to lead the church. Thus, one orders the church through the consideration of (1) offices and (2) assemblies. In fact, early Reformed orders were divided into two major sections at the outset (they would often add a third on "customs and usages," but the third section was clearly secondary): offices and assemblies.

This reflected a historical development. When John Calvin proposed a church order for the Genevan church in 1541, he began with a detailed description of the four offices mentioned above.[3] It

---

3   Calvin, John, "Draft Ecclesiastical Ordinances, September & October 1541," in *Theological Treatises*, trans. J.K.S. Reid (Philadelphia: Westminster Press, 1954), p. 58.

was the later French Reformed church that developed the presbyterial system.[4] The Dutch church began to develop this system when the Synod of Wesel in 1568 provided for provincial synods and classes already in its second paragraph (Wesel, I, 2).

Interestingly, the second paragraph of the preamble reverses earlier church orders that placed offices first and assemblies second. This ordering is reflected in the structure of the *Government*, which orders the church under the headings of the governmental units: consistory, classis, regional synod, and General Synod. The General Synod introduced the current structure in 1966: "Since the church's document on its form and method of government is essentially descriptive of the way in which the basic governmental units of the church carry out their responsibilities, the four focal points of government in the Reformed Church...were made the logical headings of the divisions of the document."[5] One might see in this order the priority the Reformed church gives to government in assembly. No office, and thus no office-bearer, governs by him or herself. Decisions are always taken in "council." All notion of personal hierarchy is hereby structurally avoided. This is a foundational principle to be remembered by all bodies as they gather. The Reformed church *gathers* in the governance of the church. We shall see this working itself out when we examine more closely the workings of the various governing bodies.

The paragraph makes a further crucial distinction when it discriminates between bodies acting as legislative assemblies and as judicatories. The difference can be confusing. In part this results from the fact that it is often the same gathering that acts either legislatively or judicially. It also results from a common use of the term, "judicatory," to refer to the various bodies. The preamble introduces the terms, "assembly" and "judicatory." When a classis, for example, functions in its normal order of administrative business,

---

4 Bronkhorst, A.J., *Schrift en Kerkorde* (Den Haag: N.V. Zuid-Holl. Boek-en Handelsdrukkerij, 1947), p. 259.
5 *Minutes of the General Synod*, 1966, p. 200, hereinafter cited as *MGS*.

it is an assembly. When, however, under certain strict circumstances (see the *Disciplinary Procedures*) it carries out judicial procedures, it is a judicatory. The *Government* is careful in its use of the terms so that the relevant body can know when it acts as either assembly or judicatory. It will be crucial to keep the matter straight because different rules apply, especially in cases where discipline is at issue.

The paragraph notes that the Reformed church recognizes four offices: minister, elder, deacon, and professor of theology. While Reformed people often argue that the threefold office (leaving aside for a moment the "fourth office") derives from the threefold office of Christ as Prophet, Priest, and King,[6] Reformed churches have found it possible to name other offices. For example, the Netherlands church created an office of "exhorter" for the mission situation in the Dutch East Indies.[7] And the Reformed church, in its Explanatory Articles, maintained an office of "Church-Master."[8] Nonetheless, the Reformed church has retained the offices as adumbrated by Calvin in the "Ecclesiastical Ordinances."

Two offices come in for special notation in this paragraph, those of deacon and professor of theology. Undoubtedly, this reflects the difficulty the Reformed church has had with these offices. The preamble explicitly states that the deacon exercises legislative function only "in the circle of the whole consistory." It was an innovation when the American church included deacons on consistories. This was a concession to the relatively small size of the churches and consequently smaller number of elders in the American churches.[9] Unfortunately, this development has allowed for the degeneration of the peculiar ministry of the diaconate, to the point where deacons function as "junior elders" in many consistories. At the same time, this sentence limits the power of a board of deacons.

6   "The Ordination and Installation of Elders and Deacons, 1987," in *Liturgy and Confessions* (Reformed Church Press, 1990), p. 1.
7   Evenhuis, R.B, *Ook Dat Was Amsterdam* (Amsterdam: W. Ten Have, 1967), vol.II, p. 319.
8   "Explanatory Articles, 1792," Article XXX, in Corwin's *Digest*, hereinafter cited in the text as "Ex. Art." with article.
9   Meeter, *Meeting Each Other*, p. 75.

That board cannot make policy on behalf of the congregation. Any decisions that have governmental implications for the congregation must be referred to the entire consistory.

> *[Par.3] The governmental functioning of these offices takes place, not apart from, but in harmony with the understanding of the mission of the church and the nature of its ministry. This basic affirmation has three consequences. First, the purpose of church government is to aid the church in the development of its own life, in order that it may carry out the mission of its Head—to announce the good news of his Saviorhood and extend his Lordship throughout the world. Second, there is only one ministry, and that ministry is shared by all Christians. The particular ministries of those who hold office arise out of this common ministry in order to serve it. Third, the ecclesiastical offices which the Reformed Church deems necessary for its own ordering are understood to be essentially functional in nature, and the term "office" is everywhere viewed in terms of service.*

The preamble interprets order as outlined above and adds the notion that the church's ministry is of a piece. While the church serves *through* its offices, its offices exist to enable the total ministry. All believers exist in ministry both through their particular vocations and together in the church. Reformed order avoids the notion that the officers minister in the stead of the church.

The concept of *office* is central to an understanding of Reformed order. "Office," in a Reformed context, finds its roots in the German *amt*. In its origins, *amt* reflects a feudal context in which the vassal is required to serve his lord. He was *obliged* to serve. By extension, one who holds office in the church stands under obligation to the Lord, Christ. In Calvinism, "the offices are associated with each other in their functions and so will serve to establish the rule of Christ in the congregation."10

---

10 Schott, E., "Amt," in *Die Relgion in Geschicte und Gegenwart*, 3d ed., ed. Erster Band (Tubingen: J.C.B. Mohr, 1957), pp. 338-40.

Nonetheless, this paragraph raises a couple of troubling issues within the ambit of Reformed order. It claims that "those who hold office arise out of this common ministry...." In a basic sense, that is true. The office-bearers emerge from the body of believers. In another sense, however, one asks whether the offices come not from the body of believers, the church, but are given *to* the church. They are called by God in Christ through the Spirit. If one hears Christ's apostolic call of Peter in Matthew 16 and understands that the apostolic nature of the church as emerging from that foundational office, then in an important sense the office bearers are set apart by Christ. This is a theological point worth pondering. If the leadership of the church grows out of the church itself, then it can no longer confess that its peculiar existence is established and led by God! Office, as such, expresses the wonder that *God* stands over and against the church.

The second difficult issue raises itself with the claim that offices are understood to be "essentially functional in nature." The phrase reflects a debate between a view that understands office as *ontological* in contradistinction from office as *functional*. In an ontological understanding, a person undergoes a change in the structure of his or her *being* upon ordination. That view has resulted in viewing office hierarchically. That is, the officer enjoys a higher ecclesiastical status than those who are not ordained. The Reformed have rejected that sort of status as unbiblical. The Reformed Church's insistence on the parity of ministry (see below) is in part a response to this concern. Subsequently, it described office in terms of the ministry the officers perform for the sake of the church.[11] The phrase is troubling, nonetheless, in the common understanding of "functional." Of course, the offices do not exist for the sake of the officers. Nor is the church fully present in its offices, as a Roman Catholic understanding might describe the church as being fully present in the person of the bishop. But the offices, in themselves, are not only functional. As *offices* (and not as office-bearers) they

11 *MGS*, 1971, pp. 203-204.

instantiate Christ's leading of the church. The fact that we have ministers of Word and sacrament is a clear indication that the church lives not by its own leading but by the Word, Christ. Remove the office and we remove what is essential to the church's very existence.

One must further ask: does nothing essential happen in the act of ordination? Do we not pray that the Spirit enlighten the ordinand? Does that mean that nothing changes within the person? Might we not speak of a "functional ontology"? In fact, the preamble uses that sort of language when it says that the offices are "essentially functional." The offices do function, but the function is not optional. Nor are those ordained left unchanged.[12]

> [Par.4] The Reformed Church in America is organized and governed according to the presbyterial order. That order is inspired and directed by certain basic principles. They are as follows:

To be governed "according to the presbyterial order" means that decisions are taken by the assemblies as the offices gather. Thus, neither particular offices, by themselves, nor individual officers are authorized to make decisions on behalf of the church. On the other hand, church governance can not be likened to either a democratic or a republican system. The officers do not "represent" a set of constituents. Nor does a general body of believers rule itself. Christ, as the sole head of the church, leads through the institution of the offices, who are guided in their decisions by Scripture as interpreted through the Spirit. Guided by Word and Spirit, church governance reflects the trinitarian nature of God.

The presbyerial system can be distinguished from an episcopal system on the one hand and a congregational system on the other. Thus, the church protects itself from a situation where one person (or a few people) can wield power. The interpretation of Scripture's

12 I have elaborated on this point in "Ministry in Context," *Reformed Review*, 51:1, 1997, pp.15-25.

leading always remains in the purview of gathered assemblies, where other minds and souls can place an individual's guidance under review. The church also protects itself from a congregationalism that can easily reflect the enthusiasms of the moment.

A remark is in order on the nature of the relations among the assemblies. The church order will be divided into "parts" that describe the various assemblies and will prescribe the responsibilities that fall to each. But Reformed history has displayed a certain tension between the privileges of the more local expressions and their relation to the "higher" or "greater" bodies.

As early as the church order of Wesel, Reformed churches of Dutch descent divided the responsibilities so that a "lesser," or more local, body would govern over those matters of which it was "capable." The "greater" bodies, the classes and the synods, would rule in matters that the lesser could not by itself. This principle was put most clearly in the Dort church order, article 30: "In those Assemblies, ecclesiastical *matters* only shall be transacted, and that in an ecclesiastical manner. A greater Assembly shall take cognizance of those things alone which could not be determined in a lesser, or that appertain to the churches or congregations in general, which compose such an assembly."

For example, the General Synod has responsibility for the theological education of candidates for ministry. Neither a classis nor a regional synod could reasonably be expected to educate ministers. Likewise, the General Synod sends missionaries on behalf of the entire church. The classes examine and ordain for ministry of Word and sacrament. While theoretically this could be done at a synodical level (and was in the early days of our church), it would be difficult to grant a local consistory such power. Similarly, the "greater" bodies are limited as to how they may intrude on the affairs of a local congregation.

A tension between "localism" and "centralism" has expressed itself throughout the history of the Reformed churches. Proponents of the "local" contend that the local church should be granted the authority to make such decisions as affect its life. "Centralists," to the contrary, argue that such freedom would destroy the coherence of the church's common witness to the gospel. Reformed order attempts a mediating position through a system of assemblies. The Synod of Wesel described certain matters as "indifferent" to be left to consistories. Such would include the mode of baptism, whether by sprinkling and whether baptism is to be celebrated before or after the service of the Word. However, "In matters which are of a different nature, and are grounded either in God's Word, or in the use and example of the apostles, or in the established custom of the churches, and that for weighty and necessary reasons, one shall not lightly stray from the agreement of the congregations" (Wesel, I, 9-11).

> [Par. 5] The Nature of the Church on Earth. *The church, which can be defined in many ways and be represented by many images, may be described as that body of people in the world which professes faith in Jesus Christ as Savior and Lord.*

One attuned to Reformed theology might find the preamble's description of the church odd. The *BCO* chooses to describe the church as a body of people "which professes faith in Jesus Christ as Savior and Lord." One might have expected something more on the order of the language of the Heidelberg Catechism, where it is the "Son of God, by his Spirit and Word" who "gathers, protects, and preserves for himself, in the unity of the true faith, a congregation chosen for eternal life" (A54). While the Belgic Confession denotes the church as a "holy gathering of true believers in Christ," it goes on to confess that "this holy Church is kept or maintained by God..." (Art. 27). In no case is it the believers themselves who, through their profession of faith, constitute the church. The Belgic goes on to "mark" the "true church" with the pure preaching of the gospel, the pure administration of the sacraments, and the exercise of church discipline (Art. 29).

One can find the historical germ of the preamble's adumbrated doctrine of the church in the preface to the Explanatory Articles of 1792, where the first sentence claims freedom for believers to gather: "In consequence of that liberty wherewith Christ hath made his people free, it becomes their duty as well as privilege, openly to confess and worship him according to the dictates of their own consciences."[13]

Still, that same document goes on to describe the church as consisting "of all, in every age and place, who are chosen, effectually called, and united by faith to the Lord Jesus Christ." Read in that light, the profession made by believers takes place within the reality of election. Nonetheless, given that the church order will be concerned with such essential matters as the "pure preaching of the Gospel, the pure administration of the Sacraments, and the exercise of Church discipline," one longs for a more adequate description of the nature of the church from a Reformed perspective.

> *[Par. 6] The Reformed churches confess that the church of Jesus Christ in the world is one church, the "Holy Catholic Church." The church is the living communion of the one people of God with the one Christ who is their Head. Their oneness in him is a "communion of the saints" with Christ and with one another in the divine blessings.*

This paragraph sets forth the ecumenical position of the Reformed church. It clearly states that the Reformed church makes no claim for itself as the "only true" church, but as one among many. It confesses that the unity of the church is to be found in neither doctrine nor in order! The oneness of the church subsists only in its Head, Christ. Thus, as the Reformed Church in America remains in communion with the One who calls it into being, it exists in "communion" with other churches which likewise subsist from the head.

13 Corwin, *Digest*, p. v.

The historical antecedents of this position are to be discovered in the preface to the Explanatory Articles. There, the division into denominations is seen to result from "many unavoidable circumstances of language, nation, or other causes of distinction...."[14] The Reformed echo Calvin's passion for the unity of the church.

This is not to claim that doctrine and order are not crucial matters. The *Constitution*, after all, includes the confessions, the *Liturgy,* and the *Government.* In ecumenical conversations, we point to these as our understanding of what it means to be the church. Nonetheless, so long as we can indicate the marks of the true church in our conversation partners, understood perhaps differently than we ourselves do, we shall acknowledge that we are, with them, in communion within the one church under the true head, Jesus Christ.

> [Par. 7] The Head of the Church. *The Reformed churches confess that Jesus Christ is the only Head of his church. The Scriptures call the church his body, and our Lord the Head of that body. He is therefore in the closest and most vital relationship to his church. As the church's true Head, he has complete authority over its life, and therefore the church must ever yield to him a ready obedience and faithfulness. Christ's headship is one of righteousness, love, and tenderness toward his people.*

This principle establishes the foundation for what will be stated in the following remarkable paragraph on the nature of the church's authority. It also makes a powerful assertion concerning the nature of the entire document under consideration. The assemblies that gather to govern the church are not simply convenient arrangements to lead a human institution that functions in the matrix of other institutions. Ecclesiastical bodies speak and act on the authority of Christ. Church order makes a theological claim. This body, as it is

14 Ibid.

so governed, is God's people who live from the "most intimate and vital relationship" with its head. The church is not a voluntary religious organization that gathers to promote the peculiar religious interests of its members.

That strong claim does not hold that the church has never been disobedient or has never erred. It has. The paragraph reminds us that we are ever to yield in obedience to the one who is the Head. It concludes with the comforting reminder that Christ's headship is one of "righteousness, love, and tenderness." This is a claim of trust that Christ will surely but gently lead his church.

> *[Par. 8]* The Nature of the Church's Authority. *All authority exercised in the church is received from Christ, the only Head of the church. The authority exercised by those holding office in the church is delegated authority. Their appointment to their special tasks is by the Spirit of the Lord, and they are responsible first of all to the Lord of the church. Their authority is of three kinds: ministerial, declarative, and spiritual. Ministerial authority is the right to act as Christ's servants. Declarative authority is the right to speak in his name within the limits set by Scripture. The church shall declare what is in the Word and act upon it, and may not properly go beyond this. Spiritual authority is the right to govern the life and activity of the church and to administer its affairs. The church shall not exercise authority over the state, nor should the state usurp authority over the church.*

Since the authority exercised by the respective offices is delegated, assemblies are cautioned against a variety of enthusiasms that can easily grip the church at any given moment. Cultural movements and conditions press in upon the church. These may reflect the working of the Spirit of God, but they must be subjected to the one authority that governs the church. Practically, assemblies remind themselves of this central dynamic when they surround their gatherings with worship. Prayers and devotions are more than a nod to God after which we are on with the business at hand. They gather us within the leadership of Christ. At times, it may be crucial to pause within the press of an agenda for prayer or reflection. It is never out of order to refer to the words of Scripture, provided that in so doing we are not using them as a club with which to intimidate an office-bearer who propounds a differing point of view.

This principle delineates three kinds of authority: ministerial, declarative, and spiritual. Ministerial authority compels the church to act. For example, the General Synod establishes a medical mission or a consistory opens a soup kitchen in the church basement. They do so on the commission of Christ and in his name. Or a consistory may decide not to allow the use of its property for a group that promotes gambling because it finds this antagonistic to the ways of Christ, or to rent its hall to a profit-making agency because that is simply not what the church exists to do.

Declarative authority not only allows but impels an assembly to speak on behalf of Christ, in advocacy of the poorer of society, for example. But there are other instances as well. When the 1979 General Synod approved the ordination of women to the office of minister of Word and sacrament, it did so because a previous synod (1958) had already declared that there were no clear biblical grounds against the ordination of women to ministry. On the other hand, assemblies are not permitted to speak contrary to Scripture. A synod must be much more cautious when considering matters about which Scripture is silent.

What, for example, does Scripture say to a consistory contemplating how it is to fix a leaky roof? Here the third kind of authority obtains, spiritual authority. One might wonder how leaky roofs fit within the rubric "spiritual." But roofs and drains are part and parcel of the life of the community of faith. Government is often about everyday, messy, matters. And they, too, are to be administered in accordance with the ways of Christ's kingdom. It is not for nothing that the entire of the Old Testament is part of the canon!

The paragraph concludes with a sentence on the relation between the church and the state. This sounds self-evident to those who live in a society with a constitutional separation of church and state. Nonetheless, it's a crucial statement that remains. This section betrays a long history of wrestling over the relation of ecclesiastical and civil authority. Article 36 of the Belgic Confession, for example, claims for civil authority the responsibility of governing human affairs and indeed to remove idolatry and false religion from a society. Furthermore, it is easy to forget the long struggle to free the church from the intervention of the state. It is not difficult to envision a change in the current state of affairs in which the state might desire to intrude on the ways of the church. We have clearly stated not only our independence, but the theological reason for it: we live by one authority, that of Jesus Christ. Conversely, some ecclesiastical currents would have the church dictate to the state how it should rule. In that case, we would violate a foundational Reformed principle that God calls women and men to serve the kingdom within the "magistracy," or the government, and that the magistracy as well as the church is fully responsible to God.

> *[Par. 9-14]* Membership Categories and Definitions. *Membership in congregations of the Reformed Church in America includes "confessing" members, "baptized" members, and "inactive" members. Reformed Church in America congregations also include "adherents."*
>
> *"Confessing" members are members who have received Christian baptism and have been received by the board of elders through profession of faith, reaffirmation of faith, or presentation of a satisfactory certificate of transfer of membership from another Christian church, and who make faithful use of the means of grace, especially the hearing of the Word and the use of the Lord's Supper.*
>
> *"Baptized" members are members who have received Christian baptism, who may or may not participate at the Lord's Table, and who have not been received by the board of elders as confessing members.*
>
> *"Inactive" members are members who have been removed by the board of elders from the confessing membership list.*

"Members" are all confessing members, baptized members, and inactive members.

"Adherents" are all who participate in the life, work, and worship of the church, but are not members.

Membership is a term that derives from an organic metaphor. One is a member as one is part of a living body. We are "members of Christ's body" (1 Cor.12). We are not simply enrolled as participants in an organization. We are organically connected, much as family "members" are connected. Historically, the Reformed recognized membership when one became a part of the body at the Lord's Table. Hence, we spoke of "communicant" membership. This was further indicated by the practice of having persons unite with a church at the time of the celebration of the Supper. When permission was granted for boards of elders to admit children to the Table in 1988, the category of "communicant" became inapplicable. This led to a new category, that of "confessing" member.

It is to be noted that membership is not limited to those who have made profession before the board of elders. Not only children but inactive members remain an organic part of the congregation and are under the care and discipline of the church. A church body will often be much larger than those who gather in its pews. At the same time, the category "adherent" acknowledges that the congregation may include in its midst many who are not, for various reasons, "members." This may include those who search for the faith. Worship is a public act and the church is a public institution.

[Par. 15] The Representative Principle. The power which Jesus Christ bestows upon his church is mediated by the Holy Spirit to all the people. Since not everyone in the church can hold an office, and since the offices differ among themselves in function, some persons will always be subject, within the proper exercise of authority, to the decisions of others. Since the whole church cannot meet together at one time and place to deliberate, representative governing bodies must be established on the various levels. The unity of the

church is preserved in acceptance of the fact that all are governed by the decisions made in their behalf by those who represent them.

The presbyterial system particularly worked out by the *BCO* clearly delimits the responsibilities of the various assemblies. Because the offices that gather act on the authority delegated to them by Christ, they are empowered to act on behalf of the church within certain boundaries. Members and officers subject themselves to these decisions. The church order will be clear that many decisions are in turn subject to review upon complaint or appeal. Thus, even within a representative system, certain checks and balances are built in. Nonetheless, a presumption of unity and authority remains.

This principle has important implications for the life of the church. Not everyone can vote on all matters. For example, the General Synod exercises original authority over matters of doctrine and polity as they relate to the seminaries (see p. 230). Such issues are not submitted to the classes or consistories for consideration. In theory, the church can change the church order to submit such issues to lower bodies, but the representative principle implies that so long as this responsibility is lodged with the General Synod, the church grants the synod the authority to act in this area. Perhaps more relevant for most congregants is that almost all decisions concerning the local congregation are taken by the consistory on behalf of the congregation. They are not subject to referendum.

It is important to be clear just what is meant by "on behalf of." One could read the "representative principle" to mean that the representatives act in the stead of those whom they represent, a sort of democratic notion. That is only partially true. The offices that gather in assembly act on behalf of the Lord of the church. Thus, "on behalf of" is better understood as "for the sake of" the church.

*[Par. 16]*Government by Elders. *The Reformed churches have sought to follow the practice of the churches whose experience is recorded in the New Testament. The churches then were*

ruled by "presbyters" or "elders," just as the synagogues from which the first Christian converts came were ruled by elders. The Reformed churches consider the minister to be an elder of a special kind, called in some churches of the Reformed order, the "teaching elder." Ministers and elders therefore govern the church together. They also assist in governing the larger church by becoming from time to time members of the higher legislative assemblies or courts of the church. Thus also the lines of authority in the Reformed churches move from the local church to the General Synod. This is so since Christ, according to the New Testament, has appointed officers to govern the church under himself. Their authority to govern derives from him even though they are elected by the people. The local churches together delegate authority to classes and synods, and having done so, they also bind themselves to be subject together to these larger bodies in all matters in which the common interests of the many churches are objects of concern.

The Reformed churches have particularly distanced themselves from a "clerocracy," the governance of the church by clergy. In fact, Reformed order avoids the term "clergy." That is, a cadre of religious professionals does not make decisions on behalf of the church. Instead, the office of elder takes a central place.

This is crucial in a Reformed understanding of the nature of the church. The church ministers to the life of all people and to the community around it. The religious professional tends to serve the church as institution, and to its members in their "religious" life. But the Reformed look beyond the walls of the institution to the culture without. Because the elder, in Reformed churches, is not a paid professional but lives and works alongside others in the community, he or she lives a life in both worlds. She is peculiarly placed to minister to those whose life she shares. At the same time, she brings her peculiar perspective within the councils of the church.

In turn, this gives a particular flavor to the ruling bodies of the church. As the church order will make clear, classes and synods are made up of elders and ministers who serve at a local level. They bring to decisions that affect the total church a perspective shaped by the countless congregations in which they serve. Thus the church, in principle, can never be fully "centralized."

Although the Reformed church maintains four offices, the preamble notes that Reformed churches consider ministers to be "elders of a special kind." Both the *BCO* and the *Liturgy* clearly keep the two offices distinct. However, the earliest Dutch order, that of the church in London (1554), recognized only two offices, elders and deacons, and described the minister as a particular sort of elder.[15]

At the same time, this paragraph betrays a puzzle. It claims that Christ appointed officers for the governance of the church. It is only with difficulty that one can find scriptural support for that assertion. The closest text may be in Matthew 16, where Jesus grants to Peter the power of the keys. This may and has been read to mean that Christ grants authority to the apostles to proclaim an apostolic faith that entails eternal consequences. However, we can claim the particular offices of the Reformed church as apostolic only derivatively. A.J. Bronkhorst lends support to this reading when he argues that Christ establishes the apostolic office in Matthew 16 and then goes on to add that the "NT displays to us also then the development of the one office of the apostles to a pluriform whole of ministries in the congregation."[16] The Belgic Confession further adumbrates the point when, in Article 30, it confesses: "We believe that this true Church must be governed in keeping with the spiritual procedure which our Lord has taught us in his Word, namely (1) that there be servants or shepherds to preach the Word of God and

---

15 Micron, Michael, *De Christlicke Ordinancien der Nederlantscher Ghemeinten te Londen* (s'Gravenhage: Martinus Nijhoff, 1956), chap. 1.
16 Bronkhorst, *Schrift en Kerkorde,* p. 62. See also A. A. Van Ruler, *Bijzonder en Algemeen Amt* (Nijkerk: G.F. Callenbach, 1952), p. 70.

to administer the Sacraments; and (2) that there be overseers and deacons who, together with the shepherds, are to function as the council of the Church."

> [Par. 17] The Equality of the Ministry. *The Reformed Church in America uses the term "parity" to describe its concept of the equality of ministers. It is not meant that authority can never be exercised by one over the other. But in every instance this authority will be delegated by the proper body, and the authority will cease to be exercised when the need for it is no longer demanded. The principle of equality pertains also among churches, among elders, and among deacons. The principle of the equality of the ministry, conceived now in its broadest sense as including the functions of the elder and the deacon, is based upon the fact that the entire ministerial or pastoral office is summed up in Jesus Christ himself in such a way that he is, in a sense, the only one holding that office. Every ministerial function is found preeminently in him. By his Holy Spirit he distributes these functions among those whom he calls to serve in his name.*

Because it is *Christ* who governs the church, and because in Christ divisions of status no longer obtain (see Gal.5:25), there can be in principle no hierarchy of authority. All ministries derive from Christ's governance. That is, of course, not to claim that there are no differences among believers. Paul's teaching on the variety of gifts reminds us of the wondrous variegation of human abilities. Those who have the gift of teaching may have little sense for governance; and those who understand administration may have little capability for preaching, for example. For that matter, some preachers are more obviously gifted communicators than others.

Nonetheless, no one is given perpetual authority, not even by virtue of office. This principle builds flexibility into the order. It recognizes that authority must be exercised at times and that authority is exercised through the agency of particular persons. A person may function, however, as authority only as delegated by a particular body. For example, an agent from a classis may say to a consistory that it may or may not financially encumber its property through a mortgage. The agent, however, ceases to exercise that authority once he or she is no longer empowered.

This is not a perpetual authority. That means that no one officer receives authority over another that adheres to him or her by nature of office. While authority derives from Christ, it is usually exercised in Reformed circles only as the officers gather in assembly.

Interestingly, the paragraph notes that equality applies not only to offices but to churches or congregations as well. One might detect in this comment the old notion that some churches carried more weight; they were located in a central city or principle town of a region. More practically for our context, this means that the "larger" church or more "prestigious" congregation does not call the shots for neighboring churches simply by the nature of the status it enjoys. Within a classis, for example, the smaller church stands on equal footing with the larger. One is not "more church" than another. The reason is quite simple. It is the presence of Christ that makes a church to be church, and Christ is as fully present in the preached Word and celebrated sacraments in the smaller as in the larger.

It should be added that this paragraph describes authority as it pertains to governance. Ministers of Word and sacrament will, by the nature of their office, exercise a particular authority that does, in a sense, rule over another. That can be so only as Christ is present in the Word to exhort, to admonish, to reprove, etc. Even in those cases, however, the minister's authority is always guarded by other officers, notably the elders, as they gather in assembly.

2
The Consistory

The *BCO* consists of two parts, the *Government* and the *Disciplinary and Judicial Procedures* (chapters 1 and 2). The division reflects the fact that the same body can engage in distinctly different activities. As shall be seen, the border is at times fuzzy and will require close attention. Nonetheless it is crucial to keep the distinction in mind, for a body acting as assembly is about differing aims and responsibilities than the same body acting as a judicatory and thus will function differently.

The government begins with the local expression of the church and its governing body, the consistory. This is most appropriate in a Reformed order. The marks of the church as delineated by the Belgic Confession are the pure preaching of the gospel, the pure administration of the sacraments, and the exercise of discipline (Art. 29). These occur, can only occur, locally. Preaching, sacraments, and discipline must happen some place. More centrally, Reformed theology reflects its understanding of God's meeting with God's people as God speaks in the Word and is present in the sacrament. That event, of itself, creates the church as God calls a people into existence. That happens locally.

One would expect that a local gathering needs some form of organization. That's true of any human group from a bridge club to a nation. Likewise, a church. We provide for a ruling body, in our case called a "consistory."

But the consistory is more than just a convenient form of organization. The consistory does not exist simply to make certain that the bills are paid or to plan new ministries. It is true that the consistory exists to act as trustees for the local congregation. Nonetheless, in Reformed order, the consistory's task revolves around the pulpit and the table and the font. We can even say that it moves from that center outward. Elders and deacons lead in the mission of the church as Christ's presence calls the church to ministry in the world. At the same time, they act as Christ's representatives to provide the appropriate occasion for the proclamation of Word and celebration of sacrament where we anticipate Christ's presence in our midst. The "Articles concerning the Organization of the church and of Worship at Geneva proposed by the Ministers at the Council January 16, 1537" open with these words:

> Right Honourable Gentlemen: it is certain that a Church cannot be said to be well ordered and regulated unless in it the Holy Supper of our Lord is always being celebrated and frequented, and this under such good supervision that no one dare presume to present himself unless devoutly, and with genuine reverence for it.[1]

If we take Reformation Geneva as our starting point, the consistory was the first assembly in Reformed order. The elders were required to gather with the ministers every Thursday to guarantee "that there be no disorder in the Church."[2] From the outset, the local church

---

1   Calvin, John, "Articles concerning the Organization of the Church and of Worship at Geneva proposed by the Ministers at the Council January 16, 1537," in *Theological Treatises*, trans. J.K.S. Reid (Philadelphia: Westminster Press, 1954), p. 48.
2   Calvin, "Draft Ecclesiastical Ordinances, September & October 1541," in *Theological Treatises*, p. 70.

had a body that gathered for oversight. The consistory that meets on the third Wednesday at First Church, coffee cups in hand, is a direct descendant of the Genevan body. The change in the relation between the church and the state has resulted in expanded duties for the contemporary consistory, but their fundamental task remains the same.

Article I. Definitions

Sec. 1. *A consistory is the governing body of a local church. Its members are the installed minister/s of that church serving under a call, and the elders and deacons currently installed in office. A consistory is a permanent, continuing body which functions between stated sessions through committees.*

The local church retains its own governance. The consistory does not represent a higher ecclesiastical authority; it does not hand on decisions made by, say, the classis for its own governance. The office-bearers are fully empowered to govern the local church. Nor can a local church devise an alternate body for its governance. If the offices represent Christ's leading in its fullness, then to do otherwise would be to betray a Reformed understanding of the nature of the church.

The consistory is constituted by persons ordained to the three of the offices of the church, minister, elder, and deacon. This requirement clearly expresses the notion that the congregation does not chose its leaders simply to represent various points of view from within its body. Its governing body will consist of those who have been ordained to particular offices.

One notes a qualifying phrase in the case of the installed ministers. It may be possible that a church may employ a minister in an assisting capacity that is installed by a classis into a "ministry" but has not consummated the pastoral relationship through installation into that church. In such cases, the minister not installed is not a member of the consistory.

Furthermore, only those currently installed shall be members of the consistory. While a congregation may have many who hold the office, not all will be installed. This is largely a practical provision. It safeguards the congregation from the accretion of power to the few who through reputation or longevity may exercise undue influence. Because this body is permanent and does not only exist at those times when it meets, the church is never without a body responsible for its life and ministry. The consistory "subsists" in various committees that it may establish that meet at times between sessions. In practical terms, this means the consistory may at times empower its committees to act on its behalf.

It is helpful here to add a note on committees. The church order is careful to avoid prescribing committees for the various assemblies. The church is ruled by the assemblies, and their responsibilities are carefully detailed in the order. *How* each assembly shapes its business remains its particular responsibility. In fact, it would be not only cumbersome but would burden the assemblies were the order to prescribe committees. This openness allows for the flexibility of the assemblies as committees come into being and are disbanded as circumstances demand.

a. A congregation is a body of baptized Christians meeting regularly in a particular place of worship.

The congregation by itself is not a church in Reformed order. Historically, for example, a municipality may encompass any number of worshiping bodies. This was true in Geneva, and later in the cities of the Reformation. In our era, a church may sponsor a congregation for the purposes of mission or evangelization. A classis that starts a new church begins by first gathering a congregation. In its beginnings, the new body is not ready to elect and ordain officers.

The definition assists in clarity of understanding. Believers are gathered in congregations. It's what we experience on a Sunday morning. While that dynamic body stands at the center of our attention, it is not, by itself, that which orders the life of the church.

> *b. A local church is a congregation properly organized, and it is served and governed by a regularly constituted consistory.*

The local church comes into existence when it is organized and a consistory is in place. Without the consistory, the local church cannot be said to exist. This is eminently practical; otherwise no body is in place that is responsible for the proper ordering of its life. However, this is so for theological reasons as well. It is the consistory that provides for those things that mark the church as church: the preaching of the Word, the right celebration of the sacraments, and the practice of discipline.

But this regulation is in place for a further, very Reformed, reason. Without a consistory, the local congregation is not responsible to the greater church. It is through the consistory that the local congregation answers to the oversight of the larger church as it cares for the preaching of the Word, and this accountability is for the protection of the congregation itself. Likewise, it is through the consistory that the congregation addresses the larger church.

> *c. A collegiate church is two or more congregations served and governed by a single consistory, constituting one church organization.*

This definition may sound quaint to modern ears. There exist few expressions of collegiate churches within the Reformed Church in America. The collegiate church has its roots in the cities of the Reformation. The church was understood to be one: the church of a particular locality. When the population grew in numbers and lived in distant neighborhoods, it was necessary to provide a number of sites for worship. The consistory continued its governance, but it provided for a number of congregations. The provision remains. The Collegiate Church in New York City continues this old tradition. Throughout its life it has had twenty-three congregations within its ambit.

On the other hand, while it may be said that *de jure* we have few collegiate systems in place, *de facto* a number of very large local churches do exist in which the number of worship opportunities exist that in effect create different congregations. They are governed as a "local church" by one consistory. Is this a contemporary expression of an old system?

> *d. A multiple parish is a group of local churches sharing the services of one or more installed ministers.*

In contrast with the collegiate system where one consistory governs a number of worshiping congregations, in a multiple parish more than one consistory govern the respective congregations but may share an installed minister. These have most commonly been called "yoked" churches and consist mostly of smaller churches whose resources prevent them from employing ministers on their own.

> Sec. 2. *A consistory combines the ministerial functions and governmental powers of the offices of the minister, elder, and deacon in the service and supervision of a local church. The whole body acts as the representative of the congregation. The elders, together with the minister/s, constitute a board of elders with specified responsibilities and powers. The deacons constitute a board of deacons with specified duties and authority.*

The consistory is responsible for the life and work of the local church. In fact, it is fully responsible. No other body within the congregation can assume its power. A church may, for example, have a board of education responsible for the church school, youth group, adult education, etc. That board may be granted responsibilities that will affect the ministry of the congregation. Nonetheless, the consistory remains responsible for the actions of that board. Nor can the congregation arrogate to itself the responsibilities of the consistory. The consistory is well advised at times to consult the congregation for its wisdom (and in the case of the calling of a minister is enjoined to do just that), but the decisions remain those of the consistory alone.

The section opens with the intriguing combination of "ministerial functions" and "governmental powers" of the offices. In so doing, the order reminds the consistory that the offices exist for ministry. The body is about something more than managing the life of an institution. It is enjoined to care for those ministerial functions that adhere to the office of the minister: the proclamation of the Word; to the elder: the spiritual care of the congregation; and to the deacon: service to the least and the broken. The consistory will spend its time fretting about budgets, tending to property, supervising personnel, but all for the sake of the ministry of the church.

Not all church orders combine these functions in one body, not even all Reformed orders. In some of the earliest Reformed orders, only ministers and elders constituted a consistory. (In part, this was because the deacon had sufficient work; his office had not atrophied to its current state! The board of deacons met separately to be about its appointed business). Nevertheless, as early as 1574, the Dordrecht order provided that in localities where too few elders were available, deacons were permitted to sit on the consistory.[3] The Explanatory Articles of 1792 used the same reasoning to grant deacons a place on the consistory of the American churches [Ex. Art., XXVII].

It is possible and desirable to divide these functions into different bodies. It's not often that gifts for ministry and administration are combined in one person. Still, our order places them together in one body, thereby indicating that all are to be placed in service of ministry. Because a consistory is a gathering of differing people within different offices, the requisite gifts can be combined within one setting.

This section introduces a further distinction within the consistory. Each church will have a separate board of elders and board of deacons. These boards will meet separately and will exercise particular functions within the congregation. The order will clearly

---

3 "Acta" of the Provisional Synod of Holland and Zeeland, 1574, Article IV, in Kerkelyke Handboekje, hereinafter cited in the text as Dordrecht, 1574, with article.

lay these out. It will be important for the consistory to keep the various responsibilities clear.

Attending to this distinction is of special note when we keep in mind that the consistory is the most intensive gathering of offices within the Reformed order. Only here do the three offices convene. This leads to the temptation to confuse the work of the differing offices. In many consistories, deacons have become little more than "junior elders," a step along the way to the "higher" office. The result is the devaluation of the office of the deacon with its particular focus. We then lose the power of the consistory as a dynamic convergence where Word, spiritual care, and service are understood as distinct but nonetheless inseparable.

> **Sec. 3.** *Ministers are those men and women who have been inducted into that office by ordination in accordance with the Word of God and the order established or recognized by the Reformed Church in America. They are equal in authority as ministers and as stewards of the mysteries of God. Ministers shall ordinarily be confessing members of only the Reformed Church in America, except as otherwise provided in Chapter 1, Part II, Article 12, Section 1. No person who has relinquished the ministry for which installed or who has been suspended or deposed from ministry shall exercise that office.*

The church order defines the three offices that gather in the consistory beginning with that of minister of Word and sacrament. Section 3 does little more than to delimit those who may be designated as ministers. Only those who have been ordained under prescribed circumstances may fill that office. It is the *church* meeting in appropriate council that sets apart persons for this office. This will occur within the responsibility of the classis. The procedure is an ordered oversight by which the local congregation is assured that the person residing in that office is appropriately educated and called to proclaim the Word. The procedure protects the congregation from its own enthusiasms for persons who through personal suasion can convince a local congregation that he or she can function as a minister.

Normally, ministers will be ordained by a classis through the order in the church's *Liturgy*. The exception allowed in this section will be determined by a classis, and is set out in Chapter 1, Part II, Article 12. The order so intends to protect congregations from an easy enthusiasm for candidates from outside the church who present themselves for call to local consistories. This needs special attention, for churches without a pastor are most vulnerable, often when they find it difficult to find a candidate for their pulpits.

The final sentence of this section is to be noted for its assumption concerning the office of minister within a Reformed understanding. Ministers are ordained to the office that proclaims the Word and celebrates the sacraments. That happens in a local circumstance and is guarded by those who *together* with the minister are responsible for Word and sacrament, either the officers of the consistory or of the classis. Thus, ministers are not ordained to a "general" office. At times, various Reformed bodies have considered ministers with wider portfolios as with, for example, an office of "evangelist," or "exhorter," or "missionary." The RCA has retained this office within the context of the local church. Just so, a classis is not free to ordain a candidate unless she or he has a call to a local church, or within other prescribed conditions (p. 172ff.). This restriction further prevents ministers from functioning independently, carrying their ordinations as license to function as ministers in whatever circumstances they find themselves.

Because this section stands under the heading of the "Consistory," ministers of local congregations will be members of the consistory. The order allows that ministers not installed to a particular local church may serve on its consistory as elders. However, when a minister serves as elder, he functions not as minister but as elder. He is subject to discipline as an elder in that role and is not to function as an additional minister.

Ministers fit within two categories, of which the order will outline in the following two sections: ministers of local churches and specialized ministers.

> Sec. 4. *The office of the minister in the local parish is to serve as pastor, teacher, and enabler of the congregation, to build up and equip the whole church for its ministry in the world. As pastor and teacher, the minister preaches and teaches the Word of God, administers the sacraments, shares responsibility with the officers and members of the congregation for their mutual Christian growth, exercises Christian love and discipline in conjunction with the elders, and is careful that everything in the church is done in a proper and orderly way. As enabler the minister so serves and lives among the congregation that together they become wholly devoted to the Lord Jesus Christ in the service of the church for the world.*

The minister is ordained to the office of minister of Word and sacrament. She is installed as pastor and teacher of a local congregation. This section describes her function in the office within a local church, and uses three terms—pastor, teacher and enabler—to denote that function. Three matters are of note.

While the section describes the office of minister as a *function*, it is crucial to recall that the minister is ordained to the service of the Word. As the Synod of Wesel put it, it is "necessary for the welfare of the congregations, that first of all care be taken to place men pious, learned, and experienced in the interpretation of Holy Scripture as ministers and pastors; so that none can doubt that thereto is required a knowledge of the languages, discipline, and established practice in the interpretation of the Scripture" [Wesel, I, I]. The National Synod at Gravenhage, in 1586, states as the first characteristic of the office of minister that he is to be one who continues in prayer (first!) and in the service of the Word, then the distribution of the sacraments is mentioned. This is "first of all" central for the simple reason that without the presence of Christ, without the Word present in preaching and sacrament, the church simply does not exist.

First, the goal of the functions are the equipping of "the whole church for its ministry to the world." One detects here the Reformed notion that the church's task is not its own life but takes place within the trajectory of God's kingdom, the scope of which is the "world." For example, while preaching occurs within the walls of a church and has as its audience largely the members of the congregation, the Word is intended to be heard beyond the walls. Reformation Netherlands began with the phenomenon of "hedge preachers," preachers who held forth out of doors where all could hear. While this occurred within circumstances that excluded preachers from the churches, it expressed the Reformed understanding that proclamation intends to shape the life of the entire culture. The minister pastors and teaches a congregation that is intended to function as a missionary institution within its culture.

Second, the minister functions alongside other officers in the church. This is explicitly stated in terms of the exercise of "Christian love and discipline." The psychology of ministry is such that it is easy for the minister to arrogate authority to him or herself. She is the one ordained to speak for God! Who are other officers to question one who speaks on such authority? Such an attitude results in divided congregations, situations that might have been avoided had the minister worked within the collegiality of offices intended by the order.

Third, the section concludes by stating that as enabler the minister serves and *lives* among the congregation that they may become the more devoted to the Lord. The ministerial office does not limit itself to what is spoken from the pulpit, as central as that is. The minister's life is itself witness. The tragic consequence of ministerial malfeasance is not only the disrepute of ministry, but also broken lives within a congregation where hearers can no longer open their hearts to the pulpit where they come hungering for a word from God.

It must be emphasized that while this section enjoins the minister to function in a broad setting, the particular task of the minister should not be forgotten. While the minister can execute her peculiar responsibility for the preaching of the Word and the celebration of the sacraments only within the circle of the elders, these responsibilities devolve peculiarly upon her. She, in her person, represents the ecumenical presence of the entire church. Except under very peculiar conditions, this is the minister's task alone, and the preaching of the Word and the celebration of the sacraments are two of the marks of the church. The congregation rightly expects its minister to spend most of her energy on these tasks.

> Sec. 5. *The office of the minister in a specialized ministry is to serve as pastor, teacher, and/or enabler of the people among whom the minister works, to build up and equip those people, and to serve with the whole church in its ministry in the world. As pastor and teacher, the minister proclaims the Word of God in word and deed and administers the sacraments when appropriate under the authority of the classis. As enabler the minister so serves and lives among the people that together they become wholly devoted to the Lord Jesus Christ in the service of the church to the whole world.*

Specialized ministers function in a variety of roles: chaplains in the military, chaplains of institutions, counselors, teachers, administrators, etc. Specialized ministers understand their role as twofold. First, they minister to those with whom they serve, prison inmates, for example. Second, they further the work of the church in its ministry to the world. They minister on behalf of the church. Thus, specialized ministers are not "independent contractors." They retain their organic connection with the church, and they are responsible to the church as the church is responsible to them.

While the placement of the definition here is for convenience and clarity, specialized ministers retain their *ordered* connection with the church through the classis. It is to be expected that where possible they maintain personal attachment to a local congregation. But their *ministerial* responsibility is to the classis that will be enjoined to supervise their ministry.

It is important to note that specialized ministers retain their office by virtue of their functioning as ministers of Word and sacrament. The order allows considerable flexibility by inserting the phrase "and deed" in the context of ministry of the Word. That recognizes that many specialized ministers will find little opportunity for proclamation in their work. One notes, however, that the celebration of the sacrament is to happen under the authority of the classis. This does not entail a classis looking over a minister's shoulder every time he or she celebrates the sacrament. It does mean, though, that the classis authorizes the minister to celebrate the sacrament in his or her situation.

At the same time it would at least be helpful and encouraging for the classis to provide opportunities for the minister to exercise his office, where possible. Specialized ministers can, for example, fill pulpits and celebrate sacraments in classis churches.

> Sec. 6. *Proper ecclesiastical designation of ministers should accord with the nature of their ministry, such as pastor, teacher, professor, missionary, chaplain, president, executive secretary, or director.*

"Proper ecclesiastical designation" emphasizes the point made above that the minister functions within particular circumstances. By making such designations with care, the church can exercise proper oversight of the work of its ministers. It remains responsible for their work. It further assists the classis especially by retaining appropriate connections with its ministers.

> Sec. 7. *Elders are confessing members of the local church who have been inducted into that office by ordination in accordance with the Word of God and the order established or recognized by the Reformed Church in America.*

This section is both delimiting and permissive. It guards against non-members, those who are not within the discipline of the church, from functioning as elders, and thus serves as protection for the local congregation. It is permissive as it allows members who have been ordained as elder in other orders, usually a presbyterian order, to function as elder. Thus, the church "recognizes" the ordination to office from other churches. This is a not unimportant expression of a Reformed ecumenical posture.

The injunction that elders be ordained sounds almost tautologous to the Reformed. To be an elder is to be ordained; that's the only way one is an elder. It is to be underscored, however. For the Reformed order recognizes in its threefold ministry minister, elder, and deacon, *all* as offices, all as part of the ordained—or ordered—ministry of the church. Thus, one must be careful in the use of language. It might be correct to denote elders as "laity" only so long as all, ministers included, fall under the heading of the "people of God." But it would be incorrect to consider either elders or deacons as "lay members" of a board, the consistory. Both offices are part of the "ordained ministry."

The reference to the "order established...by the Reformed" church signals that for a full understanding of the constitutional nature of both this office and that of the deacon, one needs to consult the orders established in the *Liturgy*. Thus three parts of the constitution, government, liturgy and standards together, delimit the fuller description of the offices.

> Sec. 8. *The office of elder is, together with the other installed elders and the installed minister/s serving under call, to have supervision of the church entrusted to them. They have charge of all matters relating to the welfare and good order of the church. They have oversight over the conduct of the members of the congregation and seek to bring that conduct into conformity with the Word of God. Elders exercise an oversight over the conduct of one another, and of the deacons, and of the minister/s. They make certain that what*

is preached and taught by the minister/s is in accord with the
Holy Scripture. They assist the minister/s with their good
counsel and in the task of visitation. They seek to guard the
sacraments of the church from being profaned. An elder may
administer the sacraments, if authorized by the board of
elders.

Reformed order grants broad power to the office of the elder. Although parity obtains among as well as within the offices, the elder may fairly be denoted as the central office in a Reformed order. At the local level, elders exercise the broadest power in legislative, disciplinary, and judicial matters.

Legislatively, they have charge of *all* matters "relating to the welfare and good order of the church." Elders are responsible for the good order of the church. While the first sentence pairs the elder with the minister, and while the minister (in section 4 above) is charged that everything be done in a "proper and orderly way," in practice this task is often left to the minister as the resident paid professional. That is to denature the order and a Reformed church thus degenerates into a "clerocracy."

The elder is charged with oversight of the life of the members of the congregation. From the outset, care of the congregation required a great deal from the office. This task is easily misunderstood to mean that elders are moral busybodies prying into the private lives of congregants. One needs to keep in mind that membership in the Reformed church centers around the Lord's Table. Members are not simply individuals who have pledged loyalty to an ecclesiastical confession. They are very members of Christ and live within a new reality. Their baptism signifies their union with the head of the church. Elders are those persons who live out this organic connection as they review the life of the congregation. What would it mean for someone who publicly flaunts Christ's way to gather at the Table? Must not someone ask serious questions, both for the sake of the communicant and of the Table itself? That task belongs to the elders—in concert.

The responsibility for the supper is clearly present in the history of the office. The Dort order (Article 23) includes under the tasks of the office of the elder that "before, or after the Lord's supper, as time and circumstances permit, and shall be most for the edification of the congregation, to assist in performing visitations, in order particularly to instruct and comfort the members in full communion, as well as to exhort others to the regular profession of the Christian religion."

In Amsterdam, for example, immediately following the acceptance of the Reformation in 1578, the consistory planned that all the households of the city be visited prior to Communion. A look at the numbers involved soon convinced them of the impossibility of the task! Nonetheless, the consistory persisted with further plans.

Just here the task of visitation is to be included in their commission. The order of Wesel anticipates that a sort of "house to house" visitation occur weekly, and especially prior to the celebration of the Lord's Supper. The requirements of office were broadly conceived and included careful inquiry into the life of the families, whether family education in the faith was occurring, whether morning and evening prayer was practiced within the home, and the like. The elder was to admonish the fallen, comfort where necessary, bring reproof at other times, and encourage parents to send their children for catechetical instruction (Wesel, IV, 2). To accomplish this, the congregation was to be divided into "neighborhoods," each elder taking responsibility for a particular area. The order of Gravenhage (1586) puts it more succinctly: the elder is to comfort and to educate the members of the congregation and to admonish them to the Christian religion.[4] Middelburg, a few years earlier, focused more clearly on the Lord's Table when it had the elder help prepare those who otherwise could not approach the Table.[5] The old practice of *huisbezoek* ("home visitation") has degenerated into "pastoral calling,"

---

4   "Kerken-Ordeninge" of the National Synod at Gravenhage, 1586, Article XXI, in Kerkelyke Handboekje, hereinafter cited in the text as Gravenhage with article.
5   "Acta" of the National Synod at Middelburg, 1581, Article XVI, in Kerkelyke Handboekje, hereinafter cited in the text as Middelburg with article.

understood as a responsibility of the minister. The result has been not only a ceding of the Reformed understanding of the congregation under the care of elders. It has also divorced the practice of pastoral care *and* that of discipline from its proper place—the Lord's Table.

The oversight of elders extends to each other and to the other offices. They represent, in their office, the responsibility of the offices to Christ. That includes, in a particular way, the conduct and the teaching and preaching of the minister. Thus, elders are responsible that the content of both scripture and the confessions be honored.

In recent years, the Reformed Church in America has expanded the responsibilities of the office of elder to permit elders, under certain circumstances, to preside at the Lord's Table. This permissive action was taken that congregations not be bereft of the sacrament when circumstances prevent the availability of ministers. This action needs to be taken cautiously. The authorization is very simple: the board of elders designates one of its members to preside. This is not ordination to a new office. The elder is not thereby permitted to preside at any other table than that of the local congregation.

> Sec. 9. *Deacons are confessing members of the local church who have been inducted into that office by ordination in accordance with the Word of God and the order established or recognized by the Reformed Church in America.*

> Sec. 10. *The office of deacon is one of servanthood and service after the example of Christ. In the local church deacons are chosen members of spiritual commitment, exemplary life, compassionate spirit, and sound judgment, who are set apart for a ministry of mercy, service, and outreach. They are to receive the contributions of the congregation and to distribute them under the direction of the consistory. The deacons give particular attention and care to the whole benevolence program of the church. They have charge of all gifts contributed for the benefit of the poor and distribute them*

*with discretion. They visit and comfort those in material need
and perform such other duties as the consistory may assign
to them.*

In the office of the deacon, Reformed order expresses the church
in service to God's kingdom in the world. Because this is an
ordained office, the Reformed understand it to be nothing less than
the work of Christ. The office of deacon does not simply imitate
Christ; it expresses organically Christ's continuing work. While
recent Reformed practice has devalued the work of the deacon, the
office remains, and current initiatives to revive it correct a
longstanding lacuna in the life of Reformed churches. The sometimes
heard complaint that Reformed order is too inward looking fails to
recognize that the missional nature of the church is inscribed in its
order.

The office of deacon has had a distinguished history. It was
deacons who cared for schools, hospitals, widows and orphans, and
others. Robert Alexander has shown, for example, that the original
"social work agency" in Albany, New York, was the board of
deacons of the Reformed church.[6] A Reformed church in Den
Bosch, the Netherlands, displays a memorial tablet that originally
graced the entrance to its "Diakonie." It was a separate building set
aside for the use of the deacons in their work. A poem inscribed on
the stone concludes with this line: "There one preaches belief and
here one does the work.." The deacons represent the church in
service not only to the community, but to the weakest in its
immediate society.

In fact, Wesel sees the deacons' task as so great that the order
divides deacons into two parts. One is to care for the money
received for the poor, both in alms and in bequests. The second part
of the deaconal task is to care for the sick, the imprisoned, and the
weak. That will require, says that order, uncommon knowledge of

6   Alexander, Robert, *Albany's First Church* (Albany: First Church in Albany, 1988), pp. 34-
     37, 217-18. See also Venema, Jenny, trans. and ed., *Deacon's Accounts 1652-1674, First
     Ditch Reformed Church of Beverwyk/Albany, New York* (Grand Rapids: Eerdmans, 1998).

the means of comfort and "of God's Word"! Furthermore, those deacons were to inform the elders of those within their "neighborhoods" who were sick or weak and who required the comfort of ecclesiastical care. The deacons' task was pastoral (Wesel, V, 6-7). In fact, Wesel only received the distinction made already by John Calvin.[7] Middelburg adds that the service of extending financial support to the weak includes not only the residents of the community but "vreemdelingen" (strangers) as well! (Middelburg, XVIII).

In the American experience, the deacons' task received a second focus. In earlier expressions of the Reformed church, financial support for the provision of the local parish came from sources outside the congregation. In some cases support came from the government; in other instances a local aristocracy may have supported the church. With the separation of the church from the state, the American church received support from its own members (although this was not often in terms of contributions; one need only recall the system of pew rentals). The deacons were then charged not only with monies contributed for works of mercy, but also for the maintenance of the institution. The Explanatory Articles note this shift and give their reason:

> As many difficulties are known to have arisen in the minds of Deacons, respecting the application of monies collected by them for the churches, to any other purposes than those of immediate charity; it becomes necessary to explain this subject, and remove the difficulties, by declaring that the design and object of the collection are not only the relief of the poor, but also the necessities of the congregation.— Charity extends to the souls of men as well as their bodies; and procuring the gospel for the poor is the highest benefit (XXVII).

7 Calvin, John, *Institutes of the Christian Religion*, trans. Ford Lewis Battles (Philadelphia: Westminster, 1960), pp. iv, 3, 9.

One notes in their reason that the missional nature of the church is included *within* the provision for worship in the local congregation. Congregations are expected to be gatherings *open* to all sorts and conditions.

Furthermore, because the deacons have charge of the entire benevolent program of the church, service and mercy are not given by church order to a committee. The task is not an option for a congregation, to be disposed of or added as fashion might dictate.

This is especially emphasized in the context of the "poor." Churches, through their deacons, are expected to be cognizant of and ready to respond to the poor within their precinct and beyond.

Deacons, too, are commissioned to visitation. In their case, it is the visitation of "those in material need." Thus, all three offices are commissioned to a ministry that extends beyond the walls of the local church.

> Sec. 11. *A great consistory of a church consists of all confessing members of that church who have served it, or are serving it, as elders and deacons on its consistory. The great consistory may be convened by the consistory when matters of special importance relating to the welfare of the church demand consideration. Members of the great consistory have only an advisory vote.*

Elders and deacons have been ordained to their respective offices. Their ordination does not cease when they no longer serve actively on the consistory. They remain officers of the church. Thus they comprise a greater body within a local congregation. This section allows a sitting consistory to consult with them in "matters of special importance." One might surmise that within a Reformed order many congregational meetings would be supplanted by gatherings of those who have been ordained to the ordered leadership of the church, especially when we recall that the church is ruled by Christ through the offices.

The section, however, carefully limits the role of the great consistory. The sitting consistory remains fully responsible for the life of the congregation. The great consistory cannot, for example, organize itself, call its own meetings, and make decisions. To do so would create a condition pregnant with the possibility of chaos and strife. Who is in charge? Thus, the great consistory gathers only at the call of the consistory, and its voice is only advisory.

Article 2. Responsibilities of the Consistory

Sec. 1. *The consistory shall act in all matters calling for judgment and decision which are not specifically assigned to the board of elders or the board of deacons.*

This broad description of the consistory's responsibilities assures that it will be the consistory that takes appropriate judgment on behalf of the congregation. The consistory cannot cede its task to any other body within the local church, the congregation included. A committee on education within the church may, for example, decide on the appropriateness of a particular curriculum. However, the consistory is responsible for that decision and would be advised to act upon the recommendation of the committee. In just this manner, the church is governed by the offices that gather.

Sec. 2. *The consistory shall provide a minister, or ministers, for the church. It has the authority to call persons to the ministry of the church if the charter of the church has not made other provisions. The consistory shall endeavor to learn the mind of the congregation with respect to any person who may be called to the ministry of the church. The judgment of the congregation in such matters shall be considered to be of significant weight, but not binding. The instrument of the call to a minister shall be signed by the members of the consistory. If the call is approved by the classis and accepted by the person called, the latter's name shall be published in the church on three successive Sundays, so that opportunity may be afforded for the raising of lawful objections. (For organizing churches, the classis may waive the three successive Sundays requirement.) If no such objections are*

raised, the classis or its committee shall install the minister
according to the office for installation in the Liturgy.

On its face the consistory's responsibility to provide the local
congregation with the ministry of Word and sacrament seems
obvious. Someone must do so; and since the consistory is charged
with the leadership of the congregation, where better should this
duty be lodged? Yet, it was not always so, and the clause "if the
charter of the church has not made other provisions" betrays an
older approach. The consistory's freedom to call a minister is the
result of a historical process. There were many congregations in the
Netherlands Reformed Church in which the local noble held the
right of appointment of the local pastor. Early struggles over
church order had much to do with whether to allow the magistracy
(the town council) the right either to appoint or to have voice in the
appointment of the pastor. Indeed, the magistracy held the right to
confirm (or veto) a candidate chosen by a consistory, although the
civil authorities seldom wielded the power. All this had to change
in the American situation, of course, and the local church, as
consistory, called the pastor.

This historical development aside, and perhaps despite its intention,
this section expresses something essential in Reformed order. The
choice of the minister of Word and sacrament is central to the life
of the congregation, for it has to do with that which constitutes the
life and being of the church: Christ's presence in the preached Word
and enacted sacraments. Elders and deacons acting not simply as
representatives of the congregation but as officers who represent
Christ are charged with calling that officer who proclaims the Word
and who presides at the sacraments in their particular locality.

This responsibility expresses Reformed order in yet another way:
the *congregation* does not call the pastor. The mind of the congregation
is to be of "significant weight." The minister will minister in *this*
congregation. Elders and deacons take care that the person called
to minister will "fit" with this congregation. That too is to care for

the Word as it is proclaimed, for the hearers participate in the dynamic of the proclaimed Word.

It is important to note that no other ecclesiastical assembly appoints a minister to a congregation. The consistory does so as the local assembly. Nonetheless, the greater church participates in the process. While the weight of the decision remains fully with the consistory, the classis plays a significant role. It must approve the call. Its approval is no mere formality. The classis has among its responsibilities the supervision of its churches. There are occasions when a consistory desires to call a minister whose ministry or person would be unsuitable for a congregation, or whose doctrine or conduct the classis cannot approve. In such cases, the classis acts for the benefit of the local congregation (although the local church seldom sees the matter in that light at that moment).

The classis is further involved as it installs the minister as pastor and teacher of the local congregation. Thus the constitution of a pastoral relationship comes not in the agreement between the minister and congregation, but in the action of the greater church in the person of the classis. The pastoral relationship is between the congregation and the pastor, but it subsists, as it were, within the classis, and it can be severed only by the classis. Two clauses in the final sentence deserve note. The first almost disappears from view (largely because this particular classical responsibility is lodged here in the *BCO* and not under the classis's own part). Either the classis *or* its committee shall install the minister into the congregation. This directive frees the classis from the requirement to obtain a quorum for the installation. That requisite may be difficult in classes that extend over large geographic distances.

Secondly, the installation is to follow the order in the *Liturgy*. Classes are not free to conduct freeform liturgical acts in installations; they bind themselves as *Reformed* churches through a common form of worship.

Sec. 3. *A consistory may call one or more associate ministers. The form of the call to an associate minister shall be the same*

*as that to the senior minister, except that the word "associate"
shall be inserted before the words "pastor" or "minister,"
wherever they occur in the text of the call. The associate
minister shall be a member of the consistory. (On the
"assistant minister, see Part II, Article 7, Section 9.)*

The order provides that a congregation may have more than one
installed minister. Such will be the case in larger congregations
where ministerial demands exceed what can be fulfilled by one
person. However, the order makes a clear distinction between
"associate" and "assistant" ministers. The associate minister will be
called and installed in the same manner as the senior minister.
Classical approval is required and the associate enjoys the same
status of "call." That is, he or she remains under the call until it is
appropriately dissolved by the classis. Furthermore, as an officer,
the associate is a member of the consistory. The same is not true of
the assistant. While classical approval is required for the *hiring* of the
assistant, he or she remains under a contract which shall be
reviewed annually by the classis!

*Sec. 4. A consistory may contract with one or more assistant
ministers to serve along with its minister(s) serving under a
call. The contract(s) shall follow the guidelines established
by the classis. The assistant minister shall be installed by the
classis as a minister under contract, but shall not be* ipso
facto *a member of the church or the consistory.*

Added in 1997, the section intended to clarify the role of so-called
"staff" ministers who may work within a church, but who are not
called, and thus not installed as either "minister" or "associate."
The order allows congregations to extend their ministries in the
employment of a number of ministers without installing them as
pastors and teachers. One needs to be clear, however, that the
minister so employed is engaged in the ministry of the office to
which she is ordained. One fears a proliferation of "professional"
ministers who certainly perform valuable ministry but for whom

ordination is not necessary. Such a trend would not simply devalue the nature of ordination, but also the ministry of God's people as a whole.

The relationship of the assistant to the church is peculiar in that the assistant need not be a member of the congregation, nor is he or she a member of the consistory. By definitions of the order, she is a specialized minister to the church.

The contract would, of course, be between the consistory and the assistant minister. Of itself, this is odd, for it allows a different kind of relationship between minister, church, and classis than is adumbrated by call/installation. While the contract itself is under the review of the classis, it is further not clear whether the contract must be renewed annually. Other places in the order that denote the minister under contract (pp. 180, 194) mandate that a contract must be reviewed annually by the classis.

> Sec. 5. *A consistory or its minister may request the classis to terminate the minister's relationship to that church. (See Chapter I, Part II, Article 13, Section 8).*

The process for the *dissolution* of the pastoral relationship will be considered under the work of the classis. The order includes it here to signal to the consistory that in its responsibility for the ministry of Word and sacrament within a congregation, it may legitimately decide that the ministry of its current pastor no longer serves the cause of the local church. We shall discuss precisely what those conditions may be when we review the section noted in the parenthesis.

> Sec. 6. *The consistory shall provide services of worship and other activities and organizations in the church's life for the spiritual benefit and growth of Christ's people.*

As offices gathered, the consistory is charged first with provision for that which is essential to the life and being of the church— worship—and worship understood as the preached Word and enacted sacraments. Again, this does not happen as a matter of convenience or efficiency (somebody must do it), but as those charged with spiritual offices. God acts through the consistory to provide nothing less than Christ's own presence at a local place and time, and to invite the prayers and praise of a gathered people in response. Thus, the consistory has not only as responsibility, but as awesome privilege the task of providing a place in the local community where Christ meets his own. The task is appropriate to offices that have as their root the Word and the Table of our Lord.

The section adds that the consistory provides "other activities and organizations" within the life of the congregation. These are appropriately left unspecified, for while the congregation cannot exist without worship, it can continue without a church school, a youth group, a mission society, and the like. That is not to advise consistories *not* to provide such activities, but it allows each consistory the flexibility to minister appropriately in its time and place. At the same time, the section underscores that "other" organizations are responsible to the consistory and the consistory in turn is responsible for them.

Might one detect something of the preamble's claim that the purpose of the church is to "minister to the total life of all people" in this provision? The offices of minister, elder, and deacon are set within the trajectory of the kingdom. The church's worship, for example, is not directed solely at those within the church, but toward those without. The ministry of elder and deacon are for the sake of society. In this way the foundational Reformed notion that God's intentions find their goal in the kingdom through the church's ministry is expressed.

> Sec. 7. *The consistory shall be guided by the following requirements in their provision of services of worship.*
>
> a. *The order of worship on the Lord's Day shall be in accordance with the* Liturgy *of the Reformed Church in America, or with the principles set forth in the* Directory for Worship*, as the*

consistory may direct for the edification and profit of the congregation.

The order is clear that the design for the liturgical gathering of the congregation is not the prerogative of the minister, nor of a "worship team" or committee. Worship, too, emerges from the gathering of the offices in the leadership of the congregation. As we have seen, their very offices are founded around pulpit and table. Practically, this means that while a minister (or a committee) may propose the structure for worship, the consistory needs finally to take responsibility in its action.

An observer will most likely be struck by the variety of worship shapes and styles among congregations in the Reformed church. One moves from an ordered worship directly from the *Liturgy* to more free-wheeling evangelistic or "seeker" styles. Indeed, the Reformed have allowed for a great deal of freedom in worship. Nonetheless, this freedom is restrained within a tensile unity that directs that worship must follow certain principles. We recall that these principles are set out *constitutionally* in the *Liturgy* and its accompanying *Directory*. Thus, a consistory is not free "do as it wishes" or even as it deems most helpful, if in so doing it transgresses the boundaries set out by the constitution. Indeed, from the outset, Reformed churches maintained a fixed liturgy especially in the matter of the sacraments. The Synod of Wesel is exemplary when (Chapter VI, 18) it requires the reading of the order from the Ecclesiastical Liturgy at the Lord's Table.

> *b. The sacrament of baptism shall be administered, if possible, at a time and place of public worship. "The Office for the Administration of Baptism" shall be read.*

> *c. The sacrament of the Lord's Supper shall be administered, if possible, at least once every three months in every church. "The Office for the Administration of the Lord's Supper" shall be read. All baptized Christians present who are admitted to*

the Lord's Supper are to be invited to participate.

The consistory establishes the time, place, and order for the celebration of the sacraments within the guidelines of the order. Baptism, an occasional service that occurs when appropriate, is ordinarily to take place within the setting of public worship. Its celebration thus accords with the Reformed understanding of baptism as entrance into the communion of faith. The order allows exceptions for those instances where the baptized is precluded from attending public worship. In any case, it is a matter for consistorial decision.

The local congregation is required to celebrate the Lord's Supper at least four times a year. Unfortunately many Reformed churches have not only disregarded John Calvin's desire for weekly celebration, they have used the "four times" rule as the maximum. The order simply requires that the sacrament be celebrated at least four times a year and allows it to be celebrated as many times as the consistory judges appropriate.

Furthermore, the order requires that the appropriate offices from the *Liturgy* be read at the administration of the sacraments. Consistories and congregations are not free to construct their own liturgical expressions around the sacraments. The General Synod has, at times, allowed other orders to be used in occasional circumstances. Examples include the so-called "Lima Liturgy" and the "Communion Liturgy from the Churches of Christ Uniting."

Since the Reformed Church does not practice "closed" or "close" Communion, the order requires that all baptized Christians admitted to the Lord's Table be invited. The order expresses a deeply ecumenical recognition that the church is greater than the Reformed communion, and that the church is constituted around the table of its Lord.

In 1988, the General Synod urged boards of elders to consider admitting baptized children to the Table.[8] The task is taken up in

8   *MGS*, 1988, pp. 380-86.

no place in the order beside the notation under "Membership Categories" in the preamble. There it is noted that "baptized members" may be admitted to the Lord's Table. One presumes both through the duties of their office and the General Synod's action that it is the board of elders' task to determine just how and when baptized children are to be admitted.

A board of elders is well advised to consult the report of the General Synod's Commission on Theology that provides the theological rationale for allowing children to participate at the Lord's Table.[9] The admission of children to the Table is founded on a Reformed understanding of baptism, rooted as it is in the biblical notion of covenant and church. In baptism, the child is received as a member of the church. Membership is around the Table as the believer there participates in the presence of the living Christ. While Reformed churches had for many years understood confession of faith to function as admission to the Lord's Table, the Theological Commission maintained that nothing in Scripture, the early history of the church, or Reformed theology required confession of faith for admission to the Table. Indeed, it was the history of the western church as it moved toward a full-blown sacramentology that understood confirmation as a sacrament administered by a bishop and that further adumbrated a doctrine of transubstantiation that kept children from the Table. The Reformed church clearly distanced itself from that sort of sacramental understanding. Nor were children to be excluded because they could not articulate an adult understanding of the nature of the Table. Rather, as part of the community of faith who are already members of the body of Christ, children can express a faith in the love of God in Jesus Christ and thus can gather authentically around the Table. The board of elders, in its responsibility for the local communion of the church, then can make proper provision for the participation of children at the Table.

9 *MGS*, 1988, pp. 380-85. See also the Theological Commission reports of 1977 and 1984.

In fact, deliberative action on this particular matter can renew the congregation in its commitment to the education of the baptized.

d. The hymns used in public worship shall be in harmony with the Standards of the Reformed Church in America.

It may surprise many to see the regulation of hymns included under the responsibilities of the consistory. However, the use of hymns in Reformed churches has a long history. The first Reformed churches restricted the musical expression of the congregation to the psalms of Scripture. The 1578 Synod of Dordrecht, for example, limited singing to the psalms (as set by Peter Dantheus) and such hymns as may be found in Scripture (LXXVI). Dort itself (LXIX) limited singing to the psalms and the songs of Mary, Zacharias, and Simeon. The Explanatory Articles likewise prescribed psalms, allowing for French hymns compiled by Beza and La Moret and German hymns published at Marburgh and Amsterdam. It also allowed hymns compiled by Livingston! (LXV).[10] It was not until the nineteenth century that the Netherlands church allowed the singing of hymns, and then the introduction was not greeted with acceptance by all.

The provision surprises further because many people assume that the selection of hymns is left either to the minister or those responsible for music. That may indeed be the usual practice; however, the consistory retains responsibility for the content of the hymns.

Music and consequently the hymnody of the church possesses a particular power to move the congregation. Its hymns are a form of its prayers. And hymns with their music imprint themselves on the human soul. They become vehicles for the theological formation of believers. A consistory would need to be careful in the American culture with its treasure of evangelistic hymns. It is all too easy, for

---

10 John Henry Livingston (1746-1825), often considered the "father" of the Reformed Church in America, is best known as the driving force behind the Explanatory Articles and the first indigenous liturgies, and he was the first professor of theology.

example, for the congregation to sing merrily about the choice the individual must make for Jesus, thus skating on Arminian thin ice!

The issue becomes all the more acute as a congregation moves away from Reformed hymnals. The current era further boasts the ability legally to use copyrighted hymns that are printed in the weekly worship folder. The consistory's responsibility only appears to grow.

> e. The consistory of a church may invite or permit ministers of other denominations whose character and standard are known to preach for them. Ministers of other denominations or their counterparts whose character and standard are not known shall not be engaged to preach in a local church until they have furnished to the consistory written evidence of recent date of their good ministerial standing and of their authorization to preach the Word. The consistory shall then determine whether to issue an invitation to preach. Ordinarily, the preaching of the Word shall be performed by an ordained minister or a theological student appointed pursuant to the Government of the Reformed Church in America, Chapter a, Part II, Article 7, Section 7. In special circumstances, an elder commissioned by the classis as a preaching elder may preach. However, a consistory may authorize, in occasional or special circumstances, other persons to preach.

The consistory's responsibility for the life of the congregation around pulpit and Table will include those times when the congregation's minister is absent (or the pulpit is vacant). This subsection grants permission for the consistory to engage a non-Reformed church minister. However, it may do so only with full knowledge of that minister's character or written evidence of his or her ministerial standing. In so doing, the consistory protects the congregation from those who may be popular (or simply available) but whose theological or personal proclivities hinder the right proclamation of the gospel. It is thus incumbent upon a consistory to have appropriate knowledge of those engaged to preach.

In 1998, the order was amended, giving permission to consistories to allow elders commissioned by the classis to preach.[11] This permission is closely circumscribed. See the comments under Part II, Article 14, of the *Government*.

The consistory is, however, allowed by this subsection to invite other persons to preach in *occasional* circumstances. One might suppose that this provision allows for such events as laity Sundays, youth services, and missionary visits. The consistory is advised for the sake of the order of the church to keep the occasional nature of this permission in mind.

> f. *The points of doctrine contained in the Heidelberg Catechism*
> *shall be explained by the minister at regular services of*
> *worship on the Lord's Day, so that the exposition of them is*
> *completed within a period of four years.*

Perhaps few prescriptions in the *BCO* have been observed more in the breach than in fact than this requirement. While it has existed since the inception of the Reformed church, synodical and classical minutes have continually complained of the infrequency of its observance. Ministers and consistories often console themselves with the rather weak assertion that since the preaching follows Scripture it per force covers the points of doctrine in the catechism.

In fact, the Reformed church's history had allowed for an easier fulfillment of the requirement. The second service, often an afternoon service, was set aside for the catechism. The morning, or principle, service was directed more "outward" to the larger community and the sermon remained rooted in the evangelical promises and demands of Scripture. The second service concentrated more on the life of the local congregation and was more appropriate for a didactic or doctrinal purport that shaped the congregation around its confessional identity.

Nonetheless, the provision remains. As the covenant to maintain a common liturgical life binds the Reformed churches in its

11 *MGS*, 1998, p. 70.

liturgical expression, the catechism provides a covenantal life doctrinally. When one recalls that the catechism functioned as the hermeneutic through which the Reformed read Scripture, this provision is appropriate for a consistory that is responsible for what is preached from its pulpit. Indeed, in an era when many Reformed churches question their identity as "reformed," a consistory would be well advised to consider this prescription seriously for the life of the congregation.

> Sec. 8. *The consistory shall make provision for the private administration of the sacraments in instances of sickness or other emergency. At least one elder shall be present with the minister on such occasions. At least one other elder shall accompany an elder administering the sacraments privately.*

Consistent with its theology, Reformed churches celebrate the sacraments in the gathered congregation. God's meeting with God's people is not a private event but happens in a true communion. Nevertheless, occasions arise when it is not possible for a person to be present in a congregation. He or she remains a part of the congregation as the consistory includes her in its sacramental life.

We note that it is the consistory that makes this provision. Common practice has the minister arrange for private Communion. Perhaps that is more practical. However, the consistory as officers of the community retain their responsibility for font and Table. In so doing, they tend to the life of the congregation through nothing less than those "means of grace," the sacraments.

The prescription that at least one elder accompany the minister, or that an elder accompany another elder administering the sacrament, further expresses the Reformed understanding that the sacrament happens in the gathered congregation. The attending elder stands in for, or represents, the congregation in the celebration of the sacrament.

> Sec. 9. *The consistory shall have the care and supervision of the church's property and financial interests. They are the*

trustees of the church's property, unless the act of incorporation of the church or the statues of the state in which the church is incorporated, make other provision. The consistory shall not sell, transfer, lease, mortgage, or otherwise alienate or encumber any real property of the church on which there stands a building designed for worship or religious instruction, or as a residence for the minister, unless the approval of the classis of which the church is a member has been secured. Further, the consistory shall not incur a total indebtedness which exceeds two-thirds of the prior year's expenditures for congregational purposes, as reported to the General Synod, without the approval of classis.

In most instances, the consistory functions as a board of trustees for the congregation. This has not always been the case in Reformed order. Some orders institute a separate board of trustees that cares for the real property of the congregation. And some RCA congregations have a separate board of trustees as allowed within the provisions of this section. At first glance, such division of labor seems to offer a clear distinction in the consistory's task. The consistory is not weighed down with mundane problems with roofs and sewers, with the complications of financial support for the congregation. The consistory can focus its energy on the task of ministry.

However, such division raises a fundamental challenge to the church order. For it would admit a separate body that exercises real power in the ministry of the congregation, a body that is *not* made up of officers. If Christ leads the church through the offices, then the offices need to concern themselves with *all* the tasks of the church. Furthermore, to claim that matters of real property fall outside the purview of the offices would be to import an invalid dualism into Reformed life. The church as spiritual body is not a *disembodied* reality; its life includes buildings and money. How a church constructs its building, how it raises and spends its money, how it cares for its property are all fully theological matters, and thus they come under the guidance of those charged with leadership, the consistory.

Although the consistory remains trustees of a congregation's real assets, it does so in responsibility to another assembly, the classis. The classis exercises oversight of a consistory that intends to encumber the property used for the purpose of congregational life. A classis will act as "check and balance" on a consistory's decision to sell, transfer, or otherwise encumber its property. The order does not intend to hinder the ministry of a local church through this provision. Rather, this acts as a caution that protects a consistory from what may be its own over-enthusiasm.

Sec. 10. *The consistory shall be guided by the following requirements in its supervision of the election of elders and deacons to membership in the consistory:*

a. *The elders and deacons shall be chosen from the confessing members of the church in full communion who have attained the age of twenty-one years or, at the discretion of the consistory, eighteen years. They shall be elected by a vote of the confessing members of the church.*

b. *Notice of a congregational meeting for the election of elders and deacons shall be made in the usual place of worship on two Sundays preceding the date of such meeting. When an election has been omitted at its usual time, the consistory shall designate another time for that purpose, at an early date. They shall furnish notice of the meeting in the usual way. Election to vacancies on consistory shall be provided for in this same manner.*

c. *Elders and deacons in churches already organized shall by chosen by one of the following methods:*

(1) *A double number of candidates shall be nominated by the consistory.*

(2) The confessing members of the congregation shall nominate
and choose the whole number to be elected with or without
advisory nominations by the consistory or other
representatives of the congregation.

(3) The method approved by the church's charter.

(4) The method approved by the church's bylaws, subject to
approval by the classis.

d. The method employed by a church shall not be changed
except by permission of classis.

The one task not allowed the consistory by the church order is its
self-selection. Elders and deacons are to be elected by the local
congregation. Election of consistory is the primary manner by
which members of a congregation participate in leadership.

The consistory is charged, however, with arranging the election,
and the order carefully delimits how this is to occur. It denotes
which congregational members may participate in the election. The
order requires that proper notice of elections be given in order that
the elections be fair and open. And the order further describes the
allowable methods for nomination to the offices.

However, fundamental fairness of election is not the only and
perhaps not the primary issue at hand. It is election to office. Those
elected will be ordained as spiritual leaders of the congregation. The
detail conferred on the election expresses the theological seriousness
at hand. The congregation, through the work of the Holy Spirit,
claims: "These persons are to be set aside by God's Spirit not simply
as representatives of the desires of the congregation but as ministers
of God."

The relation of assemblies comes into play yet again in the
classical oversight of elections. The classis does not involve itself in
each election. The classis is granted neither the power nor the
responsibility; they fall outside its authority. The consistory remains

responsible for its *method* of nomination and election, subject to the approval of the classis.

> e. The elders and deacons shall be elected for a term not to exceed five years, the length of the term being at the discretion of the consistory. A classis may, under extenuating circumstances and at the request of a consistory, grant permission for an extension of the term of office of elders and deacons, subject to classis review at least once every five years.

> f. When a vacancy is to be filled, the person elected shall serve the remainder of the unexpired term.

> g. In order to avoid an entire change of consistory at one time, a part of the whole number of elders and deacons shall be elected annually.

> h. When a consistory is enlarged, a part of the whole number of elders and deacons to be added shall be elected annually.

The setting of the length of terms of service outlined in these sections indicates that a consistory cannot indefinitely perpetuate itself. The order does not in itself require a rotation of a consistory so that it will always have new persons as members. Section 11 below allows for re-election and does not require members to "rotate off" a consistory. Still, the congregation is privileged not to re-elect those nominated. The membership of the consistory remains in the hands of the congregation.

> Sec. 11. The names of the persons elected as elders and deacons shall be published in the church on three successive Sundays preceding their installation, in order that any legitimate objections may be presented to the board of elders for its judgment.

Election alone does not confirm the process to ordination for elder or deacon. There may exist "legitimate objections" to an ordination that a simple tally of votes will not disclose. If, for example, an electee has been involved in a way of life that would bring dishonor upon the church and the gospel, but the behavior in question is such that it remains known to only a very few, the church would err by ordaining him or her. A man may quietly and secretly beat his wife or his children, a habitual activity that his family hesitates to make known. Should such a person be granted the office of elder? In such a case, it may be incumbent upon one with knowledge of the pattern of behavior to make it known to the consistory. Thus not only is the office protected, but the church as well.

The section is clear that an objection be "lawful." A person cannot object to an electee simply because he disagrees with the electee, nor because she doesn't like the officer-elect. What then constitutes a lawful objection? The *Liturgy* talks about a "scriptural reason" why an electee may not be ordained. The burden, then, is on one bringing the objection along with the consistory to show that an objection fulfills a "scriptural reason."

One can, of course, put forward other "lawful objections" from the *BCO* itself. The person may, for example, not be a confessing member of the congregation! Or she may have consistently and unrepentantly neglected her vows as a member of the congregation. The person may have fostered division and strife within the congregation, for example, and thus not sought for things "which make for purity and peace" within the church.

> Sec. 12. *Elders and deacons may be re-elected, but they shall not be reordained to the same office. They need to be installed only when the terms of service are not consecutive.*

Ordination to office happens once. In the order for ordination, the church prays that God may enlighten the ordinand with God's Spirit. The ordinand *becomes* an elder or a deacon. He or she retains that office for life unless particular reasons intervene, as would happen for example if she were deposed from office. The perpetuation of office in her person is what is often called the *indelibility* of ordination. This provision further signals that consistory members are not simply administrative leaders of a congregation, but maintain a spiritual office.

> Sec. 13. *A consistory shall recognize as valid only such ordination to the office of elder or deacon in another denomination as is able to meet the following conditions: intended to be within and to the ministry of the catholic or universal church; performed by a duly organized body of Christian churches, and by the authority within such body charged with the exercise of this specific power, accompanied by prayer and the laying on of hands.*

An ecumenical stance lurks within the consistory's responsibilities. Churches engaged in ecumenical discussions struggle with the "mutual recognition of ministries." Can a denomination recognize as valid the *ordained* ministry of another denomination? At issue usually is the question of who presides at the Lord's Table and who inhabits a pulpit. However, the Reformed Church *already* recognizes the ministries of elder and deacon as ordained and grants a consistory power to recognize them as such, provided the ordination in question meets certain conditions. Those conditions further signal that the ordinand be set apart for ministry within the church catholic, and thus is not ordained only within a sect. Furthermore, such ordinations are recognized as they conform to the conditions set forth not by the Reformed Church, but by a sister church. However, the ordination occurs insofar as it is accompanied by prayer and the laying on of hands, that is, in the conferral of authority by the *church* through the power of the Spirit.

> Sec. 14. *The president and the clerk of the consistory shall keep a careful register of all baptisms and marriages, of all admissions to confessing membership, of all dismissions to other churches, and of the deaths of members.*

Sec. 15. The consistory shall make a statistical report at the meeting of classis immediately preceding the stated meetings of the regional and General Synods. The report shall comply with the requirements of the General Synod and shall be accompanied by such comment on the spiritual state of the church as the consistory may deem proper.

Sec. 16. The consistory shall forward to the appropriate congregation or classis stated clerk within one month the names, addresses, and pertinent information regarding persons moving from the bounds of the local church.

The duties outlined in these sections sound essentially administrative, almost secretarial. However, they are given to the consistory because in each case they include the care of the church for its integrity as a community. It takes care to keep track of those who gather around the Lord's Table. Furthermore, by so doing, it exercises responsibility to other congregations. How else can it attest to membership when another church requests a transfer of membership? More than sloppy record-keeping is in the balance.

By requiring a statistical report, the order reinforces the relationship between the assemblies and the accountability of the local church to the greater church. The comment on the "spiritual state of the church" reminds the consistory of its task. It also enables the greater church as expressed by the classis to exercise its superintendence of the congregations. The reports are a systematic way by which the local congregation opens itself not simply to view by the greater church, but to mutual assistance and prayer.

The requirement to forward names and addresses of members who have moved acknowledges that while members are always members of a local church—they gather around *this* table—they are therefore members of the Church of Jesus Christ. Responsibility to those members entails that provision be made for *them* to become part of a local communion. That can happen only through a local church where they now reside. This provision assists in that process as it alerts a local church to those who reside within its boundaries that they may extend an appropriate invitation to members of the church now within their peculiar ambit.

Article 3. Officers of the Consistory

Sec. 1. *The minister shall be president of the consistory and shall preside at all of the its meetings except where otherwise provided. It shall be the duty of the president to state and explain the business to be transacted, to enforce the rules of order, and, in general, to maintain the decorum and dignity belonging to the church of Jesus Christ.*

It may seem odd that the order requires that the minister preside at consistory meetings. Presidency of the body, after all, seems administrative and might well be executed by an elder or deacon more gifted to the task. Furthermore, it appears to allow power to accrue to the minister, thus reinforcing just that sort of clericalism that tempts the church. Three reasons may be ventured for having the minister as president of consistory. First, he or she presides at the Lord's Table. The consistory table derives its place and reason for existence from the Table *par excellence*. At the Lord's Table, the minister, in some sense, represents the headship of Christ over the community. Likewise, the consistory recognizes at its table that Christ remains the head of the assembly. We recall, though, that it is only "in a sense" that the minister stands in for Christ. He is not Christ's vicar; the offices remain in parity. Thus, the minister is not free to declaim *ex cathedra* the way and will of God. The consistory continues, together, as a gathered body to seek the will of its Lord.

Second, the minister, in his office, stands behind the pulpit and so the congregation acknowledges the priority of the Word for its life. That symbol, too, is taken into the consistory. The consistory gathered is no less under the discipline and power of the Word than they are within the sanctuary. Still, the limits observed in the first reason still obtain.

Third, the minister represents the church catholic. He or she does so in her person. Thus she expresses the ecumenical connection with the larger church. She does so as a member of the classis. The congregation lives in organic connection with all other churches.

The power of the minister as president stands as a symbol in a Reformed order that expresses the insight that God's meeting with God's people in worship creates a community that is also an institution. The community takes a particular shape. That shape will find its way into a consistory that is about its business as it maintains the "decorum and dignity belonging to the church of Jesus Christ." One order has the president of the classis (which applies *mutatis mutandis* to the other assemblies) commanding silence from those who are "too hasty in speech," or who "haggle" (Middelburg, XXVI). The church witnesses to its Lord no less in the gathering of its councils than in, say, its public worship or acts of mercy.

That said, the order does not prohibit other officers from taking leadership in the consistory meetings. The order only states that the minister shall preside. The precise shape of that presidency may vary from consistory to consistory. Thus even when an elder is "in the chair," the minister remains responsible as the presiding officer.

> Sec. 2. *The consistory shall elect one of the elders to the office of vice-president. If there is more than one installed minister serving under call the consistory may elect the associate minister/s to the office of vice-president in addition to the elder vice-president. The order of seniority of the several vice presidents shall then be determined.*

In many congregations, the minister comes from "outside." She did not emerge from a community that draws its life from generations who live together in the same place. That has changed in a mobile society; the minister maybe resident longer than many of the members! Still, the provision for a "senior" officer from among the elders institutionally places in authority one whose office emerges from the congregation's life and thus signals that the leadership of the consistory is not restricted to the minister. This is the more emphasized when the order allows that associate ministers may be elected vice-president, but only in addition to the elder vice-president.

The peculiar *role* of the vice-president is left unspecified. It will differ among the churches. The consistories will determine, often informally, the role of its vice-president.

> Sec. 3. *The consistory shall have a clerk whose duty shall be to keep a faithful record of all the proceedings of that body, and to furnish official notices in writing to all persons directly affected by decisions of the consistory.*

The clerk (who may be either elder or deacon) is not simply a "secretary" for the assembly who does little more than record minutes. The actions and decisions of the consistory affect the life of the church and are expected to be open to inspection. Only so can the body retain an institutional memory not only for its own sake, but for the care of the congregation. This is especially crucial in matters of dispute. The clerk's record will become the official record of the consistory's action if it is complained against. Thus, the consistory should designate one who can take extreme care in recording its actions.

This provision is very old in Reformed orders. Already in the 1574 Synod of Dordrecht the order required that a consistory keep a "certain book" that in which was carefully noted the actions of the consistory (Dordrecht, VI). This requirement cared for the life of the congregation by means of a leadership careful in its institutional life.

Article 4. Transaction of Business

> Sec. 1. *The consistory shall be guided in its transaction of business by such rules of order as it shall adopt from time to time, and which are in accord with the* Government of the Reformed Church in America. *Elders and deacons shall have an equal voice.*

The business of the church is to be conducted in good order. The church order allows each consistory to adopt its own rules of order to guide its deliberation. That is to be advised. However, local rules of order cannot conflict with the government as outlined in the *BCO*. This assures that the local congregation acts within the life of the *Reformed* church.

Sec. 2. *A majority of the consistory members regularly convened shall constitute a quorum for the transaction of business.*

This section appears self-evident. Still, it protects the congregation from direction from a few. The full *consistory* retains responsibility as the gathered offices for the governance of the local congregation.

Sec. 3. *All consistory meetings shall begin and end with prayer.*

Prayer is not a formality, a nod to the divine after which the consistory can get down to business. The consistory gathers to lead the church in the name of Christ; this is the community gathered as a spiritual body in essence. Thus, its meetings are surrounded by prayer; all deliberations are transparent to the work of the Spirit. Indeed, through debate—difficult and even acrimonious—and vote the church believes that the Spirit is active. Thus, prayer is part and parcel of the gathering of this body. *How* and what form prayer takes is left to each consistory. The order only states that prayer shall be a part of the consistory's business as it opens and as it closes its gathering, thus opening the entire meeting to the presence of God.

Sec. 4. *A member of the consistory shall not have the right to protest against any act or decisions of that body, but shall have the right to redress by appeal or complaint to the classis. Any member of the consistory shall also have the right to request that the names of all consistory members, with their votes for or against a matter in question, be recorded in the minutes of the consistory for the information of all; however, that request maybe denied by a two-thirds majority of the consistory.*

The consistory gathers and acts as a body. Reformed order maintains that assemblies are gathered bodies where decisions happen in mutual discernment of God's will for the church. No one officer, including the presiding officer, can raise him or herself above the body to maintain that she alone bears God's desire for the church. This is especially crucial as we look toward the congregation. An officer convinced that he is in the right may easily be tempted to put the case before the congregation, building pressure "from below" for the body to change its position. This would be to violate a Reformed understanding of how God leads the church, and, further, it would precipitate disorder within the congregation.

That does not mean that a member of the consistory has no redress. The actions of all assemblies (excluding the General Synod) are subject to review by a greater body. The provision of complaint or appeal protects the right of the minority to be heard in instances where the minority is convinced that the consistory erred in a fundamental manner. However, this complaint is laid not before the congregation, but the classis. The method for redress can be found in chapter 6, *Disciplinary and Judicial Procedures.*

> Sec. 5. *A consistory regularly convened may invite a minister of its own classis to preside at any meeting of the consistory when, in its judgment, circumstances make the presiding of its minister inadvisable.*

The church order presumes that a consistory shall not meet without a minister present. One might reasonably argue that such a requirement enables a classis to maintain proper oversight of a consistory; the installed minister himself is a member of the classis and subject to its discipline. However, more is at stake. The consistory as gathered offices of elder, deacon, and minister represents the fullness of Christ's leading. If any office is absent, the consistory no longer exists in its fullness. We recall what was argued above about the symbolic nature of the minister as president of the consistory.

The prescription in this section is perhaps most relevant in those cases where a dispute arises between a minister and the consistory. A consistory could easily deem that it best meet in secret, or in an informal setting where it can discuss matters concerning its minister that cannot be done in the minister's presence. The order requires that the consistory meet in regular session and that another minister be invited to be present. Thus the order attempts to assure that all will be done in order and for the good of the church.

> **Sec. 6.** *The president shall call special meetings of the consistory when they are deemed necessary and shall do so promptly when requested by at least three members of the consistory.*

The consistory is enjoined to meet *regularly* (Sec. 2 above). This is generally assumed to mean that a consistory will hold *stated* meetings, meetings held at times determined by the body that occur in a regular rhythm. However, the press of business is often such that a consistory must meet at a special time. The order permits special meetings; a consistory's own by-laws may include further provision for how a special meeting is called. The calling of the special meeting ordinarily occurs through the office of the president. However, there may be instances when the president is reluctant to call a special meeting. He must do so if at least three members of the consistory request the meeting.

> **Sec. 7.** *The consistory shall submit the minutes of its meetings to the classis whenever the classis shall require it.*

This is yet another instance where the consistory's accountability to the greater assembly comes into play. The consistory, as a spiritual body, lives under the discipline of another body, the classis. The classis may ordinarily not desire to take cognizance of the work of each of its consistories. Often, however, in periods when a local church faces difficulty, a classis may find it wise to maintain closer vigilance over the life of a consistory. Thus its record does not remain within the "possession" of the consistory but must be laid open to the classis.

Article 5. Responsibilities of the Board of Elders

> Sec. 1. *The board of elders shall meet at stated times at least four times a year for the transaction of business which is their particular responsibility. A majority of the board regularly convened shall constitute a quorum. The minister shall preside at all meetings except where otherwise provided. The meetings shall begin and end with prayer. Minutes of meetings shall be kept and shall be submitted to the classis at least once a year.*

The nature of the offices are such that both elders and deacons are granted a separate body by means of which the offices can execute the responsibilities peculiar to the offices. The consistory as gathered offices expresses the union of the offices in ruling the church. The separate boards protects the offices from confusion.

The board of elders is peculiar from both the consistory and the board of deacons in that it not only functions as an assembly, but as a *judicatory* as well. That is, it is charged with the practice of discipline (see chapter 6). Its duties in the life of the congregation are clearly detailed in this article.

The nature of the work of the office is of such central importance to the life of the congregation that it is not left to meet at its own pleasure, but must meet at least four times a year in *stated* session. The spiritual oversight of the congregation is not accidental or haphazard. Thus the order takes pains that a Reformed congregation enjoy the pastoral oversight not simply from its installed minister, but from the elders gathered.

The importance of its work is further stressed by the requirement that the board of elders submit its minutes to the classis each year. In the case of consistories, a classis may from time to time request their minutes. This is not an option in the case of the board of elders.

In this way the classis can exercise appropriate oversight of the spiritual leadership of the local congregations.

> Sec. 2. *The board of elders shall be guided in its supervision of the membership of the church by the following requirements:*
>
> a. *It shall pass upon the qualifications of those who desire to make profession of faith. It alone has authority to admit persons to membership and to transfer members to other churches. It shall consider requests for infant baptism, providing at least one parent or guardian is a confessing member of the church to which the request is presented. A request for baptism from a parent or guardian who is not a confessing member of the church to which the request is made shall first be submitted for approval to the governing body of the church where the parent or guardian has membership.*

The elder stands at the hinge-point between the sacraments and the world that God so loved. The sacramental life of the congregation is at the core of the office. If we recall that membership in the congregation is primarily membership at the Table, then the elder's task of caring for both the body itself and its members will likewise focus on their participation at the Supper.

While the order has elders pass on qualifications of those making profession of faith, it is helpful to keep in mind that profession historically emerged as a requirement for admission to the Lord's Table. Although elders may allow baptized children to partake of the supper, the Reformed church has retained the process by which the baptized make public profession. This may, and must, be seen to center on the Table. For in making profession, a person places him or herself under the discipline of the church, thus becoming accountable to the body of Christ. And it is the Supper, the presence of the Lord in the Spirit, that realizes this coherence.

Elders, then, tend the "gates" of the church. Gatekeeping, however, ought not be understood as sectarian in nature.

"Qualifications" may include understanding of the beliefs and practices of the church as well as the sincerity of the profession of faith in Jesus as Lord. However, the elders are not admitting members to a denomination but gladly hearing the profession of faith in Jesus as Christ and welcoming the new member to the Table.

Welcoming members into the church includes the sacrament of baptism. In baptism the baptized is "received into the visible membership of the holy catholic church." Just so, the board of elders has authority over the administration of baptism and all requests for baptism must be placed before the board.

The requirement that a parent or guardian be a member of the church has caused pain in some areas of the church. Why should the church refuse the sacrament, especially to an infant who has no say in the matter? At issue is a Reformed understanding of baptism in which the baptized is not simply brought into relation with Christ, but is brought there through the communion of the church. The vows taken by parents *and* congregation make little sense otherwise. This section does permit a *guardian* to stand in for the parent. A board of elders may judge, for instance, that while the parents are not within the body of the church, a grandparent or another adult will take responsibility that this child will be raised within the life of the church and so may be educated in the life of the faith.

At the same time, the order makes provision for those who are not members of the particular congregation to request baptism for their children. This may happen, for instance, when the extended family is a member of the congregation while the parents live and worship elsewhere. The order provides that this can happen within the ambit of the *church* as it relates itself to the church of origin. In that way the entire church participates not only in the baptism, but in the baptismal life of the new member. The baptized has become part of the church in its local expression.

> b. It shall receive as confessing members of the church only
> those persons who have made a profession of their faith in
> the Lord Jesus Christ before the board of elders, or who have

made a reaffirmation of a previous profession of faith, or who have presented a satisfactory certificate of transfer from another Christian church.

While it is to be emphasized that baptism is the entrance into church membership, the order provides for "confessing" members (see the preamble to *Membership Categories and Definitions*). Such members are admitted by profession of faith in Jesus Christ. That profession is essential. The profession need not be elaborate, especially for persons who find the sometimes erudite theological formulations of the Reformed beyond their capacity! Nonetheless, the board is prevented from admitting persons who simply want to be part of the congregation as an institution or a community but who cannot make this fundamental Christian affirmation. New members are, after all, being joined with Christ!

Reaffirmation by faith is a handy provision that allows the board of elders to recognize, first, that a person has at some time in her life confessed her faith in Jesus Christ and is not new to the church. Second, it recognizes that the person has drifted from the life of the community. She can make a public profession that is not her "first" but that acknowledges the full journey of her life of faith, including the celebration of union with a congregation. Other instances may present themselves in which the person uniting with the church is a member of another ecclesiastical body that does not recognize certificates of transfer. In that case, reaffirmation expresses explicitly that the person is not *entering* the faith, and thus it acknowledges the legitimacy of the original church membership.

Transfer of membership further acknowledges that someone uniting with a particular congregation is already a member of the church of Jesus Christ. He or she simply unites with the particular local congregation.

c. It shall publish to the church the names of persons received as members and enter them on the church roll.

It would seem obvious that the local congregation would be cognizant of members received in a service of worship. That may not be the case in large congregations with multiple times of worship. The provision discloses a further understanding of the church, however. It acknowledges that a congregation is greater than simply those who worship regularly. It includes not only those who cannot come to worship—students, shut-ins, military personnel, and also those who are inactive but still part of the church. Publishing the names of new members also recognizes that those becoming part of the church are members of a *community* of persons.

> d. It shall place on the inactive list the name of any confessing member whose relationship with the church has ceased for one year or who for one year has not made faithful use of the means of grace, especially the hearing of the Word and the use of the Lord's Supper, unless there are extenuating circumstances making such faithful use impossible. After making due effort to notify the member of such action, the board shall seek diligently for an additional period of one year to recover that member. If there is no renewal of an active connection with the church in spite of these efforts, the board may vote to strike the name of the member from the church membership. Due effort shall be made to notify the member of such action.

Confessing membership assumes that the follower of Jesus Christ will participate actively in Christ's body as it is about its primary task, the praise and worship of God. Reformed faith does not acknowledge a person's direct relationship with Christ outside the community. Or more correctly, while the person is drawn into a deeply intimate relationship with Christ, that relationship is mediated through the community. The elder is ordained to care for the spiritual life of the congregation and its members, and thus has, with the gathering of elders, a primary commission to oversee the life of the members in community.

This task, usually undertaken by the board of elders with regularity, is perhaps the most evident and most usual disciplinary expression of their office. It is a remarkable care as the board reviews each member's presence it the life of the community. When taken seriously, it demands much time, effort, and prayer in ministry not only to the congregation as a whole, but to its members.

The interpretation of this subsection has sometimes puzzled boards of elders. One notices the "or" in the first sentence. What constitutes a "relationship with" a church besides attendance at worship? Is it financial contribution? Or might it be attendance at church school? Or activity in some other area of the church? The "or" allows for a relationship outside of presence at worship. On the other hand, given the elders' responsibility, should presence at the Table be devalued in that manner? Likewise, "faithful use" poses the question as to the interpretation of "faithful." The matter is left to each board of elders.

The board's task is not finished with the placement of a name on the "inactive list." Responsibility implies an active attempt to "recover" the member. This often proves a difficult and disheartening task, but one through which the elder represents Christ in seeking the lost. The onus is not left on a lapsed member but remains on the church as it represents the Lord who searches persistently for his own. Furthermore, the task evidences that a community or communion is at work. A family, for example, does not allow a member simply to drift away without making a strenuous effort to recall the lost one back to her or his fundamental identity as a member of the family. A board of elders may responsibly and perhaps more pastorally discharge this task by working with lapsed members before designating them inactive.

This subsection allows the board to strike the name of a member if she or he does not renew active relationship with the church. This, however, is a permissive clause; the board may decide to retain a member as inactive. To do so is consistent with a Reformed understanding of baptism.

e. It shall seek to impress upon members of the church who move from the bounds of its ministry the duty of obtaining a certificate of transfer to another church.

Since membership is membership around the Table, and since that further implies living in discipline with a communion of faith, the elders care for members who have moved by helping them find a new communion in which to live and worship. The board does not force the issue with an "automatic" transfer but is charged with communicating the desirability of transfer. The church remains cognizant of its members as it does not simply forget those who disappear from its midst.

f. It may permit a confessing member of a congregation or classis of the Reformed Church in America who is serving as a missionary outside of the United States or Canada to hold membership also in an indigenous church.

This subsection is the only place where the order allows a member to exist under two disciplines at the same time. Ordinarily, one is a member of Christ through a local church, and only one. However, missionaries serving outside the bounds of the Reformed Church in America cannot be "active" at Word and sacrament due to geographic circumstance. It is, then, permitted for them to unite with a local congregation where they serve.

g. It shall remove from the church roll the name of the following members: one who has transferred to another church; one who has united with another church without securing a certificate of transfer; one whose membership has been terminated by a procedure of discipline; one who has had a prolonged inactive status; a deceased member; and that of a licensed ministerial candidate upon becoming the installed minister of another church.

The principle adumbrated above, that one is a member of only one congregation, is clearly set forth here. Instances occur when members join another congregation without informing the local church. The board has no option then but to delete their names from the rolls. Other instances are then stated.

> *h. It shall not penalize nor permit to be penalized any member for conscientious objection to or support of the ordination of women to church offices; nor shall it permit any member to obstruct by unconstitutional means the election, ordination, or installation of women to church offices.*

The General Synod made a judicial ruling in 1979 to allow women to be ordained to the office of minister, and in 1980 it added the so-called "conscience clause" to the *BCO*. This clause released those who could not support women's ordination from having to participate in an action contrary to their understanding of Scripture.[12] Interestingly, it is the responsibility of the board of elders to execute this action in the local church. Practically, the clause means that an elder or deacon need not participate in the ordination of women as elders or deacons. It may also mean that members of a consistory cannot be penalized for refusing to recommend a woman as a candidate for ministry to a classis.

However, the clause states just as clearly that one cannot be penalized for *supporting* women's ordination, as may happen in some sections of the church where support for women's ordination is a minority stance. Furthermore, the board may not permit any church members from obstructing the election, ordination, or installation of women to church offices. That does not mean that a board need support women's ordination. However, if a congregation elects a woman to office, the board not only cannot obstruct the ordination, but it is positively charged to assure that ordination and installation occur!

> *Sec. 3. At each regular meeting, the board of elders shall seek to determine whether any members of the congregation are:*

12 *MGS*, 1979, pp. 64-70, and *MGS*, 1980, pp. 274-76.

a. *in need of special care regarding their spiritual condition and/
or*

b. *are not making faithful use of the means of grace, i.e.,
attending worship and participating in the sacraments and
shall provide the means of extending Christian ministry to
such persons.*

The responsibility prescribed here underscores the role of the
office of elder because it requires the board at *each* of its regular
meetings to inquire as to the spiritual health of the congregation
among the members themselves. The elders thus have always
before them their ministry to the members of the congregation.

It should be remembered that this provision originated around
the Lord's Table, thereby reinforcing our contention that the
offices emerge from the Lord's presence that calls the congregation
into existence each time the Spirit gathers it around pulpit and
Table. The Constitution of 1833, for example, put it:

> Particularly before the celebration of the Lord's Supper, a
> faithful and solemn inquiry is to be made, by the President
> [to the elders], whether to the knowledge of those present,
> any member in full communion has departed from the
> faith, or in walk or conversation has behaved unworthy the
> Christian Profession? That such as are guilty may be
> properly rebuked, admonished, or suspended from the
> privilege of approaching the Lord's Table, and all offences
> may be removed out of the church of Christ [Ch.II, Art. II,
> Sec. 5].

The tone of that section sounds harsh to modern ears, and the
amendment of this provision sounds more "pastoral." But that is to
forget that discipline is fundamentally pastoral, and that true
pastoral care occurs as it tends to a member's relationship toward
God, most centrally focused in the common meal. Furthermore,
the meal instantiates the *communal* nature of the member's faith.

Nonetheless, the provision requires the elders to remain cognizant of the spiritual life of the members *and* to extend ministry to the members. It may again be emphasized that this is not the task of the minister alone or even primarily, but of the elder. Furthermore, this ministry happens not by an officer alone, but as the offices gathered in communion.

This requirement makes the board of elders a ministerial body, often deep in prayer for the congregation. The meetings of the board of elders thus become a profound expression of the presence of Christ's ministry within the local community.

> Sec. 4. *The board of elders shall exercise Christian discipline with respect to any who continue in sin without repentance. All members of the church are subject to the church's government and discipline as administered by the board of elders. The board of elders shall admonish, or rebuke, or, if necessary, suspend from the privilege of the Lord's Table any who should be so disciplined. It shall be the privilege of the board of elders to receive the penitent into the fellowship of the church again.*

> Sec. 5. *The board of elders shall be guided in the exercise of Christian discipline by the requirements stated in the Disciplinary Procedures.*

The process of discipline is divided in the order between these sections and those set forth in the *Discipline*. The process demands care, for the board functions at one time as an assembly and yet again as a judicatory. The distinction must be kept in mind, for in the earlier stages of discipline the board acts pastorally as an assembly. The *Discipline* states clearly that "admonition and rebuke are pastoral in nature and are exercised by an assembly in the ordinary course of its proceedings" (p. 266).

In fact, the exercise of discipline presupposes prior function of the board. It will have, under the preceding sections, already have taken cognizance of the life of the church's members and will have acted pastorally to lead members back to appropriate life within the community of faith. The board turns to a more formal exercise of discipline with those who continue "in sin without repentance."

Membership in the church, indeed membership in Christ around the Table and under the Word, means that members have opened their lives to Christ's leading. Nor is Christ's leading an *individual* affair, something that happens in the privacy of one's relationship with God. Christ leads through his embodied community. Upon making public profession, the member promises "to accept the spiritual guidance of the Church, obeying its doctrines and its teaching...and to walk in the spirit of Christian love with the congregation, seeking the things that make for unity, purity, and peace." Spiritual guidance occurs institutionally through the offices that are ordained to that purpose and that gather to lead not only the church as a body but its members as well.

One exception must be noted to this section's assertion that *all* members of the church are subject to discipline, at least as administered by the board of elders. Ministers are members of the congregations they serve. However, ministers are subject to the discipline of a classis, and the responsibility of the board of elders toward them is strictly circumscribed in the order.

The final sentence of section 4 deserves to be emphasized. The board of elders enjoys the *privilege* of receiving the penitent into communion. In just this manner, the order makes clear that discipline is not for the sake of punishment, nor even to cleanse the body of impure elements. Discipline is for the sake of both the community and the member and finds its goal when the member has been received into the body once again. The loss of a member is a painful tear in the body. The congregation is less, as a communion, for the loss; and the member has forfeited her place at the Table where she receives the bread of life, the enjoyment of Communion with her Lord and with her sisters and brothers.

Article 6. Responsibilities of the Board of Deacons

Sec. 1. The board of deacons shall consist of those deacons who are in active service. The number of deacons shall be determined by the needs of the congregation and the evident gifts of those being called by God for the ministry of mercy, service and outreach.

From the outset, Reformed orders have provided for, or at least assumed, the gathering of a board of deacons to administer the ministry of the office of deacon. However, until quite recently, the board of deacons enjoyed a truncated place in the *Government*. In an attempt to recover the office of the deaconate, the General Synod of 1988 initiated a series of amendments that added both this section and the following to the *BCO*.[13] The clear intent was not only the strengthening of the office but the recovery of the ministry of service.

The deacons express the ministry of the church to the broken and the needy. This is not an "accidental" ministry of the church, one that *adds* something to the essential nature of the church's life. The church places it at the center of its life by denoting the deacon as an office. Furthermore, the board is not to be compared to a "mission committee," or even a Sunday school that may be a part of the church's life but that under other conditions may not apply.

While the office of deacon has atrophied in recent years, and while its ministry has often been reduced to tending the finances of the local congregation, the order reflects the Reformed notion that the church exists to serve not only as it proclaims gospel and invites the lost into communion with Christ, but as it *lives* gospel in service. Here, almost surprisingly, Reformed order displays a mission orientation the possibilities of which have scarcely been explored.

The article in question opens with a surprising, often unnoticed, section that states that the number of deacons is to be determined

13 *MGS*, 1988, pp. 234-42.

by need. This sounds very different from a church's usual practice of setting in its by-laws the number of deacons to be elected, usually a number equal to the elders. By making the number a function of need, the order expresses the basic nature of the deacon, which is service.

But the number is not only a function of need, but of those gifted for the service of ministry, service, and outreach. One can envisage, then, that a congregation with a greater number of such persons *grows* in its ministry as it finds new opportunities to serve and to express (as the next section puts it) the "social concerns of the church."

Just so the order describes a congregational way of being as it moves outward from the pulpit and Table. The faithful place their gifts before the Lord in the setting of the Supper, and they are thereby transformed to service of the world, now in service not of the church, but of the Kingdom, proleptically present within the worshiping congregation.

> Sec. 2. *The board of deacons shall serve those in distress and need. The deacons shall minister to the sick, the poor, the hurt, and the helpless, shall aid the victims of the world's abuse, and shall express the social concerns of the church. They shall oversee and carry out their work as those concerned with the redemption of humankind. Their focus is turned outward in service and ministry both to the world and in the church.*

In much of the church catholic, the deacons have performed a *liturgical* ministry. The Reformed view of the church, in contradistinction, has the deacon move outward from the liturgy in concern with the "redemption of humankind." This was clearly Calvin's understanding.[14] Here is clearly displayed the Reformed notion of the church active in the sanctification not of the person,

---

14 See Eugene P. Heideman, *Reformed Bishops and Catholic* (Grand Rapids: Eerdmans, 1970), p. 39.

but of the culture and society that shape the nature and lives of persons. The church is more than a "salvation cult." It turns outward not simply to call persons to Christ, but to call the surrounding world—in its government, business, education, cultural movements, etc.—to the evangelical demand to place primary care on the least and the last, the broken and the maimed.

A board of deacons that takes this commission seriously will engage in more than assisting a family that has lost a home to a fire, or an impoverished woman down on her luck. It will engage its thought and effort in an entire range of works of mercy: assisting the homeless, providing space for twelve-step programs, feeding hungry people, encouraging quality health care for all sorts and conditions. The task is overwhelming. But a board so engaged will turn a congregation into a full locus of mission.

Nor is the board restricted to acts of mercy. Its expression of a church's social concerns will turn toward acts of prophecy as well. It can assist the church as it speaks to those in power, be it in government or in business. If, for example, a congregation holds invested funds, the board can influence those corporations in which it is invested toward shaping their policies to the demands of the gospel. A local congregation may, under appropriate conditions, speak to issues before a local school board or planning board.

> Sec. 3. *The board of deacons shall keep minutes of its meetings when it meets at stated times for the carrying out of its ministry. A majority of the deacons regularly convened shall constitute a quorum for the transaction of business. The meetings shall begin and end with prayer. The board shall render an account in consistory of its ministry, including its collection and distribution of the benevolence contributions of the congregation.*

The work of the deacons is as crucial as that of the elders (although rarely granted this place of importance in the practice of Reformed churches) and thus is enjoined to meet at stated times for the performance of its task. Further, the order requires as much care in its meetings, confers the same injunction that their work be done as a gathered body, and builds in accountability to the congregation as the deacons report their work to the entire consistory—the body that expresses the full ministry of the church in the gathering of all the offices.

Article 7. Union Churches

Sec. 1. *Particular churches of this church may unite to form union churches with one or more particular churches of other reformed bodies, with the approval of the classis.*

The order expresses the Reformed commitment to ecumenism in its most pointed form as it grants provision that a local church can enter organic union with a local church not of this particular denomination. This section is clear that such union is allowed with a church of a "reformed body." Although this section does not further specify, the order itself presumes that a reformed body will exhibit an analogous order. One might venture to add that a reformed body will share the RCA's constitutional commitment to the extent that the other church coheres with the theological understanding as articulated the *Standards* and expressed in the *Liturgy*.

The provision for union churches gives flexibility to the churches for ministry. They have found expression often in rural areas, where the maintenance of individual congregations is difficult, and in urban areas where particular ethnic ties bind smaller congregations or in circumstances where the union of congregations serves the ministry of Christ.

The order is careful, however, that such unions not be entered hastily, but with the concurrence of the greater church through the classis. Thus the entire church involves itself in ministry in its local expression.

Sec. 2. *The following Plan of Union shall be adopted by the union church so formed:*

a. *The following Plan of Union is adopted by the _____Reformed Church of_____, effective as of the date when each of the congregations have approved the plan by a two-thirds majority of those present at a regularly called congregational meeting with such notice and quorum as is required by the constitution of each church, and when the classis (presbytery) of jurisdiction of each church has approved the particular union and this Plan of Union.*

So cautious is the order in the case of union that it prescribes in detail the plan of union that must be entered both by the congregation in the RCA and the other congregation. Furthermore, approval requires not only a super-majority of each congregation entering the union, but the approval of the appropriate body of jurisdiction for both churches.

b. *The purpose of this union is to provide for the worship of Almighty God and instruction in the Christian religion by a united congregation which will share the property, real and personal, of the uniting churches and provide for the services of a minister or ministers for the united church.*

A union church intends to strengthen the ministry of Christ as expressed most centrally in worship. The real union—it becomes one in possession of the mutual assets of the congregations— serves to strengthen the purpose. Very often union enables the new entity to express fully the work of the local congregation where before it had been difficult or impossible.

c. *The united church shall be known as the Church of _____.*

d. *The united church shall be subject to the constitution of each church as set forth in subsections r, s, u, and v.*

One practical complication of becoming a united church is the attention required to the constitutional nature of the denominations under which it now exists. The sections noted will clarify how judicial matters are to be handled, and which denominational jurisdiction claims authority in matters of conflict or dispute.

> e. The consistory (session) of the united church shall submit its records annually, and whenever requested, to each assembly (judicatory) of jurisdiction.

This differs from the case of a consistory of an RCA congregation. In this case, the consistory must submit its record for annual inspection to *both* bodies charged with supervision of the local consistory.

> f. The membership of the united church shall consist of those who were members of the uniting churches, plus those received by the consistory (session) of the united church.

The members of the congregations remain members of the church. This is full organic union. In addition, the ruling body of the new congregation is empowered to receive new members. One interesting note, however, is that it is not the board of elders, but the consistory that receives the members into the union church.

> g. The consistory (session) of the united church shall report an equal share of the total membership to each assembly (judicatory) and jurisdiction, and such membership shall be published in the Acts and Proceedings (Minutes) of the general assembly, with a note to the effect that the report is that of a union church, and with an indication of the total actual membership. A similar report of church school enrollment, baptisms, etc., and financial expenditures shall be made by the consistory (session) and noted by each general assembly in its minutes.

While this provision appears to be clerical in nature, it expresses the reality that the congregation remains a body within both greater churches. It is and remains a *responsible* gathering of believers.

> h. *Initially the officers of the united church, elders and deacons, shall be those officers in active service of the united churches, who will undertake to perform their ordination responsibilities under the constitution of each church, as indicated in subsections d above, and r, s, u, and v below.*

> i. *At the first annual meeting subsequent to the effective date of the union, new classes of officers, to replace the officers noted in subsection h above, shall be elected by the united congregation according to the constitutional procedure in force as a consequence of subsection v below.*

These subsections allow for the ordered leading of the congregation in accordance with Reformed order and provide a means by which the new ruling body will be elected.

> j. *The pastoral relations of the ministers of the uniting churches shall be dissolved automatically by the action of the classis (presbytery) of jurisdiction in approving this plan, but they may be eligible to be ministers (pastors or associate pastors) of the united church according to the will of the united congregation and subject to the approval of the classes (both the classis and the presbytery).*

The pastors of the uniting congregations do not per force become pastors of the new body. The pastoral relations must be dissolved and the new body may, but need not, call the pastor or pastors to become a minister of the new congregation. This provision clearly denotes that the union congregation is a new body, engaged in a fresh ministry. Furthermore, the requirement of approval by both supervising ecclesiastical bodies ensures that the greater church will be involved fully in the new ministry.

k. The minister/s of the united church shall be full and responsible members of each assembly (judicatory) of immediate jurisdiction and shall be subject to discipline as provided below in subsection s.

It is an ecclesiastical question of import that asks which communion will be "home" to the minister of the united congregation. This provision requires that both supervising jurisdictions accept the minister as a minister in full standing within that body. Thus the order ensures that the union will be a full ecclesiastical union. The question of discipline is handled below in subsection s.

l. The united church shall cause a corporation to be formed under the appropriate laws of the state where permissible. The corporation shall include in its articles or charter the substance of subsections b, c, and d above.

m. All property of the uniting churches, real and personal, shall be transferred to the corporation formed in subsection l above, The new corporation shall be the legal successor of the corporations, if any, of the uniting churches, and it shall be bound to administer any trust property or moneys received in accordance with the provisions of the original establishment of the trust. All liabilities of the uniting churches shall be liabilities of the united church. In any state where a church corporation is forbidden, the purposes of this subsection shall be achieved in harmony with the law of that state.

n. Trustees of the corporation (or unincorporated body) shall be elected in harmony with civil law according to the constitutional provisions outlined in subection d above, as interpreted by subsection v below.

These subsections ensure that the new body will exhibit appropriate responsibility to its predecessor bodies, and that it can function as a fully constituted body responsible to the civil requirements. In distinction from an RCA congregation, this subsection requires a board of trustees (although that board, if in conformity to subsection v, may be the consistory of the united church).

> *o. While recognizing the basic right of any giver to designate the cause or causes to which the gift shall go, the consistory (session) of the united church shall annually propose to the congregation a general mission or benevolence program which shall be divided equitably among the officially approved causes of each denomination. The proportions shall be as the consistory (session) shall decide in response to the request of the higher assemblies (judicatories).*

The united church is required to honor its membership in both denominations through an equitable benevolent posture to both. However, this provision places on the united church a requirement absent for RCA congregations. Nowhere are RCA consistories required to propose a benevolent budget to the congregation for approval. Nor are RCA congregations bound to "officially approved causes." United churches appear to stand under a greater burden.

> *p. Per capita apportionments or assessments shall be paid to each classis (presbytery) of jurisdiction on the basis of the total communicant membership of the union church, equally divided among the denominations involved.*

This subsection intends that a united church will not be overburdened in its financial obligation to the greater church, but shall participate in a fair manner. However, this is a curious addition to church order. Nowhere does the order note that apportionments or assessments need be made on a per capita basis. A classis, for example, may raise funds on which it is assessed in any manner it deems appropriate.

> *q. All members of the united church shall be under the discipline of the board of elders (session) according to rules agreed upon in harmony with the constitution of each denomination*

> *where they coincide, and in harmony with the mandatory provisions of the constitution of the one denomination where the others are permissive, and at the choice of the board of elders (session) where they may be contradictory.*

This provision clarifies how discipline will be handled in the united congregation. It will be incumbent upon the uniting body to determine how its discipline is shaped in accordance with this rule.

> *r. Appeals or complaints against the actions of the consistory (session) shall be made to one assembly or judicatory only (presbytery or classis) at the choice of the members, and all subsequent appeals or complaints shall be in the courts of the members' original choice, and the decisions so finally made shall be binding on the consistory (session) and on the members.*

Judicial procedures shall be followed in only one denomination, that choice being made by the one making the complaint or appeal. However, the complainant (or appellant) cannot change the rules in the middle of the game as she or he might be tempted by an adverse ruling. Thus, this provision clarifies the route of judicial redress.

> *s. The minister/s shall be subject to the discipline of the classes (presbytery and classis) provided that when either shall begin an action, it shall invite a committee from the others to join the commissioner, prosecutor, or prosecuting committee in formulating and pressing the charges. In the event of appeal the case shall be finally decided by the highest court to which the appeal is taken in the church which commenced the action, and that decision shall be equally binding on the classes (both presbytery and the classis).*

In contrast with members, the minister is subject to both supervising ecclesiastical bodies. She or he is a member of both and thus subject to a dual discipline; however, the order provides that discipline shall be handled jointly. As with the previous subsection, this provision clarifies that discipline will occur within one denomination.

> t. *The minister/s shall participate in the denominational pension plan of one of the churches. If already participating in a plan, the minister/s shall remain in that plan. If there has been no participation in a pension plan, the minister/s shall choose which denominational plan to join.*

> u. *Complaints against the administrative acts of the consistory (session) may be taken under the constitutional provisions of only one denomination, according to the choice of the complainant, and once being complained to one assembly (judicatory), no other denomination shall accept jurisdiction in the same matter.*

> v. *Wherever the constitutions of the denominations differ, the mandatory provisions of the one shall apply in all cases when the others are permissive. Wherever there are conflicting mandatory provisions (except as provided by subsection q above), the consistory (session) of the united church shall petition the assemblies (judicatories) of immediate jurisdiction to overture their respective highest courts to resolve the conflict either by authoritative interpretation or by constitutional amendment.*

This subsection addresses the possible inconsistency between the constitutions of the denominations. It provides a solution where mandatory provisions are present in one in contrast to permissive provisions in the other. However, in the case of conflict of mandatory provisions, the united church is required to petition both supervising assemblies to request a ruling, and that from the highest court in each denomination!

> w. A union church may be dissolved by a two-thirds vote of two congregational meetings, held not less than one year and not more than two years apart, subject to the concurrence of the classes (presbyteries) involved. In case of dissolution of a union church, all property of the united church, real and personal, shall be divided equally between the classes (presbytery and the classis) of jurisdiction.

A union church may come to an end, provided its congregation votes in accordance with the conditions of this subsection. However, this is not a return to the previous status of two separate congregations. The dissolution would be the end of the church's existence as a congregation. The property is not divided between the former congregations, but between the two greater churches in supervision of the united church.

> Sec. 3. No provision in this chapter shall be construed as modifying or amending the constitution of this church in its application to any but union churches organized under this chapter, their members, officers, or ministers.

The addition of this section makes clear that Article 7 delimits a special case. One cannot derive church order principles from provisions under this article that thereby transfer to other congregations within the RCA. This article builds flexibility into the order for the sake of Christ's ministry. In those places where modification is made to the order, it is done so only as an exception and for the sake of ministry in those particular places so allowed by the relevant classis.

3

The Classis

As maintained, the order of the Reformed Church in America centers on the various assemblies. The order supposes a certain horizontal relationship between the assemblies as it clearly adumbrates their responsibilities and authority. The "greater" assemblies intervene in the life of the "lesser" only at those points prescribed by the order. Nonetheless, the classis exists, on the one hand, as the central assembly, and on the other hand as perhaps the most powerful assembly. The locus of the classis in Reformed thinking is perhaps best described by Explanatory Article 38:

> The Reformed Dutch Church holds the middle station between two extremes. On the one hand, she denies all superiority of one Minister of Christ over another; and on the other, considers independent, unconnected congregations, as unsafe and inconvenient. In order therefore to unite both council and energy for the promotion of the spiritual interests of the church, consistent with the liberty and dignity of the Gospel Dispensation, her government is administered by Classes and Synods....In

this Assembly, an immediate representation of all the churches within those limits is formed; and a power of regulating the common measures for promoting religion, preventing error, and preserving peace within such district is lodged...

The gathering of churches into classes began with the French Reformed, who thereby instituted the *presbyterial system* (and thus expanded on the consistorial system of Geneva), and was imported into the Dutch church at the Synod of Wesel, 1568. This was a church in formation (or re-formation), and since it required an authority beyond the local congregation for the maintenance of good order, it needed to replace the hierarchical system from which it was turning. This happened, in part, through the assistance of neighboring congregations. Furthermore, since the only offices remaining in the church were those centered in the gathered congregation itself, it could not rely upon an office to function as ecclesiastical authority. The classis, then, performed that function.

The presbyterial system offered a number of advantages. First, the church was understood as a *local* expression. The church did not subsist in bishops, in an office often distant from the local community. The church existed as it was called into existence by Christ through Word and around Table. That happened in the local congregation where the offices existed to represent Christ's leading that emerged from pulpit and table.

Second, the classis preserved the horizontal nature of ministry and inoculated the church from clericalism. The classis existed only as the offices of minister and elder, equal in standing, *gathered* to exercise ministry.

Third, the classis was itself local, as it gathered representatives from neighboring churches. At the same time it prevented the local church from assuming to itself all power. The classis reminded the local congregation that it lives in communion with other congregations.

Article 1. Classis Defined

*The classis is an assembly consisting of all the enrolled
ministers of that body and the elder delegates who represent
all the churches within its bounds. The classis is a permanent,
continuing body which functions between stated session
through committees. Voting rights shall be limited to elder
delegates and those enrolled ministers who are actively
serving as ministers either under the jurisdiction of or with the
approval of the classis.*

Common parlance derives the word "classis" from the same
Latin word that means "fleet" (or, if you will "army") and goes on
to describe the classis as a fleet of churches. The church order of
Dort supports that notion by describing the classis as "composed
of neighboring churches"[1] That changed, however, with the
Explanatory Articles, which maintained that a classis consists of "all
the Ministers, with each an Elder, and one Elder from every vacant
congregation within a particular district" (Art. XXXVIII). The
classis is *not* the churches gathered, but officers *from* the churches
gathered. Thus it becomes an ecclesiastical assembly.

Nor does the classis consist of *only* those officers who represent
local congregations. In fact, the minister does not represent a
congregation, but is a minister of and within the classis by virtue of
his or her declaration of the formulary for ministers of Word and
sacrament (Form. 3) within that classis. Elders are delegates who
represent the various congregations or consistories within the
bounds of the classis. Thus, while in principle the classis consists of
equal numbers of ministers and elders, in fact, a classis may have
more ministers than elders (the obverse is also possible).

The classis is a "permanent, continuing body." That has not
always been so. Until the twentieth century, a classis existed as an
assembly only while it met. It would elect a president each time. One

---

1   "Articles of Dort, 1619," Article LXI, in Corwin, hereinafter cited in the text as *Dort*
    with article.

of the president's tasks was the calling of the following gathering. That has changed. The body now exists between sessions in the body of its committees. Although the order does not and should not prescribe a committee structure for a classis (or any other assembly), this article seems to suggest that a classis will need at least one committee. Most often that occurs through a provision for an executive committee. The power and authority granted to that or any other committee is left to the wisdom of the classis.

"Voting rights" has presented a puzzle to a number of classes. The article is clear in the case of elder delegates; the elder must be authorized by the local consistory. However, which ministers may vote? The article states that only ministers "who are actively serving" may vote. The question turns on the phrase "actively serving." Some classes, especially those with a large number of retired ministers on their rolls, interpret that to mean that the minister must be installed in a local congregation, serve as a minister under contract, or serve in a specialized ministry. Otherwise, such is the fear, retired ministers may form a voting interest that outweighs that of those "active" in ministry. Other classes interpret "active" much more broadly. A minister is active who actively ministers! That is, he or she engages in the ministry of Word and sacrament in some form. The order is not univocal on this matter and thus it may be inferred that the determination is left to each classis.

At the same time, the order is explicit that ministers who serve actively are only those who do so under the jurisdiction or with the approval of the classis. The provision thus expresses the classis's responsibility for its ministers. Ministers may be enrolled who are engaged in a secular occupation that does not meet the requirements for specialized ministry, and who do not function in the office. Such ministers do not retain the privilege to vote.

Article 2. Responsibilities of the Classis

Sec. 1. *The classis shall exercise a general superintendence*

over its enrolled ministers and over the interests and concerns
of the churches within its bounds, and shall enforce the
requirements of the Government of the Reformed Church in
America.

The order will describe in detail the superintendence of ministers
and churches. However, "general superintendence" remains a
broad category and is open to misunderstanding. Just when and
how may a classis involve itself in the life of its congregations?
General principles of Reformed order would hold that the "greater"
body should not intervene at will in those matters for which
consistories are competent and to which they have been granted
explicit authority. On the other hand, classes remain responsible for
the life and ministry of the local church. Sadly, and sufficiently
often, instances arise when congregations, consistories, and ministers
find themselves in conflict. The classis is charged with responsibility.
How shall that responsibility be exercised? Classes do well to devise
ordered procedures for intervention that respect the integrity of the
congregation even as they allow the classis to lend appropriate
assistance. When classical by-laws include such procedures, they
provide minister, congregation, consistory, and classis with clarity
within mutual accountability.

Remarkably, the order gives the classis the responsibility to
enforce the requirements of the *Government.* When a local consistory
or minister violates the government, the classis is fully within its
authority to intervene. A local consistory cannot plead independence.
It stands accountable to the greater church for its life and action.

Sec. 2. *The classis shall exercise original and appellate
supervisory power over the acts, proceedings, and decisions
of the boards of elders and consistories, both in temporal
matters and in those relating to church discipline.*

Original supervisory power indicates that the classis is the "first
court" to which consistories and boards of elders are responsible.
A classis may nullify an action that a consistory takes when, for

example, it financially encumbers its property without receiving the necessary approval of the classis. The presbyterial system discloses its power at just this point. Consistories and boards of elders live under the broader authority of the classis. The classis, of course, does not intervene simply because it may disagree with a decision of a particular consistory. The classis must show that the lesser body has in some manner fundamentally violated a Reformed understanding of the church. In any case, the consistory or board of elders retains the right of redress to a "higher court," in this case the regional synod.

Appellate supervisory power indicates that the classis is the court to which consistories or boards of elders addresses a complaint against an action of an assembly or an appeal against discipline in a board of elders. The procedures for complain and appeal will be discussed under the *Disciplinary Procedures.*

> Sec. 3. *The classis shall form, dissolve, and disband churches, and shall form or dissolve combinations of two or more churches.*

A classis *alone* is granted the power to form and dissolve churches. While current practice often has regional synods perform the "legwork" of gathering congregations, only the classis can constitute the congregation. This preserves the integrity of the congregation in communion not with the "greater church" but with neighboring congregations. The congregation is, at its outset, a manifestation of the greater church locally expressed.

Clearly, the local church does not have the authority either to form itself nor to disband itself. The Reformed order is of a *presbyterial* polity. That is, congregations cannot birth themselves. A congregation emerges from the action of God and cannot presume to organize itself. Of course, the classis itself can no more presume God's action to itself than the congregation. However, presbyterial polity asserts that congregations emerge from the life of the church. The classis as gathered offices signals that the congregation lives from its head, that is, from the Christ who calls it into being.

The procedure for forming and dissolving churches will be detailed in Section 7.

> Sec. 4. *The classis shall have the authority to transfer a local church to another denomination, together with all or part of its real and personal property.*

> Sec. 5. *The classis shall have the authority to receive under its jurisdiction as a local church, any congregation signifying such desire.*

The local church *cannot* reserve to itself the ability to transfer itself to another denomination, nor does the church retain authority over either its real *or* personal property. The local church exists in and of itself—it is the locus where the Word calls together a people—and at the same time subsists only in relationship with the entire church. The greater church does not work from a distance. It exists in the presence of the neighboring churches. In their persons, the officers of neighboring churches will know the circumstances, the members, and the officers of a congregation in question. This is one place, among others, where the classis mediates between centralism and localism.

Conversely, the classis alone can receive a local church under its jurisdiction. While in theory one could imagine a greater assembly doing so, the local church exists within the context of neighboring churches; the classis is the "closest" body and thus most capable of judging the circumstances of a church's application. At the same time, the principle by which Reformed order works, whereby assemblies are grouped by geographic proximity, augers that for a greater body to rule in this case would be to "jump lines." The Reformed Church has not, as a rule, maintained non-geographical jurisdictions.

> Sec. 6. *The classis shall exercise general supervision over all students of theology subject to its jurisdiction.*

> Sec. 7. *The classis shall examine students of theology for licensure, and licensed candidates for the ministry for ordination. If individual members of the classis find that their consciences, as illuminated by Scripture, would not permit them to participate in the licensure, ordination, or installation of women as ministers, they shall not be required to participate in decisions or actions contrary to their consciences, but may not obstruct the classis in fulfilling its responsibility to arrange for the care, ordination, and installation of women candidates and ministers by means mutually agreed upon by such women and the classis.*

> Sec. 8. *The classis shall ordain, install, transfer, suspend, depose, declare demitted, declare inactive, and declare retired ministers.*

The authority to ordain to ministry defines a locus of power within the broader church. In the Reformed churches, this power is divided between the local consistory, which is granted the power to ordain to the offices of deacon and elder, and the classis, which alone may ordain ministers. It is crucial to retain such a distinction lest the Reformed degenerate into a type of clericalism always too near the surface.

Still, it must be admitted that in a very real sense, the Reformed have centered on the ministry of Word and sacrament both historically and theologically. Understanding that the Word creates and sustains the church, the Reformed have understandably taken great care as to whom should be granted the privilege of the pulpit.

The matter begins with the care of candidates for the office of ministry, named here "students of theology." The order's description of this task will be described in Article 8. Here it may be noted that while the classis exercises a general supervision, the General Synod shares this responsibility both by overseeing theological seminaries and by electing persons to the office of professor of theology. Nonetheless, as the final decision to ordain remains with the classis, the greater power, and, one might add, the greater responsibility, remains with it.

The authority to examine by the classis alone is relatively recent in Reformed order. The Explanatory Articles provided that the particular synods retained the power to examine and to license candidates for ministry. The power was shared with the classes (Exp. Art., XLVII). That power had dropped out by the 1833 constitution; however, a provision remained from the Dort order that required a synodical *deputatus* to represent the synod, and thus the greater church, at each examination.[2] The examination of the candidate was of such importance to the greater church that the responsibility was, at least symbolically, shared. By the 1874 constitution that provision had been dropped. Henceforward, the power to admit persons to the pulpit has remained the prerogative of the classis.

As with the offices of elder and deacon (see p. 86), the order includes a "conscience clause" concerning the ordination of women to the office of minister. Here the clause applies to individual members of the classis. Those conscientiously opposed, by virtue of their understanding of Scripture (and that alone), are released from participation in licensure, ordination, or installation of women as ministers. They may not obstruct or, as one might infer, cause to be obstructed the ordination of women. One can easily envisage problems in classes where a large number of members can appeal to this clause. In that case, the classis is obliged to make appropriate arrangements to which both the classis and the women in question must agree. The shape of those arrangements is left to the parties noted. One could suggest that in certain circumstances another classis may be involved, especially since the order provides for the cooperation of classes in ordinary circumstances (p. 156ff.).

Ministers are not only members of the classis as an assembly. Their ecclesiastical identity *as* ministers, as those ordained, resides

---

2   Dort, XLIX, and the "Constitution of 1833," Chapter II, Article IV, Section 4, in Corwin, hereinafter cited in the text as "1833" with chapter, article, and section.

within this assembly. Nor are they only responsible to it; the classis itself determines their ecclesiastical relationship. There is little room for an individualism that expresses itself in concern for one's own career within the church. The minister is called by God, through the Spirit, as expressed within the configuration of the church. Thus the *church* must act on a minister's particular standing, from ordination to "retirement." While a request to approve an installation comes from a consistory and a request to transfer, to be demitted, or to be "retired" comes from an individual, the classis must make the appropriate declaration in each case.

Sec. 9. *The classis shall approve and disapprove all calls, and effect and dissolve the relationship between ministers and churches.*

By Reformed order, a local church *calls* a minister to its service. We have seen that the provision of a minister is a primary responsibility of the consistory—the offices of deacon and elder gathered as a body. The order assumes the work of God's Spirit not only through the offices, but through the members of the congregation whose advice the consistory seeks. However, the presbyterial system adds the approval of the classis. So crucial was the confirmation of the greater body that Wesel, anticipating the formation of classes, advised that until classes were constituted, the approval of ministers and elders of other churches was prescribed (Wesel, II, 3). By the Dordrecht synod of 1574, the approval of the classes or three neighboring churches was required (Dordrecht, 1574, XII).

At issue is both the protection of the congregation and the welfare of the church. A congregation can become so enamored of a candidate or so desperate to fill its pulpit that it overlooks danger signals. The classis is able to be more dispassionate in its care for the welfare of the congregation.

But classis does more. The relation between a minister and congregation is not simply contractual. A peculiar bond is effected when a classis declares, in the service of installation, the pastoral relationship between the minister and the congregation to be constituted. So firm is that relationship that it cannot be broken without a stated procedure and without the action of the classis.

In this way, too, the minister is not an "independent operator." She lives and ministers within the church, not at the direct behest of an ecclesiastical authority, but in an ordered relationship within it. At issue is the ministry of the church, not the career of an individual.

> Sec.10. *The classis shall exercise all ecclesiastical functions in accordance with the* Government of the Reformed Church in America *which are not specifically delegated to other assemblies.*

This catch-all clause was added with the major revision of the *BCO* in 1968. Could situations arise where provision had not been made for an assembly to take appropriate responsibility? Certainly no order, no set of legal regulations, can cover all eventualities. In any case, this section gives to the classis powers not given to any other assembly. Not even the General Synod can assume to itself the privilege of entering ecclesiastical areas that are not specifically granted to it. This provision continues the Reformed concern that the greater power not reside at the level of the governance of the entire church. At the same time, it protects against a congregational polity that would grant to the local expression of the church too great an authority. The governance of the church remains close to that place where the Word is preached and the sacraments performed, but it does not finally devolve to either the congregation or even its consistory.

Article 3. Elder Delegates

> Sec. 1. *A church with three hundred or fewer confessing members shall have one elder delegate, and an elder delegate*

for each additional three hundred confession members or fraction thereof. A church shall not have more than four such elder delegates. A church without an installed minister shall have an elder delegate who shall not be counted as one of the above delegates. A collegiate church shall have at least one elder delegate for each of its constituent congregations.

Sec. 2. The congregation in a multiple parish may take turns sending to classis one or more additional elder delegates so that the number of minister and elder delegates is at least twice the number of such congregations.

Sec. 3. The elder delegate to classis shall be chosen from the entire body of elders in a church, whether or not presently a member of the board of elders.

The order is careful that congregations be privileged to possess sufficient representation to that configuration of the greater church to which they are most intimately connected and to which they are most directly responsible. Larger churches are granted a greater number of elder delegates. Multiple parishes, most of the time served by one minister, are granted an additional delegate, as are churches without an installed minister. By taking this sort of care, the order assures that the classis is an ecclesiastical body, indeed a *presbyterial* (consisting of presbyters or elders) body, and not a *clerical* synod.

Because elders remain officers even when not actively serving a consistory, they are eligible to serve as representatives to the classis. This permissive clause makes clear, however, that an elder does not simply represent the interests of the local congregation. She or he sits in classis as an officer of the church, as one who acts as one who represents Christ, the head of the church.

Sec. 4. The elder delegate shall be a member of classis from the date of election or appointment and shall continue in that responsibility to classis until the effective date or appointment of a successor. If, however, confessing membership in the church represented shall be terminated during the period of appointment, the delegate shall cease to be a member of the classis.

The classis was defined as a "permanent, continuing body." We have seen that it bears particularly broad and crucial responsibilities in the governance of the church. It will thus require a peculiar commitment of officers who bear primary responsibilities in other areas of church life. It is crucial, therefore, from a practical perspective, that the members of the classis be available for the ongoing work of the classis between its sessions. This could not happen if elder delegates were themselves not members for a particular term.

But another practical and ecclesiastical reason presses. If the classis is to be a body in which the office of elder is more than a symbolic presence, it will require elders who commit themselves to this peculiar work of the greater church. The office of the elder brings not only a peculiar but an essential presence to the classis. It is thus advisable that the church enjoy the leadership of the elder in the classis, a possibility that can only be strengthened by term of service.

Article 4. Sessions of Classis

Sec. 1 *Stated sessions of classis shall be held at least annually at such times as the classis may determine. All classis sessions shall begin and end with prayer. There shall be a sermon preached, or a devotional service, or both, at each stated session. The presence of a majority of the elder delegates and a majority of those ministers who are actively serving in ministries under the jurisdiction of the classis is required.*

Stated sessions are those meetings set at a regularly recurring configuration of dates. The classis knows that it will meet on, say, the third Tuesday of September. This replaces an old practice when the classis would set its next meeting at the end of each session. The rule of order of a classis may prescribe the agenda for each stated session. The intention and general practice is for the classis to conduct the full range of its business at the stated sessions. Just so, the offices gather regularly. The classis is not an occasional body that functions only when the need arises. This is especially crucial for a church that forswears a hierarchy, for no office subsists on its own to execute necessary ecclesiastical functions.

The order then requires a classis to establish its stated sessions. The order generally does not state what must happen in any or each session (with the exception that the president of the classis must place a set of inquiries to ministers and elder delegates, p. 121). It is of interest that through the order of Dort, each classis was to have held a *censura morum*, an inquiry whether any member of the assembly had been guilty of censurable conduct within the assembly, or had "despised the admonitions of the lesser Judicatories" (Dort, XLIII). The classis was exercising its supervisory function.

The classis expresses Christ's leading of the church. It is not a simple administrative body; rather, its administrative functions are themselves spiritual. The body thus lives out of service to its Lord, the central cultic expression of which is worship. The order confirms this reality by requiring a classis to live within the context of worship. The provision is elastic. A classis need not begin with a full service of the Word; a sermon is permitted but not required. On the other hand, the provision appears to allow that little more than a sermon occur.

The order further requires a certain number of delegates and ministers be present for the conducting of business. This section avoids the term "quorum." A classis cannot revert to "quorum calls" and the like. The order simply states that a majority of *both* elder delegates and ministers actively serving is required. The classis is a *gathered* body; it cannot subsist in the presence of a minority of its officers. That is not to say that a classis cannot empower a lesser number to act in the stead of the classis on a particular occasion. However, even then it is the full body that grants a particular power in discrete circumstances. Many classes provide for a particular committee to act on the approval of calls and transfers of ministers. Those sorts of demands arise between sessions, require the action of the classis, but in many cases would require little more than a formal approval. The classis places its power in the hands of its committee.

> Sec. 2. *The president of classis shall call a special session of classis whenever special business requires it or upon the written request of two ministers and two elder delegates. At least ten days' notice of any special session shall be given to all the ministers and elder delegates of the classis. The notice shall state the purpose of the special session. The presence of three ministers and three elder delegates shall constitute a quorum to transact the business stated in the notice of such special session.*

Occasions will present themselves when a classis will need to transact business outside times set aside for stated sessions. Installations, approvals of calls, and the like occur at a variety of times. An emergency situation within a church or the need for a classis to take disciplinary action also will demand immediate attention. The order prescribes two means for the calling of the special session. The most common case has the president call a special meeting. The initiative can also come from members of the classis itself, although at least four officers, two ministers and two elders, must be convinced of the need for a special meeting.

Because a special meeting is not a stated session, and because the classis is the full gathering of the officers, the order requires that sufficient notice be given to ministers and elder delegates. The work of the classis is thus done fully together and in full openness. The notice shall state the purpose of the session, and the session shall transact only that business for which the session has been called.

In this case, the order states the minimum necessary for a quorum. The number is not arbitrarily chosen. Reformed order maintained that three ministers and three elders was the minimum to constitute a classis. Albany Classis, for example, attempted to start a new classis in Upper Canada in the early nineteenth century but could not do so because it could not install three ministers in the Canadian churches. One could not a classis make; that would be an individual. Two would build no more than a bipolar relation. Three begins to shape community. The classis is a communion, reflective of the communal, or covenantal, nature of the church so cherished by both Reformed theology and ethos.

Article 5. Officers of Classis

> Sec. 1. *The president shall preside at classis sessions. It shall be the duty of the president to state and explain the business to be transacted, to enforce the rules of order, and, in general, to maintain the decorum and dignity belonging to the church of Jesus Christ.*

Reformed order does not grant ruling authority to a person but always to gathered bodies; nonetheless, those bodies cannot be leaderless. The order provides for two "officers" but clearly limits their function and power.

The president's role is to help the body carry out its function. The president may express other roles. She or he may act in the name of the classis in an installation or ordination, for example, or bring the presence and the greeting of the classis to another ecclesiastical body. The president is not, however, an executive officer, charged with conducting the business of the classis between sessions or executing its decisions. Her primary function remains presenting and conducting the business of the classis as it meets.

A further task of the president is noted elsewhere in the order (p. 218). The president must prepare a "state of religion" report that reflects on the how the churches fare, on the state of the faith, and indeed on nothing less than the state of "religion" (see comments there).

> Sec. 2. *The classis shall have a clerk whose duty shall be to keep a faithful record of all the proceedings of the body, and to furnish official notices in writing to all who are directly affected by judicial decisions of the classis. The clerk shall also be responsible for forwarding to the denominational archives copies of minutes of the classis and subsidiary corporations, all papers pertaining to disbanded churches, and all papers of the classis should the classis disband.*

The weight of responsibility given to the classes and the attention those responsibilities require has increased the role of the clerk (usually called "stated clerk") to the point that all classes have made this a paid position, and some classes employ a full-time clerk. Clerks have become, de facto, the closest thing that a classis has to an executive officer. Still, their role remains circumscribed within the order. The clerk plays no ecclesiastical role beyond careful attention to the record. One will note, however, that the *Disciplinary Procedures* will both require and presuppose that the clerk plays a major role in coordinating the work of the classis and in keeping the classis mindful of its task within the framework set for it by the *Government*.

One of the few tasks explicitly enjoined upon the clerk involves the archival record of the classis and its churches. As an institutional communion, as a covenantal body, the church maintains its peculiar memory. The greater church provides archival resources beyond the capability of any particular classis. Thus, the classis deposits its record in a central "memory bank."

Article 6. Transaction of Business

> Sec. 1. *The classis shall be guided in its transaction of business by such rules of order as it shall adopt from time to time, and which are in accord with the* Government of the Reformed

Church in America. If state laws permit, the classis shall be incorporated.

The order enjoins the classis as a responsible and institutional body to adopt rules of order. The particular shape of those rules is left to the classis as an autonomous body. It is not and cannot be the intention of the church order to prescribe how the classis executes its responsibilities. Subsidiary committees and commissions exist only in their relationship to the assembly in question. Nonetheless, proper order and open and fair dealing for the members of the body and the local churches demand that a set of rules exist that outline how the body functions. Those rules define the contours of the body. One naturally expects that they will follow the contours of the church order, as they will institute how the classis caries out the responsibilities set out in Article 2 and detailed in further articles in this part of the order.

The classis will exist as a legal body. That is, it may from time to time own real property, hold assets, and make decisions that affect the lives and institutions within its bounds. For that reason, it is not only advisable but necessary that it constitute itself as a legal corporation able to transact business in the civic context within which it lives and works. This section is consistent with the Reformed notion that God's purpose does not begin and end with individual persons, nor with the church, but that it serves a kingdom that includes societies and cultures. The church lives within a broader society.

Sec. 2. *A member of classis shall not have the right to protest against any act or decision of that body, but shall have the right to redress by appeal or complaint. Any member of classis shall also have the right to request that the names of all classis members, with their votes for or against a matter in question, be recorded in the minutes of the classis for the information of all; however, that request may be denied by a two-thirds majority of the classis.*

See the comments on the parallel section under consistory (above, pp. 76-77).

Sec. 3. *Only duly accredited delegates to classis shall be entitled to vote.*

A particular classis meeting may consist of a greater number of persons than those granted the vote. A classis often will grant corresponding status to visitors, representatives from other ecclesiastical bodies, candidates for ministry, and others. Ministers whom the classis has determined are not in active ministry (Article 1 above) may also be present. An elder may be present who is not delegated by her consistory. In many cases, the question of vote may be of little consequence. However, care needs to be taken for two reasons. First, all actions of the classis may be reviewed by a higher body which may vacate a vote where unauthorized delegates have participated. Second, certain votes—one thinks especially of disciplinary matters—are so sensitive that only authorized members of the body should vote.

Sec. 4. *Except as otherwise provided in the* Book of Church Order, *membership on classis committees, commissions, or boards shall be open to all confessing members of the churches in the classis.*

This section was recently (1994) added to the order to allow those other than elders and ministers to serve on bodies responsible to the classis. It was maintained that gifts for the ministry are not limited to those ordained to office. This expands the classis's ability to execute its functions and expresses a broader understanding of the church. It needs to be remembered, however, that the classis in a Reformed order is a gathering of offices—elders and ministers—and it alone can take responsibility for its functions.

The exceptions mentioned generally have to do with disciplinary matters. Elders and ministers alone are ordained to exercise discipline. Thus, the classis will need to take special care in selecting committees charged with judicial business, the oversight of its ministers, and its decisions not only in cases of ordination but all matters outlined under Article 2, Section 8, of this chapter.

> Sec. 5. *The privilege of the floor shall be extended to Associates in Ministry under the supervision of the classis, provided, however, that they shall have no vote.*

Associates in ministry is a new category in the order, introduced in 1994. Associates in ministry are Christian educators who meet a set of criteria established by the church and certified by the classis (Article 14 below). They are not members of the classis; they are not officers in the church. However, they contribute to the ministry of the church and are granted a subsidiary place within the classis. They are granted the right to speak, but they cannot participate in decisions through vote.

Article 7. Superintendence of the Churches

> Sec. 1. *The president of the classis, at the same meeting at which delegates to the synods are appointed, shall address the following inquiries to the ministers and elder delegates of each church. The answers shall be entered into the minutes of classis for the information of the synods:*

The constitutional inquiry, or "consistorial questions" as the process is known colloquially, has a long history in Reformed order and expresses the care of the greater church for the life of its congregations. The questions crystallize what the church considers most important in the ongoing, yearly life of the local church. Already in the Dort order of 1578, the *praeses* of the classis was to ask whether the customary discipline was practiced, heresy and doubt countered, the poor and the schools given proper attention, the governing body (the consistory) of the local church brought help and advice, and "other similar matters."[3]

---

3 "Acta" of the National Synod at Dordrecht, 1578, Article XXIX, in Kerkelyk Handboekje, hereinafter cited in the text as Dordrecht, 1578 with article.

It should be noted that the classis places *questions* before the ministers and elders. While the questions presuppose an expectation laid upon the churches, this is not a sort of moral policing of the churches. A consistory may have valid reasons for a "no" answer on a particular question, one that the classis takes into account. It remains the responsibility and prerogative of the classis to respond in the manner it deems wise. The questions provide opportunity for the classis to catch problems aborning and subsequently to enter into conversation with a local church.

The questions, then, provide a way by which the local church lives in responsibility to the greater church and through which the classis can exercise proper pastoral authority over its congregations.

> *a. Are the doctrines of the gospel preached in your church in their purity in conformity with*
>
> > *i. the Word of God?*
> >
> > *ii. the* Standards *of the Reformed Church in America?*

The honor of place belongs to the centrality of the Word in a Reformed church. The order thus incorporates the first mark of the church in the supervision of the local church. However, the question asks about doctrine. The Reformed congregation gathers within the *school* of the gospel; it is not only called into existence by the Word, its life is shaped by the teaching the Word intends as it shapes not only the lives of the believers but of the congregation itself.

That doctrine is measured, first, by the Word. The vocabulary here discloses an ambiguity. Many contemporary readers will assume that the "Word" is an equivalent for "Scripture." Indeed, the history of Reformed doctrine grants Scripture the honor of the term Word. However, "Word" first and primarily denotes the second person of the Trinity. Are the doctrines preached in conformity to Christ? One might then legitimately continue by recognizing that the "Word" also but subsequently refers to Scripture as the disclosive revelation of Christ. Scripture mediates Christ to the church.

But the order adduces a parallel norm, the *Standards*. The church acknowledges that its confessional documents cannot claim the authority of Scripture. To do so would be to contradict the confessions themselves. Still, Reformed churches have always recognized the *Standards* as the proper hermeneutic, or key, to the understanding of Scripture. Otherwise the congregation is left to the confusion of Scripture's multilayered and many-faceted witness.

A preacher, in responsibility to Christ through the church, is not free to ignore or abandon the interpretive key of the *Standards,* especially not on the strength of his or her own discovery. To do so would not only sow confusion, it would betray the covenantal understanding of the church as living out of the Word, together.

When the Netherlands Reformed Church developed its new church order following World War II, it used two metaphors that are helpful for our understanding of the place of the confessions. Its article on the confession of the church began: "In thankful obedience to the Holy Scripture as the source of preaching and the true rule of belief....and in *communion* with the confession of the fathers [and mothers]...."[4] Scripture remained the source; the church lived in communion with the confession of the forbears. Thus, the church granted a place of honor to previous generations who have lived under Scripture without demanding agreement with them in every detail. A second metaphor stated that the church lived from the "soil" or stood on the "ground" of the confession. It is a lived faith from which the church, as an organic body, lives. The RCA's order articulates this slightly differently when it asks whether the doctrines preached are "in conformity with" the *Standards*. This is not to say that the preaching agrees in every detail, but that it is shaped within the coherence of a theological understanding articulated by the *Standards*.

4   Kerkorde, Article X, Section 1.

The questions place great responsibility on the elders who are to answer the question. It presupposes that elders are knowledgeable and articulate concerning the *Standards*. This further supposes that Reformed churches live within a system of catechesis in which the doctrines of the faith are not the preserve of the preachers but a common vocabulary of the church, in this case, in the office of elder. The elder, too, is to be theologically educated.

> *b. Are the points of doctrine contained in the* Heidelberg Catechism *explained in your church from time to time, as required by the* Government of the Reformed Church in America?

Catechesis is not simply a program for the education of youth, although the Reformed system of Christian education was originally centered on catechetical education; Sunday schools were a later and somewhat strange intrusion into Reformed life. The education in doctrine and life (for the Heidelberg especially educates on how one *lives* the faith) happens with adults.

The question neither asks nor demands that the catechism itself be taught, but that the points of doctrine be explained. It is to be noted that the "points of doctrine" at issue are those taught in the catechism; neither the Belgic Confession nor the Canons are mentioned. The preaching, then, would need to include the catechism's emphasis on sin, grace, and gratitude; on the Apostle's Creed; the Ten Commandments; and the Lord's Prayer.

This question frees a consistory from a rigid requirement. However, the Reformed church has constantly had to remind itself of the importance of this question. It cannot be assumed that the individual preacher, left to the dictates of conscientious exegesis of Scripture, will of his or her own *automatically* preach these doctrines. That would be again to deny the communal nature of a church that enjoys a covenantal relationship with the mothers and fathers in faith.

> *c. Is the education of the young people in the essential truths of the Word of God carried on by catechising, or is it*

otherwise faithfully attended to in your congregation?

The school of faith, as intended by the Reformed, begins with children. Indeed, Reformed theology of baptism supposes that children will be educated not to a conversion to the faith, but into the baptism through which they are already members of Christ and his church. The greater church asks whether this happens primarily through catechesis, but it also allows that other means may be used—one thinks of the institution and popularity of church schools.

> *d. Has the consistory prayerfully considered persons within the congregation, especially the young people, in order to identify with them their gifts for pastoral ministry, to encourage the development of these gifts, and to pray for those individuals on a regular basis?*

Added in 1996, this question intends the church to pay significant attention to the needs of pastoral ministry (by which is meant the ministry of Word and sacrament). The question supposes that a call to ministry is not an individual matter between God and the individual, but that it emerges from God's gathered people. Furthermore, the congregation participates in the call to ministry through spiritual encouragement.

> *e. Is care and visitation faithfully performed in your congregation by*
>
> > *i. elders?*
> >
> > *ii. deacons?*
> >
> > *iii. minister/s?*

Earlier versions asked whether visitation was faithfully performed by the minister. Elders and deacons were added, in accordance with their offices as outlined above (pp. 46-52). The greater church is not simply asking here about the program life of a congregation. It cares that a Reformed congregation understand itself in its mutual responsibility as a *communion* of faith. Reformed order expresses that through the ordered attention to the life of those gathered around Word and Table.

> *f. Does the board of elders fulfill the requirements contained in the* BCO, *Chapter 1, Part I, Article 5, Sections 3 and 4?*

The third mark of the church, according to the *Confession of Faith*, Article 29, is discipline. Discipline is not only out of favor in an individualistic age, but it is a difficult task, as any parent can testify. Boards of elders are tempted to forgo the task. Thus the classis asks to remind the local church of how it lives and functions as a *Reformed* church.

> *g. Do the salary, housing, arrangements for professional development, and all other benefits received by the minister/s meet the terms of the original call, subsequent revisions thereof, and the minimum standards of the classis?*

Ministerial remuneration has always been difficult. Financial survival has presented many churches with hard choices. Classes have intervened to require that ministers receive compensation that not only enables them to live without fear of poverty, but that thereby frees them to the task to which the church calls them—a full-time meditation on the Word from which the church lives. This question then goes to the heart of the church's life.

The question, further, grants a classis (and the classis alone) the authority to impose salary standards for its ministers. While a "no" answer to this question does not place a church in immediate jeopardy, a wise classis will take immediate cognizance for the sake of both the church and the pastor.

> *h. Does the consistory regularly review the performance of*
>
> > *i. the consistory?*

   ii. the board of elders?

   iii. the board of deacons?

   iv. the installed minister/s?

This question, dealing with performance reviews, is a relatively new addition. Reviews were first envisaged for installed ministers. A consistory reviewed the installed minister's work, in order to assist him or her in the execution of her duties. However, one wonders about the place of "performance" within an office whose task is not "achievement" nor "performance," but the faithful interpretation of Scripture. The order charges elders with that responsibility.

   i. Is your church fulfilling its stewardship obligation by contributing annually and significantly to the mission programs of

   i. the denomination?

   ii. the regional synod?

   iii. the classis?

Does the congregation recognize its responsibility to live in mission? Does it acknowledge that it shares in the life of the greater church as it engages in Christ's work in a kingdom that works its way in broader societies and cultures? The classis reminds the local congregation of the challenge and the invitation.

Here we note a dissonance in vocabulary. The question names two assemblies, the regional synod and the classis. Why then does it begin with the term "denomination"? Shouldn't "i" read, "General Synod?" Since it is the *synod* that lives and acts in mission, "Denomination" refers to an institution characterized by certain agencies and staff patterns.

   j. Is your church engaged in significant, regular activities which

*faithfully witness to the gospel and which challenge others to
respond to God's Spirit in a faith commitment to Jesus Christ
as personal Savior and Lord?*

Another recent addition, this question places the churches'
evangelistic task before consistories. It was intended to remind
congregations that the gospel does not create communities closed
in on themselves; rather, it opens outward in invitation to others to
gather around the Lord's Table in the joy of the reconciliation won
by Christ at Golgatha.

This question, while intended to prod the church to evangelize
persons, might open itself further within a Reformed context. Jesus
is Lord not only of one's personal life, but of all of life. Thus, the
elders and deacons witness Jesus' lordship over public life as well.
This question just might ask of consistories their engagement in
issues of peace and justice!

The questions posed to consistories in turn raise the following
question. If the questions clearly turn not only on two marks of the
church but reveal a Reformed understanding of the church, where
is the missing mark, the right celebration of the sacraments? Given
the temptation to liturgical license in a broadly evangelical
ecclesiastical culture, and the stubborn questions around infant
baptism (or requests for rebaptism), one wonders why the sacraments
are not included in the questions to consistories.

Sec. 2. *The classis shall offer guidance to a congregation for
the purpose of the continuation of pastoral functions when
the installed minister is absent for a period of more than two
months due to illness, sabbatical, or other reasons.*

When a pulpit is "vacant," a classis must appoint a supervisor to
oversee the proceedings of a consistory (see below). Two functions
are thereby discharged. First, a consistory as the gathering of the
three offices is thus fully constituted—a minister is present. Second,
the classis exercises its supervisory function of the consistory; the
church remains in relationship with the greater church now through

the supervisor. However, circumstances may arise in which a pastor cannot be present for other reasons. Poor health may remove him from ecclesiastical duties for a time; the church anticipates his return and thus the pastoral relationship remains. Or, as is occurring with greater frequency, the church grants its pastor a sabbatical leave (one could also envisage a leave of absence). The classis is charged in these instances with providing pastoral assistance to the local congregation.

This section does not prescribe the form of that assistance. Some classes may wish to appoint a supervisor, as it does with vacancies. In other cases, the classis may offer advice. Through whatever means it chooses, a classis will be well advised to ascertain that consistories function responsibly during any significant absence of installed pastors.

> Sec. 3. *The classis shall appoint one of its ministers as supervisor of all proceedings of the consistory of a church without a minister or senior minister. The supervisor shall attend all formal meetings of the consistory, due notice having been given.*

The order supposes that a minister of the classis will be present at the meetings of each of its consistories. Normally this happens in the person of the installed minister. Vacancies, however, require special attention, and the classis must appoint one of its minister as a supervisor. This requirement includes churches with more than one minister when no senior minister is present. The classis may appoint a minister on the staff of that church, provided that she or he is a minister of the classis. It need not do so, however, and it may find such an appointment to be inadvisable.

The supervisor's role historically has included not only presence at consistory meetings and assistance in fulfilling pastoral functions, but the supervisor has often assisted the consistory in calling a new minister. In fact, the supervisor is required to attest to the call by signing the call form [Form. 5]. Thus she or he represents the classis's involvement in the life of the congregation as it provides for the ministry of the Word within its boundaries.

> Sec. 4. *The classis, at the request of a church or with its consent, shall appoint one of its ministers or a minister of another classis, or of another approved body, the minister under contract of a church that is without an installed minister. The appointment shall be for a term of not more than one year. It shall be subject to renewal after proper review by the classis. The minister under contract shall perform the duties and receive the financial support which is agreed upon and shall report to the classis whenever that body shall require it.*

This section introduces a new figure into the church order, a "minister under contract." The order assumes that the normal relationship between a congregation and minister is through installation of a called minister. The church has always had churches unable to call a minister at one time or another, often for financial reasons. The order provides that such churches not be left without the ministry of Word and sacrament. Currently, with the origination of "interim" ministers, this provision has been further extended.

The minister under contract serves without call and is not installed as pastor of the church; thus no ongoing pastoral relationship has been formally established. She is "under contract." Furthermore, the contract requires at least an annual review and approval by the classis (see Sec. 8 below). This provision not only protects a congregation from involving itself in a difficult "semi-permanent" arrangement, but it provides the classis with an opportunity to review the life of the church, always keeping as its goal the installation of a called minister.

While the minister may not be a member of the classis, she remains responsible to the classis for her ministry and shall report to the classis upon its request.

One notes that although the arrangements will most likely be made between the local consistory and the minister under contract, the minister is appointed by the classis. Furthermore, while the classis may not require the congregation to accept a minister under contract, it certainly may so suggest.

The classis takes further responsibility by ascertaining who is qualified for appointment. If the minister is a member of an RCA classis, the classis will have little problem. If the minister is not from the RCA, the classis will need to decide whether the church from which the minister comes is an "approved body." The order nowhere specifies which other bodies are so approved. However, since the Reformed Church has entered into full communion with the Presbyterian Church (USA), the United Church of Christ, and the Evangelical Lutheran Church in America, a classis may safely assume that these churches are "approved" bodies. The responsibility for approval of the minister under contract remains with the classis.

Sec. 5. *The classis shall determine whether a minister under contract who is also a member of the classis shall be appointed supervisor of the church served. The minister under contract shall preside at meetings of the consistory of the church if invited by the consistory to do so, but shall not have the right to vote.*

Since the minister under contract is not installed, she is not a member of the consistory by virtue of position. The advisability of her presence as supervisor of the consistory is left to the decision of the classis. On the one hand, she brings the perspective of the pastoral ministry and thus a positive leadership in the ministry of the congregation. On the other hand, by becoming supervisor, she is in the position of overseeing the annual contract to be agreed upon between the consistory and herself. The classis might view that as a conflict of interest. The order leaves the decision to the classis as the body in the best position to judge.

Sec. 6. *The classis, at the request of a church or with its consent, may appoint a specialized interim minister to serve that church between installed ministers, subject to the provisions of Sections 4 and 5, provided the minister has been endorsed as qualified by the General Synod or its designated agent.*

This section introduces yet another category into the order, that of "specialized interim minister." The category is further delimited by this section with the requirement that such be endorsed by the General Synod. A congregation without a minister may, with or without the approval of the classis, contract with a minister who fills its pulpit and may perform many of the *functions* of an interim. However, the appointment of a *specialized* interim must follow the guidelines outlined here.

The classis may strongly suggest to a congregation that it needs a specialized interim minister. Such ministers assist churches that must face a transition following a long-term pastorate, or that require assistance in recovering from a period of conflict. The arrangement between the consistory and the minister does not occur privately, but through the appointment of the classis. Because the minister must be endorsed by the General Synod, the classis will need to communicate with the synod concerning the qualifications of a particular candidate.

Sec. 7. A classis may appoint a theological student to a church without an installed minister or a minister under contract, to furnish the service for which the student is qualified. Before the appointment is made, the student must secure the approval of the appointment by the seminary the student attends.

A theological student *may* have been granted a license to preach, and thus is "qualified" to lead in the service of the Word. The arrangement is not made between the student and the church, nor between a seminary and a church. The classis retains its responsibility for the ministry of the church, and the student is required to be appointed by the classis.

At the same time, since the seminary is responsible for the student's theological education and will attest to the church the student's "fitness for ministry," it is necessary for the student's well-being as well as that of the congregation that the seminary's approval be granted. This requirement is ambiguous, however, in cases of students attending seminaries outside the RCA. The Ministerial Formation Coordinating Agency (MFCA) is the General Synod's agent responsible for such students. A number of students under the aegis of MFCA may be available to RCA congregations. Does the order intend that MFCA approve such appointments?

> Sec. 8. *A church shall not enter into a contract with a minister or a student except by approval of classis. Between sessions of classis the approval may be given by the president and the clerk of the classis.*

The inclusion of this section is puzzling. Previous sections have required the classis to appoint ministers or students under contract. One presumes that such appointments would only happen with approval! The section does serve to underscore, however, that arrangements between churches and those who provide the ministry of pulpit (and Table) cannot occur without the approval of the body within which the congregation subsists.

> Sec. 9. *The approval of the classis shall be required before the church and a competent minister, or ministers, may contract for the purpose of maintaining public worship, under that church's direction, in a place or pulpit in any locality, or provide assistance for its own installed minister/s. In such cases a formal call is not required, though the classis shall review all such appointments annually. Ministers employed by such contracts may or may not be required to be members of the classis.*

A consistory may consider contracting with a minister for a ministry beyond that provided by either its senior or associate (both installed) ministers. A church may desire an additional minister on staff to assist in a specialized area of the church's ministry. Or it may desire to provide worship at a location other than the church's own sanctuary. The consistory may contract with such persons. However, not only is classis approval required, but the contract will be reviewed annually by the classis. It might surprise some to note that this requirement includes assistant ministers in the local congregation.

It is not necessary that ministers in this category be members of the classis, that determination being left to the classis.

> Sec. 10. *The approval of the classis shall be required for two or more churches to call a minister to serve them jointly. This relationship may be approved only if the ordination meets the requirements of the* Government of the Reformed Church in America, *Part II, Article 12, Section 1. This relationship shall be terminated only by action of classis. The right to vote shall be granted to a minister of another denomination serving a Reformed church under the above conditions if the right to vote is reciprocated under the same conditions.*

It is not uncommon for smaller congregations, often within geographical proximity of each other, to desire to call a minister jointly. This cooperative endeavor does not intend that the congregations themselves become less than independent bodies. However, they will relate in the support of a minister and the sharing of her time and energy. The advisability requires review by the classis, both to enter the relationship and to end it.

Beginning with the second sentence of this section, we are presented with a puzzle. The sentence refers to a section concerning the recognition of the validity of ordination of ministers from other denominations, a matter of tangential interest to this section. It is not difficult to imagine two or more churches in a relationship, one of which is non-RCA. Or for such a call to be made upon a non-RCA minister. But why deal with that matter here?

Furthermore, the granting of the right to vote, while permitted here, is also handled under Article 13, Section 15 under the rubric of temporary membership in the classis. Indeed, that provision does not include the restrictions placed in this section that the non-RCA denomination in question grant an RCA pastor the right to vote under similar circumstances.

Sec. 11. *The classis, in forming new churches, shall appoint a committee to meet with those persons who desire to be organized into a church. The committee shall act as a board of elders in receiving members on confession, reaffirmation, or certificate. Notice of the time and place of the proposed organization, and of the election of elders and deacons, shall be published for three Sundays in the church or usual place of worship. The ordination of elders and deacons shall follow the regular procedure. The first elders and deacons of a newly organized church shall determine by lot, at the first meeting of the consistory following upon their installation, who of their number shall serve for one year, who for two years, and who, if it should be necessary, for three or more years.*

This is the only section in the order to deal with the formation of a new church. The provision is worded oddly, perhaps a relic of past practice, when it appears to imply that the initiative lies with "persons who desire to be organized." In practice, either a classis or a synod has often begun a new congregation from the outset. However, from the perspective of *order* that gathering does not become a church until it is established by the church as a body through the action of the classis.

Several steps need to be taken for a church to come into existence. First, a body of confessing believers must be received. Since a board of elders does not yet exist, the classis, itself a body constituted by the offices of elder and minister, is ecclesiastically qualified to act as a board of elders. Second, the officers of the new congregation must be elected and ordained. The classis calls together the newly gathered congregation to elect the officers, and then proceeds to ordain and install the new officers. Thus constituted, the new church will have in place its own ruling body, authorized to provide for the ministry of Word and sacrament.

> Sec. 12. *The classis shall have the authority to supersede a consistory in the administration of a local church when, in its judgment, there are conditions in that church which make it unable to fulfill the functions of a local church as these are defined by the classis. Such conditions shall include at least one of the following:*

The classis *supersedes* a consistory when the classis itself takes over the responsibilities of the consistory (and boards of elders and deacons) for a local church. The classis, in effect, becomes the consistory. It is necessary to take such action because a church cannot exist without a consistory, without, that is, the leading of Christ through the offices.

Classes take such action only in extreme instances and under particular conditions. The order is careful to determine when an assembly may invade the life of another body. Supersession is generally an emergency action, taken for the sake of the local church. The conditions in which the classis can act are then outlined:

> a. *Failure to hold regularly scheduled Sunday services.*
>
> b. *Absence of a quorum of a governing body as prescribed by the constitution, bylaws, or rules of order of the church, for a period of three months.*
>
> c. *Lack of a governing body.*
>
> d. *Danger of loss of property by reason of foreclosure or otherwise.*
>
> e. *Neglect of the physical condition of the church properties.*

f. Insufficiency of confessing membership to fulfill the purposes and responsibilities of an organized church.

g. Long-term or rapid decline in participation or membership.

h. Inability to provide adequate ministerial services.

The conditions all indicate the inability of a consistory to govern in such a way as to responsibly constitute a church. The classis must state one or more of the reasons mentioned, and it must verify its claim. Nonetheless the process remains cautious as shown in the following section.

Sec. 13. *Before superseding a consistory, the classis shall state its intention and summon the consistory of that church to show cause why that consistory should not be dissolved and the church and its property be administered under the direction and supervision of the classis. If the classis, after having heard the consistory, continues in its intention, it shall dissolve the consistory and otherwise terminate the formal organization of that church and take such steps as may be necessary to bring that church, its ministry, and its property under the direct administration of the classis. Such a church shall not have a consistory, but the classis shall designate those persons, not necessarily members of that church, who shall exercise the functions of a consistory or a board of elders or a board of deacons as may be necessary for the administration of the church. All actions of the classis under this section shall require a two-thirds vote of a quorum present consisting of a majority of the elder delegates and a majority of those ministers who are actively serving in ministries under the jurisdiction of the classis.*

The supersession of a consistory is a serious step. Before a classis takes it, the classis must make its intention known to the classis and to the consistory. The consistory is given the opportunity to show cause to the classis why it should not be dissolved. The decision remains with the classis, however, and it may proceed to dissolve the consistory—an action that simply states that the consistory no longer is in existence. The classis then may need to take particular legal steps, especially if the church is incorporated. The classis will place the church's property under the direct administration of the classis.

As the congregation requires leadership (the church still exists albeit with a new form of leadership), the classis will appoint persons to act in its stead as consistory, board of elders, and board of deacons.

The classis will need to pay close attention to the conditions for its action. Not only must the consistory be granted a hearing, but the vote of the classis in this matter requires a "super-majority" of a two-thirds vote. Furthermore, the gathered classis must itself be constituted by a quorum.

> Sec. 14. *When the classis has superseded a consistory, it shall have the authority, in the exercise of its discretion and in accordance with the laws of the state in which that church is located, to:*
>
> a. *terminate whatever authority the consistory or any other body has as trustees of the church property;*
>
> b. *take the church under its direction by appointing such trustees as are required for the protection, preservation, management, and ownership of the property during such time as the classis shall determine.*
>
> *All actions of the classis under this section shall require a two-thirds vote of the members present.*

In superseding a consistory, the classis takes the place of the consistory. Since the consistory is charged with the care of the church's property, and, since consistory members are trustees of the church's property (see p. 65-67), that responsibility now devolves to the classis. The classis must take care in these matters, however, for churches are often incorporated, and the classis must abide by the religious incorporation laws of the state. The classis would be well advised in these instances to consult an attorney. This section does not require the classis to act; it simply grants the classis authority. However, the classis is charged with the trusteeship of the congregation's assets and thus must take careful cognizance of the congregation's property.

As a practical matter, a classis cannot do this as a whole. Thus, it is advisable to appoint trustees to oversee the assets of the congregation. That board may or may not be the same body appointed by the classis under Section 13 above (in fact, the body appointed under that section need not be accompanied by the powers granted the classis in the section under discussion). Such trusteeship is understood as a provisional matter, and thus the classis establishes the term.

> Sec. 15. *The classis shall have the authority to reconstitute the consistory of a church when, in the judgment of the classis, sufficient growth has been achieved or suitable stability created so that the church can continue ministry without classis administration. The classis shall guide the consistory selection process (Chapter 1, Part I, Article 2, Section 9).*

Supersession as a process leads to one of two ends: either the consistory is reconstituted or the church is disbanded. The first is accomplished when the classis judges that a consistory can be elected and installed that can carry out its responsibilities as required by the church order. While the body (or bodies) appointed in Sections 13 and 14 would be in the best position to recommend action by the classis, it is the classis as the ecclesiastical body that must take the action.

Reconstitution of a consistory requires a new election. The classis, acting in the stead of the consistory of the church, must supervise the election of new consistory members following the same procedure that guides consistories.

> Sec. 16. *The classis, in formally disbanding a church, shall be satisfied that each and all of the following conditions have been fulfilled:*
>
> a. *The sale and transfer of all physical properties of the church.*
>
> b. *The transfer of all financial assets to the classis, and the assumption of all financial liabilities of the church and of all organizations within it to the extent of the value of such assets.*
>
> c. *The presentation to the classis of all formal church records, and all other records and documents in its possession.*
>
> d. *The dissolution of the corporate entity of the church.*

The second result of supersession requires the classis to take careful steps in disbanding a church. As a living institution, the local church will have accumulated assets, possibly debts; it will certainly possess records of its life and may exist as a corporate entity. Practically, only the classis is in a position to insure that the required tasks are done appropriately.

There being no congregation, there exists no need for the physical facilities. Although as a corporate body the classis can own property, the very purpose for the property has disappeared—the ministry of the gospel. Thus, the classis administers the sale and transfer of the property. This often requires legal assistance, and in some states may require court approval.

What happens to the proceeds of the sale and the assets of the congregation? Since the classis assumes the former congregation's liabilities, it will dedicate some of the assets to paying those debts. A classis may need to take some pains to determine liabilities—outstanding bills to local merchants or service providers come to mind. Any financial assets will go to the classis. This is of both practical and ecclesiastical importance. Practically, where else would the assets go? To the remaining members of the congregation? But the assets belong to a *body* to which not only they but generations have contributed not for personal gain, but for the furtherance of the gospel. Ecclesiastically, the congregation is itself a member of the larger church. The assets accrued are retained for the purposes for which they were intended, God's church.

Again, it seems only practical that the classis care for church records. Included are records of baptisms, deaths, marriages, and membership, as well as minutes, financial records, and so forth. They must go somewhere, and to a "place" that is clearly recognizable, so that they can be retrieved. But the concern is more than practical, it is care for a church and for its members even after it has ceased its active life. The records of a disbanded church are to be sent to the denominational archives (p. 118).

> Sec. 17. Whenever a church is disbanded or dissolved, all real and personal property shall thereupon become vested in the classis of which the church is a member, upon the assumption by the classis of all that church's outstanding obligations, provided the laws of the state in which the church is located permit this procedure. If the classis is not legally capable of owning real property, all such real and personal property shall become vested in the next higher assembly legally capable of owning real property, upon the assumption by that assembly of all outstanding obligations of the church. The assumption of obligations shall be limited to the value of such property.

It is often claimed in Reformed circles that the classis "really owns the church's property." That notion comes from this section. It is not, however, correct. The local church owns its property—or at least its trustees, the consistory, do so on its behalf. The half-truth in the claim is that a local congregation cannot do as it pleases with its property; nor on disbanding can the property become the possession of either its members or another body established to receive the property. The congregation is and remains part of a church. A congregation cannot dispose of its life as it sees fit.

> *Sec. 18. The classis shall have the authority to transfer a local church to another denomination, together with all or part of its real and personal property, at such time as it has been demonstrated to the satisfaction of the classis that:*
>
> *a. such church can no longer function effectively in its present relationship;*
>
> *b. the effectiveness of such congregation as a local church could be enhanced if it were to affiliate with another denomination;*
>
> *c. the denomination with which it desires to affiliate furnishes written evidence that the church in question would be able to exercise a more effective ministry under its jurisdiction, and that if such church were transferred to its jurisdiction, it would be received without reservation as a church having all the rights and privileges of any of its churches.*

The Reformed understanding of church supposes that congregations exist within a covenantal communion with other churches. An independent Reformed church is an oxymoron. A congregation subsists within the church of Christ, that greater church manifest under the category of "denomination." A congregation may judge that it might better live out its call within a different denomination. For example, a congregation geographically distant from other Reformed churches might find that the Reformed understanding of classis makes little sense when neighboring churches are several hours away.

In any case, transfer of a church to another denomination remains within the prerogative of the greater church as manifest in the classis. Before transfer can be approved, the order requires that three conditions be demonstrated to the satisfaction of the classis.

The first two conditions turn on the notion of "effectiveness of function"—a notoriously ambiguous criterion. What constitutes effectiveness? The classis will first have to answer that question. Since the following section supposes that it is a consistory that takes the initiative in such a proceeding, it will be incumbent upon the consistory to satisfy the classis to the criteria set forth by the classis.

However, a third criterion demands that another denomination be prepared to accept the congregation within its life *and* that the new denomination must itself demonstrate to the classis why the church in question can function more effectively there.

> Sec. 19. *Application for leave to withdraw from the denomination for the purpose of affiliating with another denomination shall be made by written petition of the consistory filed with the stated clerk of the classis. Said petition shall state that the applicant church proposes to withdraw from the denomination, and, if such be the case, take with it all or part of its real and personal property free from any claim of the Reformed Church in America, or any assembly, board, or agency thereof. The classis shall deal with such a petition in the following manner:*

Transfer is such an extraordinary expression of ecclesiastical life, and so seriously does the order take requests for withdrawal, that it sets out a careful and detailed process. Separation cannot be taken lightly nor can it be executed in haste.

> a. *The petition for withdrawal shall be promptly referred to either the executive committee, the Committee on Judicial Business, or a special committee, as shall be determined by the classis or its executive committee.*

Although transfer is not to be done in haste, the order does require that a classis take immediate cognizance of the request. A request signals a serious matter afoot. To allow the procedure to languish in the often slow work of a classis might be to ignore serious pastoral or theological issues. Furthermore, because the request may involve a host of difficult and complicated matters, the classis as a whole is not capable of working through all the issues involved. That is why the order demands that the classis immediately place the responsibility for handling the request in the hands of an appropriate committee.

> b. *The classis committee shall meet with the congregation, with the consistory of the church, and with representatives of the denomination with which the church desires to affiliate. The committee shall endeavor to ascertain the basic facts and conditions underlying the petition, endeavor to reconcile any differences of opinion within the congregation and between the church and the denomination, explore the advantages and disadvantages of a withdrawal and the needs of both the church and the denomination, and endeavor to ascertain how Christ's Kingdom may best be served in the matter.*

This subsection introduces a new criterion, one that might well be supposed to be the central criterion: how Christ's Kingdom might best be served. Other important considerations serve this end: conditions within the congregation, implications for the denomination, attention to conflict within the congregation and between the congregation and the denomination, and the like. The classis is charged with taking great care to obtain the fullest possible knowledge of circumstances and even to bring reconciliation where the question is that of estrangement.

> c. *The committee shall endeavor to ascertain the will of the congregation at a meeting held pursuant to the following formalities:*
>
> (1) *Notice of the calling of a special meeting of the congregation, stating the time, place, and purpose of the meeting, shall be*

read from the pulpit on two successive Sundays at all regular worship services, beginning at least ten days prior to the date set for the meeting. A copy of the notice shall also be mailed to each confessing member of the church at least ten days prior to the date of the meeting.

(2) The meeting shall be held at the usual place of worship of the congregation, at a suitable hour.

(3) Only confessing members eligible to vote for election of elders and deacons shall be entitled to vote at the meeting. Proxy voting shall not be permitted.

(4) There shall be opportunity given for presentation of all sides of the issue, after which the presiding officer shall allow time for discussion. Thereafter there shall be a secret ballot on the questions of withdrawal. Tellers shall count the ballots and report the number of each in favor, the number of each opposed, and the number of each unmarked or otherwise declared by the tellers to be invalid. Certification of such figures shall be made at the meeting by the presiding officer and the clerk. The certification shall state further the number of members eligible to vote and the number present at the meeting.

(5) All of the ballots, together with the tally sheet signed by the tellers, a copy of the notice of the meeting, a statement and reading and mailing of the notice, and the certification of the results of the balloting, shall be personally delivered or sent by registered mail to the chairperson of the classis committee.

The order requires that the full investigation of the issues surrounding the request for transfer be aired openly and fairly and that all members of the congregation be given the opportunity to comment and be fully empowered to vote on the matter. It is the classis's responsibility to see that this is done. The congregational vote by itself is not determinative. However, the detailed provisions of this subsection protect the classis from hearing a report that might be distorted by the most powerful faction in a congregation. The cautions required suppose that the question of transfer may be highly controversial; therefore, they insist that the classis receive the fullest possible report of the mind of the congregation.

> d. *The committee shall file its report with the stated clerk of the classis within six months after its appointment, setting forth its findings and recommendations. Such report shall be submitted to the classis at a regular or a special meeting held within sixty days and after receipt of the report by the stated clerk.*

> e. *Any of the foregoing limitations of time may be extended by agreement between the committee and the consistory.*

Because the step envisioned is of such grave importance, the committee preparing its report is given six months to prepare. The limit ensures that the matter cannot be tabled indefinitely but offers sufficient time for deliberate reflection. The time may be extended, but only when both parties agree.

> f. *If the classis shall then determine that it is in the best interest of Christ's Kingdom that the church be allowed to withdraw from the denomination, and to retain all or part of its real and personal property free from any claim on the part of the denomination or any assembly, board or agency thereof, it shall then so declare and proceed promptly to assist the consistory of the church in (1) dissolution of the relationship of the church to the denomination, and (2) transfer of its property to a church of another denomination.*

The decision to transfer remains in the hands of the classis. It is not a congregational matter. At issue is the "interest of Christ's Kingdom," and that is to be determined by the gathered body of those ordained to lead in Christ's name.

It is important to note that in the execution of the permission to transfer, the property is not simply given to the congregation to dispose of under its aegis, but it is transferred to a church of another denomination. The classis will need to determine just what entity will receive the property, most probably in consultation with the appropriate body of the receiving denomination.

> g. If the classis shall determine that the church should not be allowed to withdraw from the denomination, the church may institute new proceedings after the lapse of one year from the denial of the original petition.

> h. Any appeal by the church, or by any other aggrieved party, from the decision of the classis on a petition for leave to withdraw from the denomination, shall be taken to the regional synod, and any appeal from the ruling of the regional synod shall be taken to the General Synod. The decision of the General Synod, and any decision of a lower judicatory that is not appealed within the specified time for appeals, shall be final and binding upon all interested parties.

In the case of denial of the request, the consistory has two options. The consistory may place the request again, but only after the lapse of a year. Or the consistory may appeal the decision to the regional synod (or on an unfavorable ruling of that synod to the General Synod). The provisions outlined in chapter 2 of the *BCO* under appeals then apply.

> Sec. 20. *The interest of the denomination in the property of a church withdrawing from the denomination shall not be completely divested therefrom until the church shall have:*

> a. repaid to the denomination or appropriate assembly, board, or agency thereof, all money that the church has previously borrowed therefrom and promised to repay, unless specifically released or compromised by the agreement of the parties;

b. taken such action as is necessary to release the denomination or any assembly, board, or agency thereof, from any secondary or contingent liability of the church and from any secondary or contingent liability of the church and from any guarantee of payment by the church;

c. paid all assessments that have been levied by the classis, the regional synod, or the General Synod, whether or not due and payable at the date of approval by the classis of the petition for withdrawal, including the required contribution to the contributory annuity fund for the minister/s of the church.

d. provided not less than six months' severance salary and housing to any minister of the church who elects to remain with the denomination, and who is not during such period receiving salary and housing from another church or agency of the denomination, or in connection with any other employment;

e. taken appropriate action to notify the general public that the church is no longer affiliated with the denomination.

It will be incumbent upon the withdrawing consistory to settle any outstanding obligations to the RCA. The provisions allow a settlement that is less than full only provided all parties agree. Furthermore, the provision protects any minister who may not be in agreement with the church's request. And it will be the responsibility of the church to make clear to the public that it no longer is part of the Reformed Church in America, thereby avoiding any confusion of its particular expression as representative of our denomination's theology, polity, or confession.

Sec. 21. *In no event shall the property of a church that has withdrawn from the denomination, or the proceeds of sale of any such property, become the property of individual members of the church, so as to be capable of being divided among them; nor may the property or the proceeds of sale thereof be devoted to any but a church-related use. In the event of dissolution of such a church within a period of five years after the classis shall have approved a petition for withdrawal from the denomination, such property, both real and personal, or the proceeds of sale of such property, shall be conveyed, transferred, or delivered to the classis from which the right of withdrawal was received.*

This section guarantees that the withdrawal of a church remains an ecclesiastical matter. The church as an entity that includes its property remains within and responsible to the greater church. In fact, this provision acts as a reserve clause by which the classis retains a residual interest over a period of five years following the withdrawal.

Sec. 22. *The classis, in exercising its authority to receive a congregation as a local church of the Reformed Church in America, shall first satisfy itself that:*

a. *such congregation truly desires to organize and function as a local church in accordance with and in all respects subject to the provisions of the Government of the Reformed Church in America.*

b. *such congregation has satisfied all prerequisites required by the denomination, if any, with which it has been affiliated, for withdrawing from the jurisdiction of that denomination;*

c. *such congregation could function more effectively as a local church of the Reformed Church in America, and would be welcomed as such by other churches of the classis.*

While sections 19 to 21 handle a request for withdrawal from the RCA, this section envisages the opposite situation. A congregation may petition to unite with the RCA. That can occur only as that congregation organically unites with a classis. It is the prerogative of the classis to receive such a congregation.

Constitutional Theology

However, as care is taken in the request for withdrawal, similar care is taken in receiving a congregation. This section articulates the ecumenical posture of the Reformed Church in America in its relation to other denominations. In the same way, the congregation will have to show that it has met any requirements for withdrawal from the denomination with which it is affiliated.

The congregation must also show that it is prepared to live fully as a Reformed church, subject to its government (It is important to note that the *Government* includes both the *Liturgy* and the *Standards* in the preamble). It is advisable that the congregation be fully informed of the import of its request. For example, a congregation unhappy in its present denomination because it profoundly disagrees over an issue within that denomination needs to understand the full nature of what membership and responsibilities ensue as a congregation of the RCA.

Finally, the local church must also show that it will function effectively as a local church in the RCA. What "function effectively" means will be interpreted by the classis. However, given the criterion of the "interest of Christ's Kingdom" in the previous sections, the classis would be advised to inquire carefully how the reception of the requesting church furthers that cause.

The section concludes with an interesting clause. The classis must satisfy itself that the congregation would be welcomed by other churches in the classis. This further manifests the principle of Reformed order that local churches live in communion with neighboring congregations. The fulfillment of this requirement may demand some pains of the classis. How would it handle a congregation that neighbors an existing RCA church, and has lived in conflict with that church?

Article 8. Supervision of Students of Theology

Earlier orders treated the process of candidature for ministry under the rubric of the office of minister. That way of ordering the issue alerts us that not only the supervision of students but the following sections (through Section 13) having to do with various aspects of ministerial supervision will reflect and expand upon the order's understanding of the office of minister.

Historically, the sections on the classical responsibility for students is of particular importance to the Reformed Church in America. It was just this issue that provoked the coetus-conferentie dispute in the eighteenth century that led to the Plan of Union in 1771. The Plan of Union in turn provided the foundation for the Reformed Church as an integral American church.[5] The story of the American church is replete with changes and care given to this responsibility.

> Sec. 1. *A confessing member of a congregation in the Reformed Church in America who desires to become a minister shall apply to the classis with jurisdiction over the church in which membership is held to be enrolled as a candidate for the ministry. This application shall be made through the consistory of the church in which membership is held.*

This section has developed over the history of RCA constitutions. The Explanatory Articles simply state that one must be a candidate before one can be called or chosen to be a minister, and that candidacy is attained by someone who, having graduated from a seminary, is then lawfully examined by the classis (Ex. Art., I & II). By 1833, the *Constitution* required that someone desiring to enter ministry furnish appropriate credentials to his theological school (1833, I,I,4). By the 1958 revision, the candidate was required to apply to the classis, with the important notation that he will apply through his consistory.

In question is the *call* of the minister. Dort stated bluntly that no person shall "be permitted to officiate in the ministry of the word, and sacraments, without being thereunto lawfully called." Lawful calling included the call by elders and deacons of a church, the

---

5 Further information on this controversy may be found in Gerald F. De Jong, *The Dutch Reformed Church in the American Colonies*, The Historical Series of the Reformed Church in America, No. 5 (Grand Rapids: Eerdmans, 1978), pp. 188ff.

examination of the person by the classis, and the approbation of the members of the congregation (Dort, III & IV). The minister is not "self-called," nor is his or her call mediated directly by God. The call comes through the church—the church as manifest in the two assemblies mentioned in this section.

The consistory, the officers who have nurtured a congregation and thus who recognize the applicant's gifts and promise, make the first inquiry, and in effect apply on behalf of a candidate to the higher assembly. The candidate by herself does not have entrée to that assembly.

It is also clear that an applicant cannot simply approach any classis he or she may desire to supervise her candidacy. It shall be the classis within which she holds church membership. This is an ecclesiastical and not an individual matter.

> Sec. 2. *Upon the consistory's recommendation, the candidate shall appear in person before the classis or its committee for examination. The classis or its committee shall inquire into the applicant's character and behavior; physical, emotional, intellectual, spiritual, and educational qualifications; and the motives which led the applicant to seek the ministry as a vocation. If the classis is satisfied by the examination, the applicant shall be received under its care and enrolled as a candidate for the ministry.*

The application begins a process that will continue some years and that will relate the candidate to the classis in a particularly crucial and intimate manner. The classis begins with an examination that is designed as a preliminary test of the applicant's fitness for ministry and his or her understanding of her call to ministry. The demands of the order at this point are quite weighty: character, motives, physical, emotional, intellectual, and spiritual qualifications all come into play. The order is fully aware that the office of ministry places heavy demands upon a candidate. One must possess not only emotional stamina but also physical capabilities; not only spiritual resources, but intellectual capabilities.

Classes are often quite reticent at just this juncture, with tragic consequences. Elders and ministers find it difficult to say no to a candidate whom they suspect cannot live up to the demands of the order; to say no would be to bind God's Spirit. But that claim refuses to acknowledge that as officers of the classis, God's Spirit uses them in precisely this process. They are taking care for the well-being, not only of the candidate, but also of a congregation and its members whose identity remains in God's future.

Following a successful examination, the classis must take a number of immediate steps. First, the classis acts to take the student under its care. Second, the applicant is received. Some classes engage in a liturgical act through which the candidate is received with prayer and the classis promises its further prayer and support. Finally, the candidate is "enrolled" or formally placed under the care of the classis. The following section thus applies:

> Sec. 3. *Immediately following the enrollment of a candidate for the ministry, the classis shall petition the General Synod on behalf of the candidate for a Certificate of Fitness for Ministry. Such a petition must be received a minimum of twenty-seven months prior to the time it is to be given final disposition by the General Synod through the board of trustees of an RCA seminary or the Ministerial Formation Coordinating Agency. However, in instances where completion of theological training takes place prior to the required period of twenty-seven months, the classis may petition the General Synod to substitute a period of ministry supervised by the General Synod through the board of trustees of an RCA seminary or the Ministerial Formation Coordinating Agency for all or part of its twenty-seven month requirement.*

From its earliest days, the Reformed Church in America required a student to present a testimonial from a professor (of General Synod) or the professorate to the classis in order to be admitted to examination for ordination. This "professorial certificate" was the confirmation by the "fourth office" and thus by the General Synod that the student had studied theology and was qualified to become a candidate for the ordained ministry. This changed in 1990 with the introduction of a "Certificate of Fitness for Ministry" replacing the old "professorial." The new system intends a proper agent of the General Synod (a seminary of the RCA or the Ministerial Formation Coordinating Agency) to have sufficient time to observe, educate, and guide candidates before judging the candidate's "fitness."

The "twenty-seven month" rule needs careful attention by the classis. The classis makes application that effects its intention over two years into the future! However, the order allows exceptions in those cases where the classis can show (and it requires the *classis* to make the request) that the candidate has been under a period of ministry supervised by the RCA agent that grants them sufficient warrant to judge the candidate's qualifications.

> Sec. 4. *The student shall be under the supervision of the classis while in seminary, but shall remain subject to the ecclesiastical discipline of the board of elders of the church in which membership is held. The classis shall show a continuing sympathetic interest by giving guidance in the candidate's study program and practical training.*

A student lives within a number of ecclesiastical relationships. He or she is, of course, a student and thus responsible to the educational institution in which he is enrolled. Further, since the seminary will grant his Certificate of Fitness, he is subject to their review and guidance. As a church member, that is, as one gathered around the Lord's Table, he remains subject to his board of elders who alone has the authority of ecclesiastical discipline. Still, the student is under the *supervision* of the classis.

This can be and has been confusing. The seminary supervises a student most closely in course selection, practical training, even spiritual growth. Still, the classis will be charged with licensure and ordination, and it is proper that the classis take care that the candidate's education and development be such that he or she will serve the church.

The order clearly does not allow a classis to enroll a student and then release her to find her own way. It enjoins a continuing and sympathetic relationship. Classes do well to design methods appropriate to their circumstances that provide such care. Some classes, for example, provide mentors for students. Others require a seminary internship before examining for ordination.

> Sec. 5. *If the candidate's membership is transferred to a church under the jurisdiction of another classis, enrollment shall likewise be transferred to that classis. However, upon completion of seminary training, the candidate shall be examined for licensure and ordination by the classis in which church membership was held upon entering seminary studies, unless in the judgment of said classis it is appropriate for examination and ordination to be administered by the classis in which the candidate is presently enrolled. The approval of both classes shall be required to permit the classis in which the candidate is enrolled to administer the examinations.*

It is imaginable that a candidate will transfer membership during the period of her or his education. His immediate family, should he have one, likely will seek a congregation that nurtures their spiritual existence. This might especially be the case if the seminary is geographically distant from the candidate's home church. The order allows the candidate to transfer his enrollment to the classis within which bounds he holds membership. That classis would then supervise the candidate's training and would administer the yearly examinations.

However, the right and responsibility of examination for licensure and ordination remains with the originating classis. That classis may cede the privilege to the new classis, provided the new classis agrees. In many, if not most, instances classes will cooperate. Why then the reservation? Is it simply to deter a candidate from "shopping" for a classis congenial to her or his theological perspective? Such behavior should certainly be discouraged, as it is the *church* that ordains, not the student who manipulates the church to fit his own theological commitments.

> Sec. 6. *The candidate shall be examined by the classis at the conclusion of each year of seminary training. The classis may also require a candidate to appear at the conclusion of any period of internship. The candidate's classis may request a classis in the vicinity of the seminary or field of internship to act in its behalf at the conclusion of the year/s between the first and the last.*

The requirement for yearly examination provides the classis the opportunity to ascertain the candidate's developing intellectual and spiritual character as well as to assess the candidate's understanding of ministry. The examination reminds the classis of its duty and keeps the person of the candidate before the classis. The classis has opportunity, prior to the time of licensure, to provide and suggest remedial measures if needed.

The order was constructed on a model of theological education that in many instances no longer obtains. It assumes a three-year (or four-year) seminary course, the usual rhythm for candidates who move directly from undergraduate education to a full-time seminary curriculum. Increasingly, classes receive candidates who, often middle-aged and older, will enroll in seminary on a part-time basis. How is the classis to determine each "year"? Does "year" mean the calendar year, or a "year's equivalent" in seminary education. The classis will need to judge in each case, taking care to be faithful to the intent of the order.

In cases of great distance, a classis may request a classis in the vicinity of the seminary or a field of internship to examine on its behalf. The examining classis, however, examines not in its own name, but in the name of the requesting classis. Further, one expects that the requesting classis would grant the provisional license.

> a. *Prior to the final year of study the classis shall satisfy itself concerning the candidate's competence in the following areas, placing the examination in each subject in the session in which the candidate is best qualified to be examined in it, as determined from a copy of the candidate's academic record furnished by the seminary: (1) Hebrew; (2) Greek; (3) biblical introduction and exegesis; (4) church history; (5) church government; (6) views of the ministry and its duties; (7) competence in conducting public worship; (8) sermon preparation and delivery; (9) Christian educational theory for and practice with children, youth and adults; and (10) personal piety and fitness for the ministry.*

The focus of topics of examination disclose the Reformed expectation for its ministers. The Explanatory Articles, for example, had students examined, with "strict attention," not only in the original languages of scripture and in the art of sermonizing, but "especially" in his knowledge of theology, his orthodoxy, his piety, and his view of the ministry (Ex. Art. IV). Biblical languages and exegesis are requisite tools for the pastor's fundamental task of preaching and teaching God's Word. The occasional proposal to eliminate the language requirement is to be deeply regretted; those who teach and preach from God's Word are simply not equipped if they cannot work within the language of the story. They allow their congregants to fool themselves into considering one translation or another to be Scripture, *tout court*. (However, one could imagine a provision by which seminary certification in the languages would suffice. The disadvantage of such a proposal would be that it would remove another opportunity for the classis to observe the candidate's facility in biblical interpretation.) Understanding of church history frees the congregation from the bonds of presentism. As has been argued throughout this commentary, church government instantiates the shape of Christ's body. Public worship and sermon preparation constitute the task of the minister at pulpit and Table, her primary locus of ministry. Views of the ministry, personal piety, and fitness all give the classis opportunity to inquire into the candidate's character and readiness to enter an office so sensitive as to merit this much space in the *Government*.

The classis will need carefully to craft examinations for each candidate, since each may follow a different curricular path.

> b. When the candidate is examined for licensure and ordination at the conclusion of seminary training, the classis shall satisfy itself concerning the candidate's competence in: (1) theology; (2) the nature and administration of the sacraments; (3) knowledge of and adherence to the Standards and the Government and Disciplinary Procedures of the Reformed Church in America; (4) the history and program of Reformed Church world mission.

Prior to this "final" examination, the classis shall satisfy itself that the candidate has received a Certificate of Fitness for Ministry (see Section 3 above). This is the candidate's ticket to the examination and should be presented to the classis prior to examination. Second, the student must produce evidence of the receipt of the Master of Divinity degree or its equivalent. If the classis examines for ordination, it shall satisfy itself as to the requirements for ordination (see Article 11 below).

The earlier examinations should reveal a Reformed understanding of ministry, and this should be all the more the case in these more central examinations. The minister should present God's Word as understood not by him or herself, but by the church. That requires not only a theological agreement in basic principle, but an ability to understand theological issues as they present themselves in the practice of ministry. A Reformed understanding of sacraments will focus the candidate on the church's central understanding of its embodied life. The confessional and governmental shape of the Reformed Church form the central commitment and ethos of the ecclesiastical body within which the minister will live out her vocation on behalf of the church. And an understanding of Reformed mission discloses a missional understanding of the church inherent to the Reformed. To ignore such deep matters is to cease to be the church in its self-understanding.

One notes here the extraordinary power granted to the classis within the order. The classis is judged competent to make theological decisions of import to congregations and to the greater church. No other ecclesiastical body can make that judgment in the case of admission to the pulpit and the Table, the very place where Christ calls the church into being.

> c. The classis will give the candidate a provisional license to preach under the supervision of the General Synod through its agent after each year of study, provided it is satisfied with the student's attainment. The provisional license granted prior to the final year shall also give the candidate the right to receive the promise of a call.

The classis grants its students access to the pulpit. That privilege is not left to a congregation or even to the seminary. However, the license is to be exercised only under the supervision of General Synod's agent (an RCA seminary or MFCA). Interestingly, and perhaps oddly, the order does not, as an earlier order did, grant the classis the authority to supervise the preaching of its students. The Explanatory Articles, for example, had every candidate under the direction not only of the synod but of the classis, and he was to preach in those places where the classis sent him. Furthermore, if that did not occur, the candidate was permitted at his own *discretion* to accept invitations to preach (Ex. Art., VIII).

> Sec. 7. The candidate shall receive the degree of Master of Divinity or its academic equivalent upon the successful completion of the prescribed course of theological studies.

This section summarizes the Reformed commitment to an educated ministry. Ministry is ministry of the Word. The office entails not only acquaintance with the content of the Bible, but knowledge of its languages, of the history of its interpretation, of a theological history and conversation that focuses on the source of the Truth that constitutes the church. While the degree in itself does not confer fitness, it is to be a necessary if not sufficient condition thereof.

Article 9. Certificates of Fitness for Ministry

The order provides a number of routes in the preparation of candidates for the office of minister. The oldest (and, one might add, the norm) has the agent of the General Synod, its professorate, educate students for ministry. That, after all, is one of the General Synod's primary tasks, and it illustrates nicely the principle of Reformed polity that the greater assemblies do that which lesser assemblies are incapable of doing. A second route, introduced in the early nineteenth century, allowed the General Synod to grant a "dispensation" from the attestation by the professorate that the candidate had completed a course of theological education. The General Synod was again the assembly that attested to the classis a candidate's fitness for ministry. This route was significantly altered in 1999, when the order was amended to eliminate dispensations for those who did not attend theological seminary and to grant to its Ministerial Formation Coordinating Agency (MFCA) the oversight of a process by which candidates who did not attend a seminary might receive the Certificate of Fitness for Ministry. A third path was added in the 1980s with the creation of the Theological Education Agency, a body that in 1998 was absorbed into the MFCA. The MFCA is itself an agent of the General Synod that, among other responsibilities, oversees candidates who attend seminaries other than those of the RCA and who are, therefore, not educated under the guidance of the fourth office. Prior to the formation of TEA, students from other seminaries could become candidates upon application by their respective classes for a dispensation from the professorial certificate.

Sec. 1. Candidates at Reformed Church Seminaries

A candidate for the ministry who has received the degree of Master of Divinity or its academic equivalent from a seminary of the Reformed Church in America, upon the successful completion of the prescribed course of theological studies, is found to be qualified and is adjudged to be a fit candidate for the gospel ministry, shall receive from the General Synod through the board of trustees of an RCA seminary a Certificate of Fitness for Ministry, which is entitlement to an examination for licensure and ordination.

In practice, a seminary faculty judges the fitness of a candidate for ministry. This is only to be expected; the faculty has closely observed the candidate's intellectual and theological development over a period of years. It has supervised students in ministry contexts and thus is in a position to judge how they will exercise the office of ministry. Most likely, the faculty will have guided a candidate through the emotional and spiritual reflection on the nature of the call to ministry. Nonetheless, as a matter of order, it is the General Synod that grants the certificate; for it is that synod as assembly that relates to the classis (and as a classis relates to a seminary or to MFCA, it relates to the synod as assembly). The faculty thus recommends candidates to the board of trustees of its seminary, as the body that acts in the synod's stead in the matter of theological education. (One might also note that the board is not to be a body constituted by classes or regional synods in its make-up, but by the General Synod.)

In essence, the entire of Article 9 sets up a "two- track" scheme for the supervision of candidates. The classis has been charged with the supervision of the candidate (Article 8, Section 4 above). The seminaries (or MFCA) works on a parallel track. The classis does not involve itself in the *seminary's* task of evaluating fitness, even as the classis itself will be engaged in a similar task. Classis and seminary are well advised to maintain appropriate communication but to honor the discrete tasks of each. The situation alters somewhat with those the order designates as "other candidates." See the comments on Section 3 below.

Sec. 2. Candidates at Other Seminaries

The history of Reformed seminaries follows the expansion of the RCA westward. The professorate at New Brunswick traces its roots to 1784 and to a famous letter from John Henry Livingston to his brother-in-law Eilardus Westerlo, then pastor of the Albany church, proposing a theological professorate that would eventually be located in New Brunswick, New Jersey.[6] Mid-nineteenth- century immigration of Dutch refugees from a difficult religious situation in the Netherlands began a concentration of Reformed churches in the Midwest. That immigration led to the establishment of Western Theological Seminary in Holland, Michigan. The twentieth century witnessed a further establishment of Reformed churches in the Far West. In the 1980s, the church began to discuss whether it would be advisable to establish a center for theological education in the Far West.

While that discussion centered on the West, it was clear that a number of candidates had chosen non-RCA seminaries in other parts of the country and were following a path that had the classes applying for an increasing number of dispensations from the General Synod. Thus, in 1985, the synod created its Theological Education Agency that would not only supervise the education of students in non-RCA seminaries but would be authorized, through its board, to grant the Certificate of Fitness for Ministry.

This was an odd development in Reformed order. In it, the General Synod transcended the order's provision of the fourth office as the means by which it conducted theological education. The order thus attempted to adjust to what the larger church

---

6   See Hugh Hastings, *Ecclesiastical Records of the State of New York*, vol. vi (Albany: 1905), pp. 4312-14.

understood was a new context. The church is still coming to terms with this new situation.

a. *A candidate for the ministry who has received the degree of Master of Divinity or its academic equivalent from a seminary not officially related to the Reformed Church in America upon the successful completion of the prescribed course of theological studies, is found to be qualified, and is adjudged to be a fit candidate for the gospel ministry, shall receive from the General Synod through the board of trustees of the Ministerial Formation Coordinating Agency a Certificate of Fitness for Ministry, which is entitlement to an examination for licensure and ordination.*

b. *The General Synod through the board of trustees of the Ministerial Formation Coordinating Agency shall require the applicant to furnish, at the conclusion of seminary studies, the following: a master of divinity degree or its equivalent from a seminary accredited by the Association of Theological Schools or a theological accrediting agency of comparable standards as determined by the General Synod Council; a transcript of the applicant's academic record at this seminary; and evidence of confessing membership in a Reformed church of the classis making petition.*

c. *The General Synod through the board of trustees of the Ministerial Formation Coordinating Committee shall examine the applicant in those areas of the academic curriculum which the Reformed Church in America has designated as indispensable for the proper exercise of the ministerial office of the church. The General Synod through the board of trustees of the Ministerial Formation Coordinating Agency shall also evaluate the record of the field education experience submitted to it by the applicant, as well as psychological tests furnished by the applicant's seminary or otherwise required by the General Synod through the board of trustees of the Ministerial Formation Coordinating Agency. If the applicant*

*has previously been asked to terminate studies at a Reformed
Church seminary, the examination shall be given by the
seminary requesting the termination of studies.*

Because this second route to ministry takes place outside the
norm established through which the church, in its fourth office,
ascertains the qualifications of candidates for the office of minister,
the order carefully and in some detail delimits the working of the
synod's Ministerial Formation Coordinating Agency. This too is a
bit strange for the order, for while it is careful to speak of the synod,
it in effect creates a synod agency, an act which is the prerogative
of the synod itself (see p. 232).

The Ministerial Formation Coordinating Agency derives its
authority to grant a Certificate of Fitness in subsection a. The next
two subsections determine how that authority is to be exercised.
Candidates must receive a Master of Divinity degree from an
accredited seminary. Thus, a candidate is precluded from attending
any number of degree-granting religious or theological schools that
do not meet a rigorous academic standard requisite for an educated
ministry as understood by the Reformed Church. This requirement
avoids a sectarian stance within the church and further expresses a
Reformed commitment to life within a culture that the Reformed
claim as the arena of God's action and purpose. This route is not
intended to allow candidates to travel a path that is either less
challenging academically *or* that seems to the candidate better to suit
his or her theological commitments—especially when those
commitments stand in contrast to a full-orbed understanding of the
Reformed faith.

It is to be noted that the parallel track described above in
connection with Reformed seminaries remains in place here as well.
The MFCA is charged with the responsibility of ascertaining the
theological validity of the candidate's education; it is not the
classis's task.

Indeed, the MFCA's task is not limited to validating or confirming
a candidate's curricular history. The agency is required to examine

candidates in "those areas of the academic curriculum which the Reformed Church in America has designated as indispensable for the proper exercise of the ministerial office." What are those areas? One finds them in two places. First, those topics required by the *Government* for classical examination disclose the areas expected to be covered in a theological curriculum. But second, one might also expect that the theological faculties of Reformed seminaries, as agents of the General Synod, themselves determine the academic curriculum. The MFCA is not free of itself to decide.

Furthermore, the MFCA is to evaluate field education, psychological fitness, and the like. Again, this is not left to the candidate's seminary, nor to the classis, but to the General Synod, much as would be the case with a candidate attending a Reformed seminary.

Thus, while the MFCA allows a student to follow a second route to candidacy, the agency clearly stands in a secondary role to the professorate. This appropriate role is underscored by the final sentence in subsection c. When a seminary asks a student to leave, she may attend another seminary, but she may not be examined and granted a certificate by the MFCA. That privilege belongs to the body originally established by the General Synod to educate candidates for the church.

Sec. 3 Other Candidates

A candidate for the ministry who has not received the degree of Master of Divinity or a degree that is its equivalent from a seminary that is accredited by the Association of Theological Schools or by a theological accrediting agency of comparable standards as determined by the Ministerial Formation Coordinating Agency may qualify for the Certificate of Fitness for Ministry provided the following conditions are met:

In 1999, the Reformed Church introduced a major change in how the church accredits candidates for ordination to the classes.

Previously, the order had allowed a process of "dispensation" by which a classis could petition the General Synod to "dispense" with the ordinary course of theological study prerequisite to the granting of a Certificate of Fitness for Ministry by either one of the seminaries or the then existing Theological Education Agency. The dispensation process had allowed a classis to acknowledge the gifts and capabilities of persons whom they judged called to ministry but who could not, because of circumstances, complete a course of theological study at an educational institution. By requiring the candidate to be examined by its agent, the General Synod assured the church that dispensation would be an exception to the ordinary rule.

A task force from the General Synod offered an extensive report in 1997[7] that created a new agency, the Ministerial Formation Coordinating Agency. Among the changes proposed was a major reworking of the old procedure for dispensations. Under the new change, classes may petition the General Synod for an alternate route for ordination of candidates. However, the change entails that a candidate who cannot attend a seminary for reasons that will be ascertained by the classis will be engaged in a compensatory course of study. Upon completion, the MFCA, in the stead of the General Synod, will grant the Certificate of Fitness. This is the "third" route to ordination.

> *a. A consistory shall assess the candidate's call, gifts, and experience in accordance with the standards' requisite for the ministry of Word and sacrament. The consistory shall apply to the classis on the candidate's behalf.*

The process for the alternate route begins, as does that for any candidate, with the local consistory. That body ascertains and acknowledges a person from the congregation whom it judges to be called to the ministry of Word and sacrament. The consistory must

---

7   *MGS*, 1997, pp. 330-52.

take cognizance of the standards applicable within the Reformed Church. Furthermore, it is anticipated that the prospective candidate will minister in that particular church, the consistory otherwise being unable to fulfill its responsibility of providing the ministry of Word and sacrament to the congregation. The MFCA is charged with the oversight of such standards and will make them available to a consistory upon request.

> b.   *The classis shall determine: (1) the candidate has at least five years' experience in leadership in the church; (2) the consistory has demonstrated compelling need for the candidate's ministry; (3) the candidate gives evidence of the call, gifts, and experience for the ministry of Word and sacrament, and (4) it is not feasible for the candidate to complete a Master of Divinity degree at an accredited seminary.*

The third route, being extraordinary, places a great responsibility on the classis. Before the classis can apply to the MFCA on behalf of the candidate, it must show that the four conditions of the subsection are met. The alternate route presumes that the candidate has already shown him or herself to have demonstrated leadership in the church in such a manner that he or she can fulfill the office of minister. A candidate's years of proven leadership demonstrate that she emerges from within the context of the church and that the desired ministry is more than a momentary or personal inclination. By requiring the consistory to demonstrate a compelling need, the classis assures itself that this exception to the rule serves not simply the ministry of the broader church, but of a particular church. The classis also must ascertain that the prospective candidate has the requisite call and gifts. In so doing, the classis will assure the church that the candidate will be able to acquire the skills necessary to proclaim the Word and to minister to the church. Thus, the classis assists the church in the integrity of the proclamation of the Word. Furthermore, it is incumbent on the classis to ascertain that the prospective candidate is not able to attend a seminary. Classes need to be cautious. Seminary education demands a great deal, as the importance of the ministry of Word and sacrament require. It is not simply inconvenience or high cost that is at issue. Typically, candidates who have reached an age where attendance at a seminary would be disqualifying would meet the fourth condition.

> c. *The classis shall apply to the Ministerial Formation Coordinating Agency for permission to a special course of ministerial formation. If that agency rejects the application, it shall clearly state its reasons. The classis may reapply.*

The classis does not by itself judge the validity of an alternate route. That responsibility is left to the General Synod through its agent. The MFCA, charged with oversight of the standards for ministerial formation, protects the integrity of ministerial education on behalf of the entire church. The agency can reject the application, but it is required to state its reasons. This requirement gives a classis the opportunity to review its application. It can engage the candidate and/or the consistory to meet any deficiency in its application.

> d. *The classis shall form a committee to care for and to guide the candidate through his or her program.*
>
> e. *The classis shall propose to the Ministerial Formation Coordinating Agency an appropriate program of ministerial formation.*

Upon approval of the application, a classis is given the responsibility of guiding the candidate through a program of remedial ministerial formation. In this, the classis is required to undertake two tasks. One is to form a smaller body that will oversee the candidate's development in skills, character, and gifts in such manner that he or she can meet the standards and demands of the office of minister. Secondly, the classis must propose a course of study for the candidate. That study must meet the standards set by the MFCA.

For example, the candidate will demonstrate capabilities in scriptural exegesis; acquaintance with the history of the Reformed Church, its standards, its polity, and its liturgy; demonstrate appropriate pastoral capabilities; and the like. This route will require both attention and time from a classis.

> f. When the candidate has completed the course of study, the candidate shall be examined for the Certificate of Fitness for Ministry by the Ministerial Formation Coordinating Agency. The method of assessment shall be culturally and linguistically appropriate.

> g. When the candidate passes the examination, the Ministerial Formation Coordinating Agency may award the Certificate of Fitness for Ministry.

The granting of the Certificate of Fitness is the responsibility of the MFCA. The classis oversees the program of formation; the MFCA, on behalf of the General Synod, grants the certificate. Thus the order maintains its integrity. In it, a classis does not by itself judge fitness for ministry, but it retains the responsibility for ordination. By establishing these parallel tracks, the greater church avoids degenerating into a situation in which any number of standards for ministry are maintained.

The requirement that the assessment of candidates be culturally and linguistically appropriate acknowledges a diversity of cultural backgrounds within the Reformed Church. An increasing number of churches live and worship in languages other than English. Likewise, cultural backgrounds differ, thus expressing a variety of expectations within congregations. One could not expect, for example, a congregation of white Dutch extraction to display the same dynamics as a Hispanic or Taiwanese congregation. Ministry will take contours peculiar to the culture of a particular congregation.

By changing the order to grant the MFCA the responsibility of awarding the Certificate of Fitness, the old possibility of dispensation by the General Synod itself was also removed. The order now gives that task to the MFCA on behalf of the synod.

Article 10. Dispensations

The 1999 change in dispensations largely removed the need for this article in the church order. However, a candidate who attends seminary may be incapable of meeting any particular requirement for the Certificate of Fitness. A classis may apply on behalf of the candidate for a dispensation. At the time of this writing, the General Synod is reviewing this article and is preparing an amendment that will make the application for dispensation coherent with the changes accepted in Article 9.

The order envisages two types of requests for dispensation:

Sec. 1. Masters of Divinity Degree Candidates at Theological Seminaries

A candidate for the ministry who is a student at a theological seminary, but because of age, lack of necessary academic preparation, or other sufficient reason, finds it too difficult to meet the full requirements for the Certificate of Fitness for Ministry, shall make application to the classis for a dispensation.

Students in this section include those attending both RCA and non-RCA seminaries. A student must first judge that circumstances are such that she or he cannot fulfill particular requirements for the Certificate of Fitness. Age, for example, may preclude a student from attaining a language competence; the demand of time would extend beyond that of reasonable expectation. The student then applies to the *classis* (not to the seminary, nor to the synod). The initiative remains with the student at this point.

a. If the classis finds the reason sufficient, it shall petition the General Synod on behalf of the applicant for a dispensation

*from any part of the seminary's academic requirements
(Article 8, Section 6a). The petition with the reasons for
seeking the dispensation shall be made by January 15 of the
year in which it is to be given final disposition by the Synod.*

At this point the initiative shifts to the classis. That body must judge the validity of the student's claim. It need not consent. It may judge, for example, that the language requirement can be fulfilled and may even offer assistance in completion of the requirement(s).

The request for dispensation then becomes an action of the classis as it petitions the General Synod; the student cannot do so because she or he has no particular ecclesiastical standing before the General Synod. The request and its reply becomes a matter between the respective assemblies.

The classis's request must include precisely those requirements from which the student requests dispensation and the reasons for the request. The classis may include why, in its judgment, the person is qualified for ministry, and why the fulfillment of the requirements presents an unreasonable burden. The classis needs pay particular attention to the deadline.

The reference cited in this subsection may lead to confusion. Article 8, Section 6a refers to the *classis* task of examination. The Certificate of Fitness is granted by the seminary (or MFCA). The requirements need not be the same, and to assume that they are is to mix inappropriately the work of distinct assemblies.

*b. The General Synod, through the board of trustees of an RCA
seminary or the Ministerial Formation Coordinating Agency,
shall inquire carefully into the reasons submitted by the
classis as to why the applicant is unable to meet the full
constitutional requirements for a candidate's preparation.*

*c. Upon recommendation of the board of trustees of an RCA
seminary or the Ministerial Formation Coordinating Agency,
the General Synod may grant the requested dispensation.*

The request for dispensation to be placed before the General Synod must first be reviewed by the synod's agent—the board of one of its seminaries or MFCA. This review precludes a precipitate action by the General Synod and recognizes that the synod meeting as a body of several hundred delegates is not equipped to pursue a careful inquiry into the request. Furthermore, the order seems to require that a board recommend approval of the request. Read carefully, this requirement intends that a request *cannot* be granted without this recommendation. That is, the board may recommend and the synod refuse. However, the order states that the synod cannot overturn a board's refusal to recommend!

Article 11. Supervision of Licensure and Ordination

> Sec. 1. *Upon classis approval of an examination for licensure and ordination, the candidate shall sign the* Declaration for Licensed Candidates *(see Appendix, No. 1) and shall be given a license to preach the gospel. The license shall be signed by the president and the stated clerk of the examining classis, shall be issued for a period of five years, and shall be subject to renewal by that classis. The license may be revoked by that classis on request of the candidate, or for due cause.*

Following the approval of an examination for licensure and ordination, the candidate signs the appropriate declaration. This should be done before the classis.

The formula for subscription (fully part of the *Constitution*) has undergone significant change. Candidates subscribed as follows in the Explanatory Articles:

> We, the underwritten, testify, that the Heidelberg Catechism, and the confession of the Netherland Churches [Belgic]; as also the Canons of the National Synod of Dordrecht held in the years 1618 and 1619, are fully conformable to the word of God. We promise moreover, that as far as we are

able, we will, with all faithfulness, teach and defend both in public and private, the doctrines established in the standards aforesaid. And, should ever any part of these doctrines appear to us dubious, we will not divulge the same to the people, nor disturb the peace of the church or of any community, until we first communicate our sentiments to the ecclesiastical judicatories under which we stand, and subject ourselves to the counsel and sentence of the same (Exp. Art., V).

The declaration articulates a clear commitment to the *Standards* as the church's doctrinal understanding of Scripture and commits the minister to the public and private defense of a Reformed theological position. The formula was changed slightly in the 1915 revision of the *Constitution*. While in the earlier declaration the *Standards* are "fully conformable" to scripture, in 1915 the order added, "Gospel of the Grace of God in Christ Jesus as revealed in the Holy Scriptures of the Old and New Testaments and as truly *set forth* in the standards of the Reformed Church in America" (1915, Art II, Sec. 11, emphasis added). By 1973, that too had changed. The General Synod, responding to an overture from the then Particular Synod of New Jersey, proposed a major revision of the formula that would affirm the "joy and meaning of Christian ministry."[8] The new formula retained the 1915 wording that the gospel is "expressed" in the standards, but it added a sentence that placed the confessions in a historical context: "I accept the *Standards* as historic and faithful witnesses to the Word of God." That change moved the church some distance from its earlier insistence that the standards were "fully conformable" and allowed candidates to accept the Standards as faithful within the contexts in which they were written.

The license granted differs from the provisional license. In the first place, this license indicates that the classis is prepared to ordain the candidate once conditions are fulfilled that allow ordination.

8   *MGS*, 1972, p. 199.

Second, the provisional license extends only between times of examination. The license now granted is the license per se and thus does not await further confirmation.

The classis will issue this license for a period of five years. After that time, the classis may renew the license. It may find sufficient reason not to do so. For example, a candidate may indicate that he or she does not intend to be ordained, in which case the reason for the license disappears. In that case, the candidate loses the right to the pulpit. Likewise, a candidate may request the revocation of the license. Further, the classis may revoke "for due cause." Due cause is a matter of interpretation for the classis. The classis may confirm that the candidate is preaching a gospel contrary to the Reformed understanding expressed in the *Standards*. Or the classis may possess evidence of character unsuitable to the office. In that case, the student has little recourse. While a member of the body may resort to a complaint against the classis's action, the student, not being a member of the body, cannot do so.

> **Sec. 2.** *The licensed candidate for the ministry shall remain under the immediate direction of the examining classis. The candidate shall visit such congregations and preach in such places as the classis may designate. If such direction is not given, the candidate may accept an invitation to preach in any church, but is not permitted to administer the sacraments.*

Classes rarely employ the provision in this section. It would provide opportunities for the licensed candidate to preach, and it would assist the classis in the provision of preachers for its pulpits. Indeed, by this provision, the candidate has little choice.

Perhaps that is what rubs contemporaries the wrong way. The order assumes that the minister is a creature of the classis. We are products of an individualistic culture in which ministers consider themselves independent of the classis. The classis may license and ordain, but classical involvement ends there (with the exception of those cases where a minister may come under discipline). The order thinks quite differently. The permission to accept an invitation to preach is clearly secondary.

> **Sec. 3.** *The licensed candidate for the ministry shall not be a minister delegate to any ecclesiastical assembly or judicatory, but may be elected an elder delegate to such bodies.*

The licensed candidate does not yet participate in the office. Thus, he cannot become a member of an assembly. The exception is that case when the candidate is an elder, and *as elder* is elected to an assembly.

> **Sec. 4.** *The candidate shall be ordained to the office of minister by the classis only after the candidate has received and accepted a call or other invitation to a form of ministry which meets all of the following requirements:*
>
> *a. A ministry which requires a theological education for its performance.*
>
> *b. Performed under the jurisdiction or with the approval of a classis of the Reformed Church in America.*
>
> *c. Intended to witness to the Word in the world or to nurture and train Christians for their ministry in the world.*

Reformed order does not ordain a person to an office except as that office stands in service to the church. That is, the office does not inhere in the person; it is not something he or she possesses. Furthermore, the person must be called *of* God, but *through* the church. One does not enter ministry, therefore, unless one is called—ordinarily by the church in its most concrete form, that is, a local congregation. Dort was clear that one did not enter ministry without being lawfully called (Dort, III). With this in mind, a classis will not proceed to ordain until it has received confirmation that the candidate has received and accepted a call.

Still, beginning with the changes in 1958, the order made provisions for ordination under other circumstances. The provisions were not clear regarding a person who had been assigned as a missionary or to a teaching position or to service as a chaplain. However, in the first two instances, ordination to the office of minister was not of itself necessary (except in certain instances). Thus in 1972, the General Synod proposed the set of criteria in the current form.[9] The change, however, reflected the functional view of ministry prevalent during that era, thus resulting in a language that emphasizes the "performance" of the ministry.

One might still wonder whether the criteria are appropriate for a Reformed order. While the criteria together (and they must *all* be fulfilled) may form a necessary condition for the office, do they provide a sufficient condition? Might one not do ministry with all the criteria (thinking especially of the first and the third) without the necessity of ordination? Indeed, is not the third the ministry of all Christians?

> Sec. 5. *The classis shall appoint a time for the ordination service of the candidate. An interval of at least fifteen days following the candidate's examination shall be allowed before the service of ordination takes place. That service shall be conducted by the classis in regular or special session with proper solemnity. A sermon suitable to the occasion shall be preached, and the promises, directions, explanations of duty, and prayer with the laying on of hands shall be according to the office for ordination in the church's liturgy. A certificate of ordination, signed by the president and the stated clerk of the classis, shall be given and the minister so ordained shall be enrolled as a member of the classis.*

The ordination of the minister is an action of the classis. It is not a private celebration, nor is it a liturgy of a local congregation. The officers of classis gather as representatives of the head of the

9 Ibid., p. 202.

church, Christ, for in a more real sense, the ordinand is set aside by Christ's self.

The service for ordination is contained in the church's liturgy and the classis is not free to choose its own way here. This is an act of the church, present in the classis, but representative of the entire church.

At the ordination, the candidate becomes a member of the office and shall enroll in the classis.

> Sec. 6. *A licensed candidate who seeks ordination in a classis other than that in which the candidate's church is a member shall apply for a certificate of dismission as a licensed candidate to that classis. The certificate shall be granted if the candidate is in good standing.*

> Sec. 7. *A calling classis may, at its discretion, examine a licensed candidate before considering approval of a call to that candidate.*

Earlier constitutions required that the candidate be ordained in the classis to which he or she was called. That changed in the 1968 revision, and the candidate is now ordinarily ordained in the classis where he or she entered under care. The order is permissive on this point and allows the candidate to seek ordination in another classis. In that case, the classis in which the candidate is enrolled must grant a special certificate of dismission (analogous to that granted to ministers who move from classis to classis) provided the candidate is in good standing.

The prerogatives of both classes are respected. The calling classis may, but need not, examine the licensed candidate before *considering* the approval of a call on that candidate. If the examination is not satisfactory, the candidate will not have received a call and thus will not request a certificate of dismission. He thus remains a member of the original classis.

Article 12. Reception of Ministers and Licensed Candidates from Other Denominations

The Reformed Church in America is a body within the ecumene. While it confesses that it is the true church it does not claim to be the only church. Thus, it makes provision to recognize as valid the ministry within other ecclesiastical bodies and to receive those who fulfill the appropriate conditions as ministers within the Reformed Church without a second ordination.

This practice began in the American experience as Reformed churches in the country existed in close proximity with other ecclesiastical bodies that shared many or all of the theological commitments of the RCA. Thus, classes began to receive ministers from Presbyterian, German Reformed, or Congregational bodies. By 1833, a provision had been established in the constitution:

> The judicatories of the church shall receive no Licentiates or Ministers under their care from any body of professing Christians, who maintain doctrines different from those of the Reformed Dutch Church, without an open and explicit declaration, on their part, that they have renounced such doctrines as contrary to the Holy Scriptures, and the standards of our church (1833, I,I,21).

> Sec. 1. *A classis shall recognize as valid only such ordination in another denomination as is able to meet the following conditions: intended to be within and to the ministry of the catholic or universal church; performed by a duly organized body of Christian churches, and by the authority within such body charged with the exercise of this power, accompanied by prayer and the laying on of hands.*

This section has a parallel in chapter 2, "The Consistory," p. 71. See the comments there. The parallel wording emphasizes the parity of the offices and at the same time keeps distinct the responsibilities of the assemblies. The consistory is responsible for the ordination of the two offices, elder and deacon, while the classis is responsible for those who within the office of minister.

Sec. 2. *A classis shall not receive any licensed candidate or minister under its care from any body of professing Christians which maintains doctrines opposed to those of the* Standards *of the Reformed Church in America, unless that licensed candidate or minister shall make a complete and explicit declaration in writing renouncing such doctrines as being contrary to the* Standards.

This very old requirement allows the church, through its classes, to protect the integrity of the pulpit. At issue, however, is not the one seeking admission, but the church from which she or he came. Does that *church* hold the doctrine in question? Despite our habit of personalizing the ministry, at issue with each minister is not his or her personal beliefs but whether the minister will preach in conformity with the *church's* doctrine (of course one supposes that the minister's personal belief coheres with that of the church, but that is an entirely secondary matter). Thus, the presumption is that the person in question is a minister of a particular church and adheres to its theological understanding. In the case in question when the church's doctrine is in conflict with that of the Reformed Church—and that is to be determined not by the examination of the person, but investigation of the doctrinal positions of the church—the classis cannot grant admission. However, if the minister from that body makes complete and explicit renunciation in writing, that is in a public and verifiable way, then the classis may receive him or her.

Sec. 3. *When an application is made for admission to the classis by a licensed candidate or a minister from another denomination, the classis shall determine whether the applicant's educational qualifications are equal to those required in the Reformed Church in America, and it shall subject the applicant to such examination before classis as shall demonstrate the applicant's understanding of the theology, history, government, and disciplinary procedures of the Reformed Church in America; understanding of an adherence to the* Standards *of the Reformed Church in America; and loyalty to its agencies.*

When the applicant meets the condition under Section 2, the classis must then satisfy itself of a number of further conditions. The classis will have at its disposal the applicant's academic record and must ascertain that it is equivalent with what is required of ministers educated in the RCA. It then must examine the candidate. However, the examination is clearly prescribed to include the applicant's understanding of RCA theology, history, government, and disciplinary procedures. The order makes an interesting shift, for while the classis endeavors to satisfy itself that the applicant displays a proper *understanding* of that which makes our church what it is, the classis must ascertain the applicant's *adherence* to the *Standards*.

Sec. 4.

a. When an ordained minister of another denomination wishes to be considered for a call from a congregation in the RCA, that minister shall furnish the stated clerk of the classis with the following:

1. a completed Minister's Profile form;

2. copies of academic degrees;

3. a seminary transcript

4. names, addresses, and telephone numbers of five persons who are qualified to comment on the applicant's ministry;

5. a statement from the applicant which attests to the

*knowledge of Reformed Church history, readiness to adhere
to the Standards of the RCA, and a basic knowledge of and
readiness to support Reformed Church agencies and
institutions.*

The previous sections dealt with recognition of the church, through the classis, of the validity of ordination. This section addresses the difficulty that emerges when a congregation begins to consider a minister from another denomination for its pulpit. At that stage, the classis may not yet be involved, and the question of the classis's willingness to accept the minister is not yet on the table. This can cause some pain when a church expends time and energy on a pastoral search only to discover that the classis could not accept the minister. Instead, the order now requires that *before* a minister becomes a candidate, he or she must enter a process by which the classis determines the person's readiness for a call by requiring her to meet the standards for the office of ministry as set out by Reformed history and order.

Before the non-RCA minister is allowed to begin discussion with a congregation—or for a congregation to approach that minister— he must begin the process by making application to a classis. The order does not specify *which* classis; one would presume it would be the classis of the church desiring to call. However, a non-RCA minister may desire to candidate within the RCA. In that case, the classis would most likely be that of her or his residence. In any case, the central point is that the minister be approved by a classis, for it alone among ecclesiastical assemblies is charged with the oversight of the office of minister.

He begins by submitting a written application to the stated clerk of the classis. The requirements are designed to parallel those for Reformed Church ministers. This is a preliminary screen to assure that certain minimal standards will be met. The classis will review the application to assure itself that the applicant has indeed met the academic requirements, has testimony to her ministry, and a provisional statement from her that she understands and is prepared to adhere to that peculiar set of beliefs and practices in the church she desires to serve.

> *b. Prior to becoming a serious candidate for a call from a congregation in the Reformed Church in America, an ordained minister who is affiliated with another denomination shall meet with the appropriate committee of a Reformed Church classis, which shall determine whether, in its judgment, the minister is able to meet the requirements set forth in the* Book of Church Order, *Part II, Article 12, Sections 1, 2, and 3 above. The committee's judgment, whether positive or negative, shall be sent by the stated clerk to the Office of Ministry and Personnel Services for attachment to the applicant's Minister's Profile form and such distribution as may be appropriate.*

A second step occurs when the minister becomes a "serious" candidate. Just when and how she crosses the line between candidate and "serious" candidate is not clear, but it is not difficult to distinguish between preliminary discussions between a congregation and a candidate and the onset of a series of interviews, hearing the candidate preach, and the like. Before this step may be taken, the candidate must appear before the "appropriate" committee of a classis. Here one presumes the classis in question will be that of the church preparing to call, because that classis will need not only to approve the call, but to receive the minister into the Reformed Church.

It may be helpful to note that while this subsection speaks of a "committee," not all classes are required to have the "appropriate" committee. This may be true especially in smaller classes. In that case, the classis may itself act as the committee.

This committee shall assure for itself that the candidate can fulfill the requirements set out in Sections 1, 2, and 3 of this article. In effect, the classis is assuring itself *before* the minister applies to be received that he shall be received when the application will be made! Interestingly, the committee's judgment in this case suffices. The order makes no mention of the classis itself making the judgment. Furthermore, the committee itself directs the communication to the General Synod. That judgment will then be available for other instances where the applicant may become a candidate. However, subsection d below makes it clear that the applicant's relationship shall be with this classis, and any subsequent examinations or discussions relating to the applicant's suitability for a call in the RCA will occur with this same committee.

> c. If the committee's judgment is negative, the classis may appoint one or more of its ministers to assist the applicant in preparation for a second meeting of the classis committee, which shall take place not less than six months after the initial meeting. The committee may also require additional formal study prior to a second meeting.

If the committee judges that the applicant cannot meet the requirements to fill the office of minister, the classis, through its committee, may choose to continue to work with the candidate toward a positive result. The committee need not take this further step, however. It may judge that the applicant's theological stance, for example, is too far from that of the Reformed Church and that the candidate shows no inclination to change. If the applicant is a proponent of re-baptism, for example, will promote the practice, and is firmly convinced of the theological correctness of such a position, it makes little sense for a classis to continue conversation.

The committee, however, may assist the applicant in developing his or her understanding of the Reformed Church. The order suggests a mentor from among classis's ministers. The committee may also require formal study.

> d. When an ordained minister who is affiliated with another denomination has met with a classis committee in order to determine whether the minister is qualified to be considered for a call to a Reformed church, and the committee is not satisfied with the minister's qualifications, any subsequent

> *meetings for the same purpose shall take place within the same classis, unless the classis specifically requests another classis to act on its behalf.*

The non-RCA minister approaches the Reformed Church ecclesiastically by means of a classis. The classis is the church as governed by Christ through the offices; therefore, a particular classis is fully authorized to act on behalf of the entire church. The applicant is not permitted to shop for a more congenial classis should a classis refuse his application. He shall continue to work with that classis.

The classis may, however, request another classis to act on its behalf. Even then, however, the second classis acts in the name of the first.

> e. *When a classis is requested to approve a call to a minister who is affiliated with another denomination, prior to its examination of the applicant it shall obtain full information from the chairperson of the committee which reviewed the applicant's qualifications, as outlined in b, c, and d above.*

It is not clear which classis is referred to in this subsection. The classis that initially examined the applicant will have been the classis in which she or he had become a serious candidate. In that case, if a call occurs from the church in question, the classis would be the same. However, should that call not develop and the applicant receive a call within another classis, the second classis would obtain the information requested. After that, the applicant *still* must undergo the examination prescribed in Section 3 above.

> Sec. 5. *A licensed candidate from another denomination shall not be ordained as a minister before serving in a supervised ministry for a period of up to twenty-four months. The classis shall petition the General Synod to provide this superintendence through the board of trustees of an RCA seminary or the Ministerial Formation Coordinating Agency, which will determine the length of the period of supervision.*

An additional requirement is made for the licensed candidate (to be distinguished from a minister from another denomination already ordained). The church will satisfy itself that the candidate is qualified not only in her knowledge of and adherence to the doctrine and polity of the RCA, but in the practice of ministry as well. Since candidates for the Certificate of Fitness have been supervised by the General Synod, the church enjoys some confidence in their readiness for ministry. The same cannot be said for candidates of whom the church has little or no knowledge. Such is to be obtained by observing the candidate in the context of ministry and training the candidate in the practice of a *Reformed* ministry.

The classis itself will not supervise the ministry. In any case, few classes are equipped to do so. This supervision will happen through the General Synod, the assembly specifically charged with theological education for the church.

Article 13. Supervision of Ministers of Word and Sacrament

Ministers of Word and sacrament serve within a local context of ministry, primarily in the proclamation of the Word that creates the church. As an office, the minister gathers with deacons and elders in the leading of a congregation. Nonetheless, the minister's ecclesiastical identity is in some primary way "lodged" in the classis. He is responsible to the classis for his life and ministry. The classis alone has the authority to discipline the minister. She must answer to the classis for her life and her belief. That state of affairs is not accidental. In its supervision of ministers, the classis works to guarantee that congregations will be served with that which is vital to their life: the Word of God. The Word is strange; it comes from without. It is not captive to the gathered community. Similarly, the minister as preacher remains always relatively alien to the congregation. She represents not only the God who is with us, for the minister surely lives with the congregation. She also represents the God who comes from without. That does not mean that because she stands over and against the congregation, nor is she free from discipline. Far from it. The classis exercises that discipline on behalf *of* the church in its local as well as in its global expression.

> Sec. 1. *A classis within the geographic area of service in which a minister serves in an RCA congregation or in a specialized ministry shall be the classis in which membership is held and, as such, shall be responsible for the installation and supervision of that minister with the following exceptions:*

All ministers are members of a classis. One cannot exist in the office in any other way. Ministry is fundamentally relational in that the minister's very essence is determined by her ordination into service in the church. She ministers within a body and is related to that body through the classis.

The locus of her classis is determined by geography. Assemblies in the RCA are established geographically. The church is the church in a particular area; God's rule is for the earth. When the minister serves an RCA congregation, the matter is clear; he is a member of the classis of which the local church is a member. In case of specialized ministry, the matter can be a bit more difficult. The classis is not determined by the geographic area in which the minister lives, but where he serves. It can easily happen in classes geographically contiguous that a minister can live within the bounds of one classis and serve in another. In that case, the minister's classis is the one in which he or she serves; that is, the ministry of the classis is defined by its location, and ministry within its bounds is under its supervision.

> a. *If a minister is serving two or more churches in different classes, the classis nearest the place of the minister's residence shall be the classis in which the minister's membership is held, and the minister shall be installed as a minister of the church in that classis; the status in the other church or churches shall be that of minister under contract.*

Since a minister can be subject to the discipline of only one ecclesiastical assembly, a choice must be made as to the classis of membership. Again, geography makes the decision simple. Furthermore, a classis also supervises the relationship between minister and congregation, so installation cannot occur in two classes simultaneously. Nonetheless, the classis in which the minister serves under contract retains supervision over the contractual arrangement.

> b. If a minister is serving in a specialized ministry in an area within the continental United States or Canada not now governed by an RCA classis, the classis nearest the area of service shall be the classis in which the minister's membership shall be retained.

A Reformed understanding of Christ's lordship over all creation has the church minister within geographic areas. While church membership may include only a portion of the population, God is active and the church serves its locality, furthering the cause of the kingdom in all realms of life. The classis, likewise, is presumed to extend over an area (often rather unspecified but nonetheless identifiable in broad scope). Thus, Reformed order does not generally recognize nongeographic classes, be they described ethnically, theologically, or by any other measure. The classis represents the church fully in its locality.

Given this understanding, the order must make provision for ministers serving outside identifiable boundaries of classes. Often the choice may be rather arbitrary, but the minister is advised to attach him or herself to a classis that can reasonably be described as "nearest."

> c. If a minister is serving in a specialized ministry outside the continental United States or Canada, the classis in which the minister was last installed shall be the classis in which the minister's membership shall be retained.

> d. If a minister is serving as a missionary, a specialized interim minister, or a chaplain within an organization that includes

> *various assignment possibilities, i.e., military bases, VA*
> *hospitals, etc., the classis in which the minister was last*
> *installed shall be the classis in which the minister's*
> *membership shall be retained.*

A classis may have difficulty actively supervising ministers at a geographic distance. This applies not only to the exceptions described in subsections c and d, but to ministers without charge who have moved from the geographic boundaries of the classis. Consequently, some classes have required their specialized ministers to make regular reports to the classis about their lives and work. Still, the distance makes the exercise of appropriate discipline difficult in particular.

> *e. If a minister is serving a united church, the classis in which*
> *the minister's membership is held shall be determined by the*
> *Book of Church Order, Chapter 1, Part I, Article 7, Section 2k.*

> Sec. 2. *The classis in which a minister's membership is held is*
> *the only classis to which the minister is amenable.*

Original versions of the provision from which this section derived read: "A minister shall be amenable solely to the classis of which he is a member." In 1977, in order to allow ministers serving in another country to be responsible also to the indigenous church, the General Synod dropped the term "solely," and added a sentence in a different context: "A minister of the Word remains solely amenable to the classis." The intention seemed to underscore the Reformed notion that the minister is responsible to the classis, and the classis alone has the power of discipline over the minister. No officer or member of the church stands under the discipline of two assemblies at the same time.

The change in 1985 that led to the present wording appears to shift the meaning of the provision. It now reads that a minister cannot be held amenable to two classes, which is right and appropriate. Unfortunately, the new version does not make clear that the minister is not amenable to any other assembly of the church.

> Sec. 3. *The classis shall be responsible for the pastoral care of each enrolled minister and the minister's immediate family. Pastoral care shall be exercised by such means as the classis deems appropriate, which shall be reported to the classis annually in order to assess its adequacy and effectiveness.*

This relatively recent (1981) addition to the *Government* reflected a concern that, while ministers were under the discipline of the classis, neither they nor their families received adequate spiritual care. Although they were members of local congregations, where one's spiritual life is to be primarily located, where one is gathered around the Lord's Table, effective care there was not possible. They were themselves the pastors! Who was to care for them? The appropriate place appears to be the classis.

How a classis is to exercise this responsibility has not been clear, and a number of initiatives have fallen short. Some classes have appointed a chaplain from among their members. Others have given the responsibility to a committee. The classis is charged with the task and the attempt. Whatever means used must be reported by, one assumes, either a committee or a person so charged to the classis at large at least annually.

> Sec. 4.
>
> a. *All ministers shall be responsible to a classis which shall oversee their function as pertains to the Office of Minister of Word and Sacrament (see also Section 2 and Section 6 in Article 13).*
>
> b. *When ministers move from one classis to another, they shall sign the "Declaration for Ministers" in the classis which they join.*

Reformed ministers can never function as independent operators. They remain responsible to a classis, and a classis remains responsible for them. Thus they are ministers of the church, and thus ministers of Christ. They are bound together in responsible communion. This becomes a particular issue with specialized ministers. Because they often do not work directly with a congregation, it is easy to lose connection with the everyday life of the church. Likewise it is tempting for specialized ministers to view their place of employment as the object of their first loyalty. Conversely, a classis, often caught up in the press of its business, easily loses connection with the specialized minister. Both the minister and the classis need continuing contact for the sake of the minister and of the ministry.

> Sec. 5. *The classis shall designate a minister to serve as a mentor to guide, counsel, and model the learning and developmental processes of each newly-ordained minister or, where deemed appropriate by classis, a minister received from another denomination.*

This recent provision (1992) intended to express the classical supervision for ministers following ordination. How shall a minister grow into the office? The classis, which has responsibility for its ministers as office-bearers, will exercise a new function by appointing one of its officers to "mentor" a newly ordained minister in the life and work of the office. The classis will presumably choose a minister it considers a model for ministry, one with skills to guide and care for another. Furthermore, a classis will take care that the mentor is appropriate to the one mentored.

Again, the order does not describe how this is to occur, and appropriately not. However, this task is easily lost amid the press of activity that faces most ministers, and the sometime independent spirit of those called to the office. Thus, a classis must take special care to monitor its execution of this responsibility.

Moreover, while this section requires the appointment of a mentor to the newly ordained, it allows the classis to appoint a mentor to a minister received from another denomination. This seems generally to be beneficial. A minister coming from outside the RCA will face special issues regarding the particular ecclesiastical culture, the practices, and the expectations within the peculiarities of the RCA.

> Sec. 6. *The installed minister shall be* ipso facto *a member of the church served. A minister not serving as an installed pastor shall become a member of a local church, but shall not represent that church in any classis or synod. A minister remains solely amenable to the classis, but if elected an elder, shall be entitled to all the privileges and responsibilities pertaining to that office.*

The statement that a minister shall be a member of a local church entered the order by 1958 and has been the source of debate ever since. Older orders seemed to assume that the minister was primarily a member of the classis. This seemed right, for the minister cannot be under the discipline of the board of elders *and* the classis at the same time. This view is rooted in the correct understanding that membership is held around the Lord's Table, and communion at the Supper implies subjecting oneself to Christ's discipline—expressed for the Reformed through a board of elders.

On the other hand, it has been argued that ministers are in fact, if not by the order, intimate participants in congregational life. Are they not members? More deeply, one could maintain that if membership is at the Table, where else is the table at which she or he gathers than in the congregation? The classis is not a liturgical body, and even on those occasions when the classis gathers around the Table, a body analogous to a board of elders does not function as the expression of discipline.

Thus the order has kept the provision that the minister is member of the congregation where he or she has been installed. However, the minister is not subject to the board of elders. The classis remains responsible for his discipline. Here the order attempts to clear up any confusion left over from Section 2 above.

This section recognizes that ministers may be elected and ordained to other offices; here the office of elder is explicitly mentioned. When serving in that office, the minister, as it were, exchanges his identity. He is *not* both minister and elder at the same time, at least so far as the order is concerned. While serving as an elder, he or she is responsible to the other elders. He or she can as an elder, so it appears, represent the church in the classis, as well as represent the classis in higher assemblies. (The order seems to be mistaken here. Churches are not represented in any assemblies beyond the classis. Classes may have churches choose elders for synods; but those elders represent not their churches but the classis).

> Sec. 7. *A minister of the classis shall superintend the proceedings of a consistory when a call is being issued to a minister. When completed, a call must be presented by the consistory to the classis, which shall approve the call before it is presented to the minister called. If no legitimate objection is offered, the minister shall be installed by the classis or its committee according to the office for installation in the Liturgy.*

The procedure for calling a minister is outlined on pp. 53-55. The order has always placed a major weight on the calling church in obtaining a minister for the church. Indeed, as we have seen, the Dort order includes the approbation of the congregation as constituent of a lawful call (Dort, IV). That appears to harken back to an ancient practice adduced by Calvin in which the congregation confirmed the bishop's election by affirmation. Nonetheless, the classis participates in its review of the call for the care and protection of the congregation. The classis is present in the person of one of its ministers, who has been assigned to the superintendence of the call. The supervisor can ascertain that the call is in good order, that the terms meet the minimum requirements set by the classis, that the consistory understands its responsibilities, and the like.

The call itself does not go immediately to the minister called, but must first be submitted to the classis, which must approve the call and attest to the same. The requirement for approval supposes that classis may *deny* a call with an appropriate reason. Only upon approval is the call then presented to the one called.

The process of call and the installation by the classis underscores the fact that the minister and the church do not exist in isolation, but always and only within an ecclesiastical relationship to which they are responsible.

> Sec. 8. *When the termination of a minister's relationship to a church is in view, a minister of the classis having jurisdiction shall be invited by the church to be present at a meeting of the consistory for the purpose of superintending the application for such action. The supervising minister shall attest such application and shall deliver it to the classis with a written report. The latter shall serve as the basis upon which the action of the classis shall be made. If either the minister or the consistory shall not join in the application, that fact shall be plainly stated in the report. In such case no termination of the relationship shall be made by the classis until a hearing of both minister and consistory has been conducted in open classis. The president of the classis shall give ten days' notice of such hearing to both parties. The warrant for the notice and for the call of the classis shall be the report of the supervising minister. A vote for termination of the minister's relationship to a church shall be by two-thirds of the members of the classis present.*

When a minister is installed in a congregation, the classis declares the establishment of a pastoral relationship. That bond remains until it is "dissolved" by the classis. The relationship between church and minister thus is not created by the parties themselves, but by the church, or more correctly by Christ through the offices gathered as a classis. Thus, when a termination is anticipated through acceptance of call to another church, retirement, or other resignation from office, the classis must be involved.

However, the application for the dissolution comes from the consistory and the minister. Under usual circumstances, both parties would agree, and the application for dissolution (Form. 8) states that both parties concur in the request. The function of the classis supervisor is primarily to attest to this fact, because it is the supervising minister who presents the request to the classis, along with a written report. That report usually assures the classis that all obligations have been met by both parties.

However, cases emerge where one or another party does not accede to the request for dissolution. This is a very serious matter that usually signals discontent between a minister and a congregation. The request for dissolution then must be adjudicated by the entire classis. In fact, the supervising minister's report that only one party has requested dissolution automatically sets in motion a process by which the president of the classis must call the entire classis together for a hearing.

The classis is to meet in open session. That is, the hearing itself cannot be held in an executive session. The matter must be publicly and openly heard. The order is unclear just how a classis would decide to agree to the request of either party.

> Sec. 9. *When a minister of a church has attained the age of seventy years, the ministerial relationship to that church shall be terminated. The classis shall terminate the relationship at a special meeting, or not later than the next regular meeting. The classis shall then appoint a supervisor over the church, unless other contractual relations approved by the classis are in effect. Those who reach the age of seventy years may continue to be employed on a renewable contract basis, the length of time of the contract being no more than one year at a time, with each renewal approved by consistory and classis. Retired ministers may be installed into a form of ministry.*

Having been ordained, a minister does not leave office when he or she "retires" from active service. What happens in ordination is not negated. Still, age will at some time prevent the minister from actively living out her vocation. How then shall the church respond? The concern has ever been present. Dort's order put it: "If a Minister becomes *incapable* of performing the duties of his office, either through age, sickness, or otherwise, such Minister shall, notwithstanding, retain the honour and stile of his office, and be provided with an honourable support by the churches to which he hath ministered; provision is in like manner to be made for the widows and orphans of the Ministers in general" (Dort, XIII).

The current order arbitrarily chooses the age of seventy as that time when the ministerial relationship with a congregation shall end. That is, the relation of an installed minister and the congregation shall be dissolved. The minister no longer serves as president of the consistory, nor is he or she, in most cases, the supervisor of the consistory. Thus the minister moves out of his or her position as an officer in the leadership of the congregation. However, the minister can still serve in the congregation, albeit under a contract and with a yearly review in effect.

Sec. 10.

a. The term "minister emeritus" is an honorary title and does not confer on its holder any obligations, rights, or privileges.

b. A consistory may, with the approval of its classis, declare to be minister emeritus a former minister of its congregation.

The Explanatory Articles (XVI) had the classis declare every minister who was no longer capable of fulfilling the function of the office an emeritus. Furthermore, the same article furthered the provision we met above from Dort that the local congregation is obligated for the financial well-being of the *emeritus* and his family, should they survive him! The current provision states clearly that the title emeritus by itself earns no such support. Indeed, this section intends to make clear that the pastor emeritus does not function in the office of minister in the church that declared him emeritus. Thus the order intends to prevent conflict with a legitimate occupant of the office of minister in the congregation.

> Sec. 11. *The classis shall keep a record book in which the declarations for licensed candidates and ministers are clearly written. Those who are received on examination or on certificate shall subscribe to the proper declaration in the presence of the classis.*

It is necessary for the classis to maintain a public record of those who have been authorized to preach, so that it can provide other classes with the appropriate attestation to the ministerial standing of those within its bounds. This is further instantiation of the church taking care to remain cognizant of those who might enter its pulpits.

It is common practice that not only those received on examination or by certificate, but all ministers subscribe to the appropriate declaration in the presence of the classis. Ministers thereby enter a peculiar relation with their brothers and sisters in the classis, promising to live within its discipline and in responsibility to Christ.

> Sec. 12.
>
> a. *A person who has been ordained to the office of minister may voluntarily relinquish the office by demission, but only after application to, and with the consent of, the classis of which the person is a member. The classis, having fulfilled its pastoral responsibility insofar as feasible, may declare the person to have demitted the office of minister, and, if so declared, shall remove the name of the member from the roll of classis, and, if requested, transfer the person to membership and care of a local church.*

A minister desiring to relinquish the office of ministry does so through the process called "demission." This is a serious step and the order is careful to state just how it is accomplished.

The minister requests the classis to take the action. The minister does not demit on his own. The office was not his to take; it was conferred upon him. Thus it is not his to "return." It will be an act of the church. Thus it requires an act of the classis to declare the minister to be demitted.

The classis will take care in doing so. It will need to inquire as to the reasons for taking such a serious step. Indeed, it may enjoin upon the minister the question of his or her call. It may look with disfavor upon someone who simply desires to better him or herself in a different "career." Dort's order put it clearly: "A Minister of the word being once lawfully called...is bound to the service of the sanctuary, as long as he liveth. Therefore he shall not be at liberty to devote himself to a secular vocation, except for great and important reasons, concerning which the Classis shall enquire and determine" [Dort, XII].

Still, the minister may impress upon the classis that her theological understanding has so changed as to make her ministry one without integrity. Or he may show that his character is clearly unsuitable for the vocation. The classis shall judge finally, after it has exercised care and gentleness in inquiry.

If the classis declares the person to be demitted, she is no longer a minister, and thus her name is removed from the roll of the classis as one authorized to preach the Word and celebrate the sacrament. It is not clear why the classis transfers the person's membership to a local church when the minister is already a member of a church. However, because the minister is member of a congregation only by virtue of his installation, that relationship ceases with the dissolution of the pastoral bond with that congregation.

> b. A minister who because of ill health, incapacity, lack of opportunity, or other reason deemed sufficient by the classis, has not functioned in that office for a period of six months may

> be declared inactive by the classis. When a minister has not functioned in that office due to lack of opportunity, the classis shall first use its best efforts to provide an opportunity for preaching and/or teaching the Word and administering the sacraments before declaring the minister inactive. This declaration shall be reviewed by the classis semi-annually. Should an inactive minister be capable of resuming the duties and functions of a minister and decline to make satisfactory efforts to do so and also decline to relinquish the office by demission, the classis may proceed with the presentation and trial of the charge of desertion of office, with the possibility of suspension or deposition from office.

The order recently added the category "inactive" to allow for ministers who cannot function due to ill health or lack of opportunity. This category allows the classis to consider such ministers in good standing. It was a way around difficulties posed by a functional view of ministry by which a minister ceased to exist in the office when he or she ceased to function.

The classis is enjoined, however, to take active cognizance and care for such ministers. In the case of illness or incapacity, the classis must review the minister's status semi-annually. If lack of opportunity is the occasion for the minister's inactivity, the classis must attempt to provide occasions for the minister to function in the office. Given vacancies in churches, vacations of ministers, to say nothing of a variety of ministries available in hospitals, jails, and nursing homes, this should not be difficult for the classis.

It is incumbent upon the minister then to take advantage of the opportunities provided and to exercise her office. Should she not, the classis can charge her with desertion of office. That is a welcome change from the rank functional view prior to 1992, when a classis was allowed to revoke the ordination of a minister who had not been active in ministry for a period of two years. That had called for an action of the classis as an assembly. The new provision makes it a disciplinary action and thus the decision of a judicatory. The minister refuses to exercise the office to which he was called; it is nothing less than disobedience to his Lord!

> c. A minister who attains the age of sixty years may, with the approval of classis, retire. A retired minister shall retain ordination and shall remain under the care and supervision of classis without being required to perform the duties and functions of a minister.

This section supposes a world at odds with late twentieth-century western culture. We assume that the individual person chooses when and how to exercise her vocation. Not so for a Reformed understanding of church. The minister is *expected* to function in her office. This subsection *permits* her to "retire" at a specified age. Nor may she do so on her own. The classis of which she is a part must approve the decision. Could a classis disapprove? Could it enjoin the minister to continue? Apparently it could!

Because the retired minister remains under the care and supervision of the classis, he is not under the care of a board of elders. This is crucial in cases of discipline. A retired minister is no less under the discipline of the classis.

> Sec. 13. When a person who has been declared demitted from the office of minister shall seek to enter upon a function appropriate to the office (Article 11, Section 4, above), the classis of membership at the time of demission shall administer such examination as it deems necessary. If satisfied by the examination, that classis shall reordain the person.

A person who has demitted from office may desire to perform the functions of the office. While the text here refers to Article 11, Section 4, it seems more apt to assume the more central function of the minister: preaching, celebration of the sacraments, working beside other officers in the leadership of the church. The person who has demitted has been debarred from those functions. To enter them again requires the action of the classis.

It cannot be just any classis. A minister cannot demit in one part of the country and reapply for admission in another part. That would violate the fact that the classis acts in the stead of the entire church. Moreover it would be inadvisable, for it is the classis in which demission occurred that is most fully cognizant of the reasons for demission and can thus be more pointed and more careful in re-examination.

The person must be reordained. The demission canceled, as it were, the ordination. The classis agreed that the candidate could not fulfill the call on him, and thus they severed the relational connection that was the foundation of his ordination.

> Sec. 14. *Ministers shall not be pressured in such a way as to lead either one who supports or one who opposes, on scriptural grounds, the ordination of women to church offices to offend against one's conscience; nor shall any minister be penalized for conscientious objection to or support of the ordination of women to church offices; nor shall any minister obstruct by unconstitutional means the election, ordination, or installation of a woman to church offices.*

This parallels the "conscience clause" on pp. 86 and 109. See the comments at those places.

> Sec. 15. *A minister of another denomination whose ordination meets the criteria of Chapter 1, Part II, Article 12, Section 1, whose good standing has been certified by that denomination, and who serves with the approval of classis as a minister under contract, an assistant minister, a minister in a cooperative specialized ministry in which classis shares sponsorship, or a minister to a congregation composed of denominational units at least one of which is associated with the classis may upon request and with the approval of classis, hold temporary membership in the classis. Such temporary members shall have the rights and privileges of membership for the period of the approved service, but may not represent their classis in the higher judicatories,*

assemblies, agencies, or commissions of the Reformed Church in America. Temporary members shall be subject to the discipline of the classis as provided in Chapter 1, Part I, Article 7, Section 2s.

Temporary members shall not subscribe to the declaration, but, in accepting temporary membership, shall agree that in their duties approved by the classis they will conduct themselves in a manner consistent with the declaration and accept the counsel and admonition of the classis.

Article 14. Commissioning and Supervision of Preaching Elders

In 1998, the RCA accepted a major shift in its order. Since the order centers on offices and assemblies, the task of preaching was concentrated in the office of minister of Word and sacrament. The designation of "preaching elders" did not add a new office, but to some extent it blurred the distinction between the office of elder and minister. Furthermore, Reformed order gave no place to "lay preachers." Because the church's very existence devolves from the Word, the church has been very cautious concerning those who are granted privilege of access to the pulpit.

Nonetheless, it had become evident that, in a number of areas, the church had begun to give place to "lay preachers." The Theological Commission gave serious attention to a question that pressed from the church.[10] Some churches had expressed frustration with their inability to find ministers to fill their pulpits. This was especially the case in small, rural congregations, and in some urban, ethnic congregations.

The Theological Commission argued carefully and hesitantly that a case might be made not for lay preachers, but for elders who could be commissioned to preach under particular conditions. The commission clearly distinguished between the preaching elder and the lay preacher. Indeed, the elder relinquished her supervisory and

10 *MGS*, 1997, pp. 275-285.

discerning role as elder when she entered the pulpit. Furthermore, the authorization of the elder to preach remained tied to the local congregation. He is not authorized to represent the church at large. And the commissioning of the elder to preach does not imply authority to exercise any other pastoral function within or beyond a congregation.

> Sec. 1. *A consistory may request the classis to commission a preaching elder for that congregation. If a preaching elder is requested where there is no installed minister, the congregation shall demonstrate that its circumstances make the calling of an ordained minister of Word and sacrament impossible.*

This article assumes two conditions under which an elder may be commissioned to preach. Under the first, a congregation with an installed minister may desire an elder to preach on occasion. The second condition obtains when a consistory is not able to call a minister. In that instance, the consistory must demonstrate that impossibility to the classis. Thus, a consistory cannot simply request of a classis that the classis consider commissioning an elder, but must first show why such is required.

> Sec. 2. *A commissioned preaching elder shall be an ordained elder in the Reformed Church in America with gifts for preaching. If the elder is not serving on the active consistory and is commissioned to a regular preaching ministry in a church with no installed pastor, he or she shall meet regularly with the consistory for the duration of the commission.*

A candidate for commissioning as a preaching elder must meet two prior conditions. First, he or she must be an elder in the Reformed Church in America. Thus, she is already ordained to a ministry within the church. She lives within the discipline of an office. Second, the consistory will need to ascertain that she possesses the gift for preaching.

The commissioned elder will meet with the consistory. That does not mean that he necessarily will be a member of the consistory (if not installed). His presence places him under the supervision and guidance of the consistory, recognizing that the responsibility for worship rests with the consistory.

> **Sec. 3.** *The classis shall examine the candidate prior to commissioning as a preaching elder, in order to determine that the necessary gifts, knowledge, and skills are present. Such examination shall be based on a program of study in the following areas: (1) New Testament introduction and history, (2) Old Testament introduction and history, (3) biblical exegesis and interpretation, (4) sermon composition and delivery, (5) systematic theology, and (6) RCA doctrinal standards. The form and content of this program of study shall be approved by the classis. The classis may waive all or part of the program of study if the elder demonstrates that such study or its equivalent has already been completed. In no case, however, shall the classis waive the examination.*

The commissioning of the elder to preach remains the responsibility of the classis. The classis is responsible that those who preach conform to the church's norm for responsible proclamation of the Word. While the consistory must make a prior determination of the elder's gifts for preaching, that claim must further be tested by the classis.

Furthermore, the candidate must follow a rigorous program of study. A desire to preach and the ability to construct a pleasing Sunday morning presentation are not sufficient. The classis must assure not only itself but the church that this candidate is sufficiently at home in Scripture, is able to exegete Scripture, and is conversant with theology and the doctrinal standards to proclaim the Word to a congregation. Thus the order holds the preaching elder to very high standards. This article does not allow easy access to the pulpit.

> **Sec. 4.** *Preaching elders may be commissioned for up to two*

*years. Representatives of the classis shall conduct a service
of commissioning in the church where the elder is
commissioned to preach. The commission may be renewed
after evaluation by the local consistory and the classis. When
the commissioned preaching elder is serving a church with
no installed pastor, commissioning shall be renewed only
when the calling of a minister of the Word and sacrament
continues to be impossible. The classis shall arrange for
regular and thorough supervision of commissioned preaching
elders. The classis shall revoke or refuse to renew a
commission for a preaching elder if the classis determines
that the Word of God is not rightly proclaimed.*

The commissioning of an elder is not an ordination to office, nor is it a licensure to preach. Thus it is granted for a limited time, up to two years. The commission may be extended, but only on demonstration by the consistory to the classis of the impossibility of calling a minister. This provision protects the church from gradually sliding into a condition whereby the commissioned elder becomes *de facto* a permanent preacher.

The requirement that the classis commission the elder in the local congregation signals to the congregation that the preaching elder is authorized by and stands under the authority of a greater body. The Word she preaches is not her own word, but can be trusted to be a faithful interpretation of the Word itself.

The presence of the preaching elder places a great responsibility on the classis. In contradistinction to ministers, the preaching elder remains under continuing supervision. This is not only a protective measure for the church, but an encouragement to the preaching elder. He is thus given recourse to a body that can assist him in his task.

*Sec. 5. Commissioning is only for preaching in a specific place
designated by the classis, under the supervision of the
classis and the local consistory. Commissioning does not
authorize the preaching elder to preach regularly in places*

not designated by the classis, nor to assume the responsibilities of the Office of Minister of Word and Sacrament, except for the preaching of the Word. Commissioned preaching elders may serve as regular delegates if appointed by their consistory, or as nonvoting delegates to classis at the discretion of the classis. In their preaching ministry they are amenable to the classis through the commissioning and supervision process; in all other matters they participate in mutual oversight with the local consistory in the same way that all elders do.

The order is careful here to distinguish between the roles of minister and elder. While a minister has been ordained, as minister, to preach throughout the church, the preaching elder can preach in only those places designated by the classis, most likely the congregation that has been unable to call a minister. On the other hand, like the minister the elder is responsible to the classis in the ministry of proclamation. Thus, the freedom of the pulpit is protected from the enthusiasms of a local congregation or consistory. However, the preaching elder remains amenable to the mutual oversight practiced by the consistory.

Article 15. Certification and Supervision of Associates in Ministry

The classis shall be responsible for certifying those persons who meet the criteria approved by General Synod as Associates in Ministry and shall be responsible for the supervision of Associates in Ministry.

This relatively new article introduces a new category into the church order, an "associate in ministry." "Associate in ministry" is not an office. Oddly, the article does not describe such associates. They were intended to be Christian educators, and they were included within the classis in order to grant them a higher profile in the church. The classis was designated as supervisor to regulate more closely their lives and conduct. However, they are not members of the classis. Indeed, since they are not officers of the church, they cannot be (and one wonders how they would be conceived in such an office). Thus, it is doubly odd that the classis would supervise them in any way.

Article 16. Relation to Regional and General Synods

> Sec. 1. *The classis shall report annually to the regional and General Synods upon the state of religion within the bounds of the classis. Such statistics as the General Synod shall require from time to time shall be presented in tabular form.*

The assemblies of the church are mutually accountable. The classis reports to both greater bodies when it comments on the state of religion within its bounds. In this manner not only does the classis take cognizance and care for the ministry under its supervision, but it involves the larger church in the knowledge of its life and work.

> Sec. 2. *The classis shall report annually to the regional synod the names of persons who have been examined and licensed or ordained, all admissions and dismissions of ministers, all changes of pastoral relations, and the deaths of ministers within its bounds since the last session of the regional synod.*

The classis is responsible to the greater church as it makes known the status of the ministers within its bounds. In that manner, all other classes and congregations can be aware of those ministers qualified to serve in the office.

> Sec. 3. *The classis shall appoint delegates to the regional and General Synods.*

This provision is so common that it is difficult to think that it might be otherwise. However, at the outset of the American church, the General Synod was composed of minister and elder delegates from each congregation. General Synod acted as a convention. By 1800, with the formation of a new particular synod (until that time the General and particular synods were in effect one), it was proposed to change the Explanatory Articles so that the particular synods sent the delegates to General Synod. That was not accepted, and the practice of having delegates sent from classes developed.

The General Synod, in consequence, is a gathering from the various classes. Neither the congregations nor the regional synods, but the classes gather each year in synod.

4

The Regional Synod

Until very recently, the assembly described in this part was called the "particular" synod. "Particular" correlates with the term "general," but the term had ceased to communicate, and "regional" more accurately describes the General Synod's division into broad geographic areas. Rather imprecisely, the regional synods comprise the next concentric circle of Reformed ecclesiastical governance beyond the classis.

Of late, regional synods have been considered the weakest assembly, and some have actively advocated the elimination of this "middle judicatory." The RCA's sister denomination, the Christian Reformed Church, has no parallel assembly. However, the regional synod has had a long role, and at times a crucial one, in Reformed history.

The Dutch church, for example, while providing for a general or national synod, in fact held none between the great synod of Dort and 1945, although the Algemene Reglement of 1816 provided a small, centralized, administrative "general" synod. In fact, the "great synods" of the sixteenth century had limited power, and their decisions were accepted only partially. Thus, the provincial synods did the lion's share of the work of the "greater" assemblies.

Similarly, the Reformed church in this country began with a powerful particular synod. Between 1792 and 1800 the church consisted of one particular synod, co-extensive with the general synod. The particular synod was charged with "original cognizance of such cases as are not merely local, and which in their consequences are supposed to affect the general welfare of the church" (Exp. Art., XLVI). Furthermore, the order of Dort allowed the synods to be in "correspondence" with neighboring synods (XLVIII). This was retained through the American church's 1874 constitution. The Explanatory Articles (LIII) explain this provision as a consequence of the lack of a National Synod in the Dutch church. The correspondence between the synods was a way of maintaining a national church. The establishment of the General Synod removed the need, but the provision remained. In fact, given the relatively limited scope of responsibilities assigned to the General Synod, the particular synods retained considerable power, even to a correspondence across the church. Technically, the church did not need the General Synod to remain "connected" as a church.

In general, the regional synods play a particular role as judicatories (see below) and in the formation of classes. In practice they also participate in the general administration of the broader church. However, it must be admitted that synods (the plural here referring to regional synods) are currently searching for their peculiar identity within the order. Nonetheless, it shall be shown that the order provides them with a broader role than is often granted.

Article 1. Regional Synod Defined

Sec. 1. *The regional synod is an assembly and judicatory consisting of ministers and elders delegated by each of the classes within the bounds determined for it by the General Synod. Voting rights shall be limited to elder delegates and those ministers who are actively serving under the jurisdiction or with the approval of the classis.*

The synod is neither a collection of churches nor of classes. The churches and classes exist within the synod and are, in differing respects, subject to the synod. The synod itself, however, is an assembly and judicatory, a gathering of the offices of ministers and elders. The synod may and often does much of its work through its particular agencies, but the synod itself is no more and no less than an assembly and judicatory. Thus "synod" as subject is properly restricted to actions taken by that assembly.

The General Synod sets the bounds of the various synods. Those bounds are determined geographically. While it has been the case that the General Synod may allot various classes to the regional synod—this being most recently accomplished by placing all the Canadian classes within one synod—that allotment is theoretically within geographic boundaries. The regional synods alone have the power to constitute classes. Thus in the Canadian instance, a classis belonging to the Synod of the Great Lakes was placed within the Synod of Canada because the General Synod determined a new geographical configuration.

The regional synod itself consists of delegates from the classes within its bounds. Thus, representation is not from the churches themselves, but following the presbyterial principle, from the next lower assembly (although this pattern will be broken significantly in the case of the general synod where the delegates represent not the regional synods, but the classes).

The determination of voting rights most significantly affects ministers. Although each classis determines which ministers are "actively serving," (see above) this provision disallows ministers from claiming a right to represent the classes simply by virtue of enjoying the office.

Sec. 2. *Each regional synod may determine the method of selection and the number of delegates from each classis within its bounds.*

Older constitutions prescribed the method and number of representatives to be delegated by each classis. The provisions always included an equal number of minister and elder delegates. The *BCO* appears to allow each synod to determine not only its own size, but to allow unequal (!) representation by elder delegates and ministers, however unwise that may appear within a presbyterial system. However, a synod may be large or small in number. Theoretically, this provision allows a synod to convene as a quasi-convention, in which each classis is allowed to send a minister and/or elder from each congregation, the delegates to be enrolled at the meeting of the synod.

Sec. 3. *The regional synod is a permanent continuing body which functions between stated sessions through committees.*

Like the classes and the General Synod, the synod no longer exists only when it is in session. It is a body to which reference can be made, appeals sent, queries posed, and the like. Its necessary functions occur through whatever committees it establishes (an exception being the requirement of a judicial business committee; see below). However, those committees themselves while acting on behalf of the synod do not *constitute* the synod as such. The synod subsists only as the gathering of those ministers and elders so delegated.

Sec. 4. *A regional synod may retain its designation as a particular synod for its legal documents.*

Article 2. Responsibilities of the Regional Synod

Sec. 1. *The regional synod shall exercise a general superintendence over the interests and concerns of the classes within its bounds.*

Classes are responsible to the greater church through the regional synod. This accords with the general principle already noted that the "greater" assembly (delimited by neighboring ecclesiastical entities) is responsible for "cognizance" of certain matters of the "lesser" assemblies. That notion has largely been lost in the peculiar manner by which the General Synod is constructed. General Synod receives representatives from the classes and corresponds directly with them. We live in a world made smaller by communication technology. Thus, the general interests of the church are easily transmitted and shared. Nonetheless, the order understood the regional synod as the vehicle by which the greater church communicated with the classes.

This was accomplished in part through the aforementioned "deputatus," a representative from the regional synod who was to be present at the examination of candidates for ministry. However, the order of Dort described their task more broadly. They were to "afford the Classis their advice and assistance in whatever difficulties may occur, to the end that uniformity, order and purity of doctrine, may be maintained and established" (XLIX).

At the least it would appear that the regional synod is charged with cognizance of the work of its various classes. It does not intrude on the peculiar privileges of the classes when it inquires into their activities, as it would if it questioned the ordered life of a classis or the theological tenor of its action. More positively, the synod stands ready to discuss ecclesiastical issues that arise within a classis and that a classis may put to the synod for instruction and guidance. A more lively interchange on such issues may, of itself, revive ecclesiastical interest in the work and presence of synods.

Indeed, while the church's world has become smaller, the synods still reflect differing cultural contexts. Ecclesiastical life in upstate New York, for example, occurs within a context quite different from that of southern California, or even metropolitan New York. The synods assist the church as it remains faithful to Christ's ministry in differing environments. In just this way, the church remains faithful to its mission as it ministers to the particularities of its context. The Word, while always transcending the local, remains particular, and each synod plays its role in leading and assisting the church in ministry in a particular context.

At the same time it is to be noted that the synods exercise their superintendence over the *classes* and not the local congregations. Because Reformed classes generally consist of a relatively small number of congregations, their resources are limited. In the circumstance, the synods have often hired staff to assist them in the church's work. Thus, synod staff have often been seconded to assist a local church work through conflict, develop program, and the like. However, this is only an assisting role and cannot circumvent the peculiar responsibility of the classes to their churches.

Sec. 2. *The regional synod shall exercise an appellate supervisory power over the acts, proceedings, and decisions of its several classes.*

The power noted here is appellate power. This section thus describes the synod's role in discipline. The regional synod cannot on its own overturn the action of one of its classes. That can occur only through the process of complaint or appeal, clearly set out in the disciplinary procedures. Nonetheless, the order is clear that such power resides first with the regional synod and not with the General Synod. The regional synod is the first and primary court to which classes and their members have recourse. The implications of that principle are technical but crucial for the work of the synod. They will be detailed further under the commentary on disciplinary procedures.

Sec. 3. *The regional synod shall form, combine, and disband classes, and may transfer churches from one classis to another within its bounds.*

The power to form classes is crucial to the life of the church and is found nowhere else within the order. It is granted to the regional synod because that synod alone is aware of the local conditions under which the classes exist and work. The regional synod alone is sufficiently "close" to understand the various "cultures" of the classes and the geographical and social realities within which the various congregations live and work.

The regional synods remain local enough to understand when classes become too small or too large to execute their responsibilities. But more, because the synods are themselves constituted by delegates from neighboring classes, they allow the classes to remain in conversation with each other over their needs and capabilities. One classis by itself cannot change its boundaries (although it can petition for change). Still, it maintains the sort of conversation with delegates from other classes through which it can appeal for change—or resist change.

> Sec. 4. *The regional synod shall create whatever organization it desires for the furtherance of the work of the gospel within its bounds, provided such organization does not infringe upon the prerogatives of the several classes or churches.*

Regional synods are peculiarly placed to assist the churches in ministry. They are sufficiently local to respond to the needs of churches in differing contexts of ministry. Indeed, they are close enough to local congregations to respond appropriately to opportunities for mission and to enable the congregations to enjoy a sense of ownership. At the same time, the synods are large enough to provide the greater resources in staff that the classes cannot. The church order recognizes and empowers synods to this work.

It is this section that is understood to grant the regional synods the authority to assess its member classes for its work in ministry. Without such authority, a synod's action to create subsidiary organizations would be held hostage to the judgment of the classes. A synod may be wise, however, in ascertaining the support of its classes for its ministry. In that way, it would honor the Reformed notion of the mutual responsibility of its assemblies.

The synods have traditionally exercised this function with church extension agents that assisted classes in the establishment of new churches. They have built camps and conference centers to assist congregations in the education of the faithful. But synods can do more. Some synods have developed educational programs that assist congregations in the nurture of children and youth. Others have developed opportunities for ongoing education of elders and deacons. Some synods have responded to the mission demands within their bounds. One synod coordinates the classes in their responsibilities to mentor pastors. The point is simple. The order provides greater scope for the regional synod than has often been recognized.

Article 3. Delegates

Sec. 1. *The delegate shall be a member of the regional synod from the date of election or appointment and shall continue in that responsibility to the regional synod until the effective date of election or appointment of a successor. If, however, ministerial membership in the classis represented or confessing membership in a church within the classis represented shall be terminated during the period of appointment, the delegate shall cease to be a member of the regional synod.*

Because the synod is a "permanent continuing body," the delegates serve not only when the synod meets, but throughout their terms. If, for example, it is necessary to call a special meeting of the synod, the classes do not appoint new delegates. Those delegates who are serving their terms will be called together. In the usual circumstance, they will be those appointed for the previous annual meeting of the synod. This requires particular care in cases of discipline or appeal.

Sec. 2. The elder delegate to regional synod shall be chosen from the entire body of elders in a church whether or not presently engaged as a member of the board of elders.

Article 4. Sessions of Regional Synod

Sec. 1. The regional synod shall meet annually at such time and place as it may determine. All regional synod sessions shall begin and end with prayer.

Sec. 2. The president of the regional synod shall call a special session of the synod upon receipt of a written request of one minister and one elder delegate from each of the classes within its bounds. At least three weeks' notice of the meeting shall be given, such notice stating the purpose of the meeting.

The provision for special sessions follows the pattern established in other assemblies, consistories, and classes. However, the provision for regional synods appears unnecessarily restrictive. Apparently the president may call a special session *only* on the request of the required number of ministers and elder delegates (noting that those ministers and elder delegates are those determined in Article 3, Section 1 above). However, especially in cases of discipline, the synod may find it advisable to meet prior to its annual meeting. Must the president solicit ministers and elder delegates to obtain permission to call the session?

Sec. 3. The presence of a majority of the minister delegates and a majority of the elder delegates is required to constitute a quorum at any session of a regional synod.

The assembly is not a legitimate body when a simple majority of its delegates is present. If a synod is constituted by an equal number of ministers and elders, a simple majority could be obtained with the entire body of ministers present plus one elder. The order recognizes that the assembly is the gathering of the offices, in this case of ministers and elders, and that the offices must be appropriately represented. This requirement, as simple as it sounds, prevents the church from becoming a "clerocracy," or as the Dutch were wont to call it, a "dominocracy."

Article 5. Officers of Regional Synod

Sec. 1. *A president shall be elected to preside at the sessions of the regional synod. It shall be the duty of the president to state and explain the business to be transacted, to enforce the rules of order, and, in general, to maintain the decorum and dignity belonging to the church of Jesus Christ.*

Sec. 2. *A copy of the minutes of every session of the several classes held since the last regular session of the regional synod shall be produced for inspection at the synod's annual meeting.*

The synod exercises its "general superintendence" in part through the review of official classical actions as set out in their minutes. This is more than a formal review. The synod pays particular attention to whether the classes execute their responsibilities as required by the church order. In this way the church remains responsible to itself and maintains its accountability to ministry.

What would occur if the synod discovered something amiss in the minutes of a classis? The order does not provide direction. One might assume that the synod at the least is empowered to raise the question with a classis. That opens conversation over the proper conduct of ecclesiastical life.

Sec. 3. *The president of the regional synod shall prepare a synodical report on the state of religion and present it at the annual meeting of the synod. The basis of this report shall be the reports on the state of religion of the presidents of the several classes.*

Interestingly, the order does not require the presidents of the classes to prepare a "state of religion" report. The classes have, however, historically presented such reports, although until the twentieth century it was often a special committee of a classis that offered those reports. The notice here apparently has a sort of reflective power, requiring reports from the presidents of the classes.

We take note of the phrase, "state of religion." One might expect a report on the "state of the church," an institutional report. Or a report on the state of the "faith," a discussion of how the peculiar religion, Christianity, fares, especially in an increasingly secular society. Perhaps that is what is intended. However, one might detect a Reformed background to this peculiar phrase. The faith was understood to be more than an institution, the church, and more than a confessional commitment of true believers. Christianity was a religion in the full sense, incorporating not only a cultic and doctrinal life, but encompassing a societal way of being. Religion, then, had effect not only on the churches, but on schools, business, and governmental life. One need only cite *Our Song of Hope*, where, under the fifth heading, "Our Hope in Daily Life," the church acknowledges the Spirit's work in government, hears the Spirit's call to a new orientation of societal life.[1] The Reformed church concerns itself with the sanctification of all of life in the society where God has called it into being and ministry.

> Sec. 4. *The regional synod shall have a clerk whose duty shall be to keep a faithful record of all the proceedings of the body and to furnish official notices in writing to all persons directly affected by judicial decisions of the assembly. The clerk shall also be responsible for forwarding to the denominational archives copies of minutes of the regional synod and subsidiary corporations.*

1. Eugene P. Heideman, *Our Song of Hope: A Provisional Confession of Faith of the Reformed Church in America* (Grand Rapids: Eerdmans, 1975), p. 8.

See comments above, p.118 . One also needs to note that Article 6, Section 4, below, outlines the responsibilities of the clerk in cases of complaints and appeals. This task is delineated further in chapter 2, "The Disciplinary and Judicial Procedures."

Article 6. Transaction of Business

Sec. 1. *The regional synod shall be guided in its transaction of business by such rules of order as it shall adopt from time to time, and which are in accord with the Government of the Reformed Church in America. If state laws permit, the regional synod shall be incorporated.*

See comments above, p. 119.

Sec. 2. *A delegate of the regional synod shall not have the right to protest against any act or decision of that body, but shall have the right to redress by appeal or complaint. A delegate shall also have the right to require that the names of all regional synod members, with their votes for or against a matter in question, shall be recorded in the minutes of the regional synod for the information of all; however, that request may be denied by a two-thirds majority of the regional synod.*

See comments above, p. 120.

Sec. 3. *Only duly accredited delegates to the regional synod shall be entitled to vote.*

Sec. 4. *The regional synod shall constitute, by election or otherwise, a permanent committee on judicial business. The clerk of the synod shall refer to this committee all appeals and complaints, with all papers and documents pertaining thereto, before these matters are presented to the synod. The permanent committee on judicial business shall consist of three ministers and two elders, who need not be delegates to the synod. The term of one member of the committee shall expire annually and a successor shall be chosen at the regular meeting of the synod for a term of five years. A vacancy occurring from death, resignation, or other cause shall be filled in the same manner for the unexpired term. The committee shall elect its own moderator.*

This is the only place in the church order that not only names a committee of an assembly, but prescribes its membership in detail. Although one might question the propriety of such procedural details in the church order proper, its presence discloses the importance the church order places on the regional synod as a judicial body. It stands as the final court of appeal for cases originating with boards of elders, and thus within the congregations themselves, and this provision ensures that the synod exists as a permanent body for such cases. Likewise, members of classes enjoy a court of appeal to which prompt recourse is available. Without the prescription of a permanent committee, synods would be left to create such a body. The immediate nature of complaints and appeals would make such a process almost impossible. A synod could not form the committee until it met, thus delaying proceedings well beyond a period of time reasonable for the parties to obtain relief or justice.

Sec. 5. *Except as otherwise provided in the* Book of Church Order, *members of regional synod committees, commissions, or boards shall be confessing members of the churches in the regional synod.*

5
The General Synod

The General Synod is the highest assembly and judicatory in the Reformed Church in America. As an assembly, it is the gathering of the offices of minister and elder from the entire church. If we recall, however, that the offices receive their peculiar roles around pulpit and Table, the General Synod resides at a distance from the heart of the church's existence. This fact has issued in a number of consequences.

For example, while we recognize that the consistory is the oldest assembly, established by the Draft Ecclesiastical Ordinances of Geneva in 1541, the General Synod has experienced a development over the centuries. Reformed churches found it necessary to form consistories. The first Dutch church in London drafted ordinances for its life for a consistory but had no synod. The synods evolved as a government for the greater church.

Thus, while the synods were necessary for the good order of the church, they did not constitute its essence. Reformed churches could, and did, exist without a national synod. Reformed people understood that *Christ* constituted his church through Word and Spirit. That happened as the living Word, Christ, called his people around pulpit and Table. The synods existed then, as the *bene esse*, for the good of the church, but not as the *esse*, the essence of the church.

It is with this understanding that the General Synod of the RCA has shaped its life over the past two centuries. At the outset, its power and responsibilities were limited. The church required a final court in which disputes could be adjudicated and which could develop or propose policy for the entire church. The infamous dispute over limited atonement in the 1820s that led to schism in the RCA could only be settled, finally, at a national level.

Furthermore, the Reformed principle that the greater assemblies perform those functions of which the lesser assemblies are incapable led to the growth of the role of the General Synod. In the beginning, it was the General Synod alone which could provide theological education for the church's ministers. The emergence of missions in the early nineteenth century required that the national body coordinate and support its mission program. As the church found itself called by God to bear prophetic witness to the powers that control nation and culture, it was the General Synod that could give voice to scripture on behalf of the entire church. And that synod alone could propose foundational changes in the way the church governs itself.

Still, within the framework of Reformed order, the General Synod enjoys limited power. Although it alone can establish denominational policy (note that "denomination" is not the same as either "church" or "synod"), the Reformed Church maintains a certain tension between central and local power. At its best, that tension is creative. It keeps the church focused within the life of the congregation even as it does not allow the church to degenerate into the sort of independent mindset in which everyone "does what is right in his own eyes."

The General Synod is an assembly. That means, first, that the Reformed Church is not governed by a person, or even a small group of persons. The church is ruled by those offices that gather from a variety of localities, often with a broad range of theological commitments and concerns. Officers from rural or suburban contexts are drawn into ministry in urban settings. Officers from churches in areas where the church has enjoyed a long establishment are confronted with the concerns of those who plant new congregations. The more moderate wing of the church must come to terms with the more conservative, and vice versa. Second, the assembly is a gathering of offices. Three of the four offices gather in the General Synod: the minister of Word and sacrament, the elder, and the professor of theology. Thus the church is protected, at least in theory, from becoming a clerocracy. The integrity of the order is maintained at the highest level.

Article 1. General Synod Defined

The General Synod is the highest assembly and judicatory of the Reformed Church in America. It consists of two minister delegates and two elder delegates from each of the classes having four thousand or fewer confessing members on the roll of its churches, and one minister delegate and one elder delegate for each two thousand confessing members, or fraction thereof, from each of the classes having more than four thousand confessing members on the roll of its churches as computed in accordance with the Bylaws of the General Synod; one elder or minister delegate from each of the regional synods; two General Synod professor of theology delegates from each of the theological seminaries of the Reformed Church; a number of furloughing missionary and chaplain delegates; and corresponding delegates provided for in the Bylaws of the General Synod. Voting rights shall be limited to elder delegates and those minister delegates who are actively serving in ministries under the jurisdiction or with the approval of an assembly. The General Synod is a permanent, continuing body which functions between stated sessions through the General Synod Council, commission, and agencies.

In the Explanatory Articles of 1792, the General Synod was constituted by delegates from the particular synods. However, even then the General Synod gathered as a "convention." All ministers, with an elder, were to be delegates to the General Synod. Thus, while the delegates represented the particular synods, each church could have two persons at the General Synod. This was changed by 1812, when the General Synod was constituted by three minister and three elder delegates from each classis. However, they were still appointed by the particular synods.

The role of the regional synods in constituting the General Synod has largely disappeared. Now, the General Synod is an assembly constituted by the *classes* of the Reformed Church. Nonetheless, while classes appoint delegates, it is to be emphasized that the delegates gather at the General Synod as officers. The classes cannot bind their delegates to particular votes. Because the church is governed by Christ and not by popular vote, the officers remain subject to the leading of Christ through Word and Spirit. Delegates of the various classes will quite naturally reflect the concerns and commitments of those sections of the church from which they come. However, the synod is autonomous in relation to other assemblies, and it is capable of coming to its own decisions.

The apportionment of the number of delegates among the classes is intended to provide fair representation for those sections of the church that enjoy larger numbers of members. At the same time, the allotment protects smaller classes, recognizing the full ecclesiastical standing of all the classes within the church.

The office of professor of theology is present through the delegates from the seminaries (see Article 3, Section 4 below). Missionaries and chaplains bring their peculiar perspectives and ministries to the assembly. In addition, a number of corresponding delegates are present to offer advice and perspective. They include representatives from the synod's own commissions, from the colleges, and from a number of agencies of the church. The synod grants them the privilege of the floor, thereby enlarging the conversation. However, they cannot vote in the assembly and are not members of the synod as such.

The synod is a permanent body. Although the delegates gather to meet usually once a year, they remain members of the synod until their successors have been appointed or elected (see Article 3, Section 1, below). This has certain implications. Before a special session of the General Synod may be called, three ministers and three elders from each of the regional synods must apply. They must be delegates of the General Synod. If such a special session were to be called, the classes would not appoint new delegates to the synod.

The synod functions between sessions through the General Synod Council, which functions as the synod's executive committee, its commissions, and its agencies. Those bodies act on behalf of and in the name of the General Synod. However, they are not themselves the synod, and they can decide policy only in circumscribed conditions (see Article 2, Section 4 below). The synod itself is the gathering of offices.

Article 2. Responsibilities of the General Synod

> Sec. 1. *The General Synod shall exercise a general superintendence over the interests and concerns of the whole church.*

This broad-ranging and rather indefinite power grants the General Synod the capability to review matters that concern the entire church. A visitor to a meeting of the General Synod will observe the synod tackling everything from Christian education curricula to evangelistic plans to missionary enterprises to ministerial pensions. The list is long and appears to grow through the decades.

Two remarks are in order. The synod is charged with reflection on those matters that concern the *whole* church. So while at times it may focus its attention on ministry in a particular area of the church, mission to native Americans, for example, it does so as the matter concerns the church at large. It may offer assistance, even establish policy as it affects the entire church. But it cannot presume upon the peculiar powers and capabilities of lower assemblies.

That leads to the second remark. This clause is bounded by powers granted to other assemblies. The General Synod could not, for example, directly involve itself in the proceedings of a consistory or of a classis. Such can occur only in matters of complaint and appeal. The General Synod can *propose* changes in the *Government* that have direct implications for lower assemblies, but then it does so only in matters that affect the church as a whole.

> Sec. 2. *The General Synod shall exercise an appellate supervisory power over the acts, proceedings, and decisions of the lower assemblies.*

As with the regional synods, this power is appellate. This section grants the General Synod the power to sit as a judicatory in cases of appeal and complaint. Because the synod enjoys this power, it can reverse in whole or in part the decision of a lower assembly, or it can remand the case to the lower assembly with instructions (see chapter 6).

> Sec. 3. *The General Synod shall form regional synods. It may make changes in their boundaries, and may transfer classes and churches from one regional synod to another.*

The changing size and shape of the Reformed Church has necessitated the execution of this power from the church's inception. Originally one particular synod, the General Synod created a second synod in 1800 and was active in shifting classes from one synod to another to accommodate changing circumstances. With the arrival of Dutch immigrants in the mid-nineteenth century, the General Synod created new synods in the western part of the church. Most recently, the old Synod of the West was divided, and a new synod, Canada, was added. Furthermore, the expansion of church extension activities required the General Synod to create boundaries to avoid confusion between synods in planting congregations in parts of the nation previously devoid of RCA churches.

> Sec. 4. *The General Synod alone shall determine denominational policy. It may delegate the formulation of policy to committees, boards, or other agencies.*

The crucial term in this section is "denominational policy." "Policy" can be defined as a "governing principle, plan, or course of action." A policy shapes the particular decisions and actions taken either by a body or by those subject to it. In the case of the General Synod, a policy would direct how it conducts its mission program or establishes pensions for ministers or addresses moral or political issues.

At the same time, the term cannot be construed to mean that the General Synod alone can determine confessional issues. The synod can propose confessional changes, but since confessions are themselves constitutional, any change would of necessity require the ratification of the classes. Likewise, the synod cannot presume upon the interpretation of Scripture, as it is ministers who are called to preach.

This section prevents various assemblies and agents from claiming that the "Reformed Church in America" as a body takes a particular position when that claim is inconsistent with the policy of the General Synod, or when the synod has not taken a policy position. This section was precisely at issue in 1992 when several complainants argued that the Synod of Mid-Atlantics took a position on abortion that was inconsistent with the General Synod. The synod agreed with the complainants and held that "when a particular synod presumes to enunciate policy, it bears the responsibility of insuring that the policy is consistent with policy already adopted by the General Synod."[1]

---

1. *MGS*, 1992, p. 104.

That ruling, however, if allowed to function as a general principle, could cause considerable mischief that would sow confusion within the broader principles of Reformed order. The assemblies, as assemblies, are fully capable under God's leading to take actions that do not agree with those taken by the General Synod. The Reformed Church does not grant to the General Synod "magisterial" authority. That is, the General Synod is not the "teacher of doctrine" to and for the churches. That role, such as it exists, is reserved for the constitutional doctrines of the church, here most particularly the *Standards*. Thus, of course, it is the case that a lower assembly cannot make policy that contradicts the constitutional documents (and if so, would be subject to appropriate ecclesiastical discipline). This section most probably should be read in such a way that the commissions and agents of the General Synod itself cannot make policy on behalf of the General Synod. Thus, for example, a commission could not by itself make ecumenical or liturgical or social action policy on its own. Nor could a seminary or even the General Synod Council itself speak on behalf of the entire church in a policy matter.

The General Synod may delegate the authority to formulate policy to its committees, boards, or agencies. It is presumed, however, that such delegation is explicit and circumscribed. This often happens as the General Synod approves the "constitution or enabling document" of all agencies, boards, and institutions officially related to the General Synod (Article 7, Section 3 below).

> Sec. 5. *The General Synod shall maintain a friendly correspondence and cooperative relationship with the highest judicatories or assemblies of other Christian denominations and with interdenominational agencies in all matters pertaining to the extension of the Kingdom of God.*

The Reformed Church does not, and has never, considered itself to be the Church in toto. Although in the period immediately following the Reformation, it considered itself the "true church" in contradistinction to the Roman church, it acknowledged the legitimacy of other churches, provided they were distinguished by the true "marks" of pure preaching, pure administration of the sacraments and the practice of Christian discipline (Belgic, Art. 29). The American experience, with its bewildering variety of denominations, emphasized the reality of a plurality of Christian denominations. This section presumes that the Reformed Church in America will discover common cause and communion with other denominations. Wording similar to this section can be found in the Reformed Church's constitution as early as 1833 (par.84). Indeed, the verb "shall" that is used in this section positively requires the General Synod to enter cooperative work with other Christian denominations.

The determination of the ecumenical posture of the RCA is granted to the General Synod alone. In 1997, the RCA, along with its Reformed partners in the Presbyterian Church, USA, and the United Church of Christ entered into "full communion" with the Evangelical Lutheran Church of America. The decision of the General Synod was final for the RCA. The matter did not need to be ratified by the classes.

This section does not prevent lower assemblies from entering into "correspondence and cooperation" in ecumenical settings. Local congregations are often members of councils of churches, as are regional synods. However, an attempt by the then Particular Synod of New Jersey to join with the Synod of New Jersey of the United Presbyterian Church was ruled out of order by the 1970 General Synod.[2] The section reserves for the General Synod the power to establish such relations at the level of the national bodies, and to establish the general ecumenical posture of the Reformed Church in America.

Nonetheless, it should be remarked that in the case of union or federation with another denomination, the RCA has in its practice

2. *MGS*, 1970, p. 117.

referred such decisions to the classes for ratification. The General Synod has offered several proposals over its life, particularly with the then Reformed Church in the U.S.A. (the "German" Reformed) and various Presbyterian bodies. Almost all have been defeated at the classical level. The only exception occurred in the late nineteenth century, when the synod proposed a federated synod with the German Reformed. That proposal was ratified by the classes. However, the General Synod, in deference to several western classes, refused to take the declarative action necessary to bring about the federation.[3]

The General Synod generally enters ecumenical relationships in two differing manners. One way, as with the Lutherans, is to enter into dialogue at a church-to-church level. At another level, the RCA has entered various councils of churches, including the Federal (now National) Council of Churches of Christ and the World Council of Churches as well as the World Alliance of Reformed Churches.

> Sec. 6. *The General Synod shall be the legal custodian of the funds, devises, bequests, and other property which is given, devised, or bequeathed directly to the General Synod of the Reformed Church in America, or to or for the use of its various unincorporated funds.*

The General Synod as an incorporated body is a legal entity. It can thus receive funds given to it by a variety of devises, including bequests. It is in turn responsible for the appropriate disposition of such funds.

> Sec. 7. *The General Synod shall have original authority over all matters pertaining to doctrine and denominational polity as they relate to the theological seminaries of the Reformed Church.*

3. Harmelink, Herman III, *Ecumenism and the Reformed Church* (Grand Rapids: Eerdmans, 1968), pp. 48-49.

The provision of theological education for candidates preparing for ministry was among the first powers granted to the General Synod. Theological education happened through the institution of the professors of theology, or the so-called "fourth office" (see below, Article 8). The synod now administers this responsibility through its agent, the boards of the seminaries or MFCA.

The boards, as agents of the synod, are granted a general autonomy in the administration of their schools. However, the General Synod reserves original authority in matters of doctrine and denominational polity. Thus, the seminaries remain accountable to the General Synod for the doctrinal content of their teaching, as well as for their relationship to the church in matters of polity. For example, the seminaries are required to grant Certificates of Fitness for Ministry that in turn grant candidates the right to be examined for ordination by the classes.

> **Sec. 8.** *The General Synod shall exercise responsibility in the oversight of standards for the preparation of candidates for the ministry of Word and sacrament.*

Since the General Synod is responsible to the church for the theological education of its ministers, and since it executes that responsibility when the seminaries (or MFCA) issue the Certificate of Fitness for Ministry, it appears self-evident that the synod would be responsible to the church for the standards for preparation. However, the placement of this section reflects a recent change. Prior to 1999, this responsibility had been lodged with the General Synod Council. On the one hand, that reflected a very odd arrangement. The council and the seminaries were each agents of the General Synod and thus each responsible directly to the synod. The system therefore provided the occasion at the least for organizational confusion. On the other hand, a more fundamental confusion was at work. The General Synod already has in place its own professors of theology, who are office holders within the church. One expects that the professors, having been elected and installed by the General Synod, would be fully capable of performing the task of overseeing ministerial standards of preparation on behalf of the synod.

This responsibility was moved from the General Synod Council to the new Ministerial Formation Coordinating Agency in 1998. It remains to be seen how that agency will relate to the seminaries (which remain as agents of the General Synod) and to the professors of the General Synod.

> Sec. 9. *The General Synod shall from time to time institute, organize, and direct such agencies and boards as shall enable the church to fulfill the command of the Lord Jesus Christ to teach all nations and preach the gospel to every creature, and to conduct its missionary, educational, and benevolent work effectively.*

On reading through church periodicals, communications from the various church offices, or in serving on a denominational committee or board, one encounters a rather daunting structure of interlocking bodies, often with acronyms understood only by the knowledgeable. One is tempted to confuse this ecclesiastical infrastructure with church order. It is important to make clear that such structures are established by an assembly authorized by the order, but they are not the order itself.

The order authorizes the General Synod to form such agencies to assist the church in its ministry in the name of its Lord. The order further permits the synod the flexibility to form—and to disband—such bodies as time and circumstances require. For example, the synod could, and did, consolidate its various mission boards into one General Program Council, which in turn evolved into the General Synod Council. The order itself cannot foresee new challenges and new opportunities, nay new demands, for mission. But the synod itself remains sufficiently flexible to meet the needs as an assembly.

And yet, because the synod is an assembly it cannot execute ministry. That would be far too cumbersome. Thus, it requires agencies and boards to execute its work. In addition, such boards and agencies, acting under the actual conditions of ministry, can communicate to the General Synod difficulties, opportunities, and possibilities heretofore unseen or unacknowledged. The boards and agencies serve the General Synod, and through it the ministry of the entire church.

> Sec.10. *The General Synod shall recommend to the churches such methods as shall effectively sustain the denominational program, and the denomination's official periodical, and which tend to secure the largest dissemination of the gospel.*

The General Synod has interpreted the controlling verb of this section, "recommend," in a strong sense. The synod has assumed the power of assessment across the church. The synod assesses classes (not local congregations) for the support of denominational programs and of the denomination's official periodical. Despite occasional protests from classes claiming that such power is not granted to the synod and is indeed reserved to the classes themselves, their arguments have not been sustained by the General Synod. The synod, then, engages the entire church, through the collective classes, in support of the denominational program.

It is important, however, to note the purpose of such financial support. The final clause of this section reminds the church that the denominational program exists not simply to maintain the church as an institution, but that it is intended to "secure the largest dissemination of the gospel." The order is placed in service of the church's purpose (see the first sentence in the preamble).

> Sec. 11. *The General Synod may cause corporations to be formed by any of the boards, institutions, or agencies under its jurisdiction, retaining original authority in matters of denominational polity. Such corporations shall be maintained*

according to the laws of the states where they are located, so that they may receive, hold, and transfer property, and facilitate the carrying out of the responsibilities committed to them.

The theological seminaries, for example, are corporations established in order that they can function as educational institutions. Because they are so incorporated, they can properly administer their property as well as receive and administer the considerable funds necessary for the execution of their particular mission. This section allows the synod to establish corporations whenever a corporate structure is demanded or desirable. The appropriate connection to the church's mission and subsequently its order is maintained by the reserve clause that retains "original authority" in matters of polity. Thus, a corporation could not, within its own autonomy, contradict the fundamental way of being or shape of the church. Such bodies remain a part of and subject to the church's mission to its Lord.

Article 3. Delegates

Sec. 1. *The delegate shall be a member of the General Synod from the date of election or appointment and shall continue in that responsibility to the General Synod until the effective date of election or appointment of a successor. If, however, ministerial membership in the classis represented or confessing membership in a church within the classis represented shall be terminated during the period of appointment, the delegate shall cease to be a member of the General Synod.*

It has been a common practice in many classes to appoint delegates to the General Synod on a rotating basis. Thus, all ministers receive a "turn" to represent a classis, and all churches can, over a period of years, participate in the larger life of the church through synod representation. This practice has had the advantage of increasing participation in the synod and with it a sense of shared ownership in the decisions that shape the life of the church. It has prevented a rule of an "elite" who are more versed in ecclesiastical politics. However, the rotation method is not required by the order. A classis may elect its members or appoint them as provided by their rules of order.

Interestingly, the order does not provide that the delegates be members of the synod from the constitution of a synod until the following synod is constituted. Thus, it is incumbent on sending bodies to notify the General Synod upon the appointment of delegates.

> Sec. 2. *The elder delegate to the General Synod, or the elder who serves on committees, commissions, or boards of the General Synod, shall be chosen from the entire body of elders in a church, whether or not presently engaged as a member of the board of elders.*

This section reemphasizes that the General Synod sits as an assembly within a presbyterial system. That is, while it is constituted as a body by delegates from lower assemblies, it does not govern as a representative body. Its members are officers responsible to the one authority, Jesus Christ. Thus, all elders are eligible to become members of the synod. This section might provide confusion, however, as it suggests that elder delegates represent local churches. They do not. They are sent as representatives of the classis to the synod. Or, when they serve on committees of the synod, they are responsible to the synod itself.

> Sec. 3. *If a delegate is unable to attend the General Synod to which appointed, the delegate shall notify the stated clerk of the sending assembly as soon as possible. Upon notification by the stated clerk, the alternate delegate shall assume the rights and responsibilities of appointment.*

It is incumbent upon the stated clerk of a sending assembly (classis or regional synod) to maintain appropriate communication with the General Synod. This section allows a lower assembly to alter the roster of its representation in cases of necessity; no penalty falls to the assemblies when their delegates are unable to attend. At the same time, the section provides a means for the General Synod to maintain the integrity of its body. It also protects the General Synod from the embarrassment and difficulty of having a delegate appear at its meeting claiming to substitute for a member unable to attend. The sending bodies are responsible for appropriate certification of its delegates to the synod.

> **Sec. 4.** *The delegates from the theological seminaries shall be elected by the professors in each school from their own number.*

The "fourth office" is present at the synod through the presence of two professors from each seminary. Unfortunately, this section could suggest that the seminaries, as institutions, are represented at the General Synod. This is not possible within the broad outlines of Reformed order. The seminaries themselves are agencies, and thus creatures of, the General Synod. They are not, themselves, assemblies. The professor, however, is an officer responsible to the General Synod and thus has a legitimate place within its governance. Consequently, it is not the seminary but the professors themselves who elect their delegates.

> **Sec. 5.** *The furloughing missionary with at least five years of service in the field shall be eligible for appointment to the General Synod from the classis of membership once during each furlough and shall not be counted as one of the regular delegates of that classis.*

Although a missionary may be enrolled as a minister of a classis and thus may be eligible for appointment by that body as a delegate to the General Synod, she or he often lives and works in a different context or geographical area. She would not, therefore, be presumed to represent the interests and commitments of the sending body. The order consequently provides a special opportunity for the missionary to be a part of the General Synod, thus offering the particular concerns of the fields of mission where the church is active. The advantage to the General Synod of having a missionary presence lies in the commission, given only to the synod, to further the mission program of the church. At the same time, the missionary's attendance does not penalize the sending body's own representation.

Sec. 6. *An active duty military chaplain with at least five years in the military service shall be eligible for appointment as a delegate to the General Synod from the classis of membership. A chaplain delegate shall be eligible once during each succeeding five-year period and shall not be counted as one of the regular delegates of the classis.*

Similar considerations apply to this section as to the one immediately preceding. One might ask concerning other chaplains (of hospitals, schools, prisons, and the like) about their ability to represent their classes. They, however, live and work within the geographic areas of the classes. They are enrolled as ministers and thus are eligible to represent the classes as provided by the rules of order of the local classis.

Sec. 7. *The General Synod shall pay travel expenses within Canada and the United States (exclusive of Alaska and Hawaii) to and from the synod's place of meeting.*

Article 4. Sessions and Meetings of General Synod

Sec. 1. *The General Synod shall meet annually at such time and place as shall have been determined at its previous session. All meetings of the General Synod shall begin and end with prayer.*

The Explanatory Articles of 1792 provided that the General Synod meet once every three years. That arrangement did not last long, and the synod was soon meeting annually. A number of attempts have been essayed to have the synod meet biennially. The synod could accomplish its necessary business at less cost to the entire church by meeting every two years. Nothing within an understanding of Reformed order requires an annual meeting. However, synods have consistently rejected such proposals. Generally, it has been judged salutary for the life of the church that its representatives gather often to participate in the life of the church. Thus, the Reformed Church is gathered from across two nations each year to superintend the broad interests and concerns of the work of the gospel.

> Sec. 2. *The president of the General Synod shall call a special session of the synod at a place determined by the president, vice president, and the general secretary of the synod upon the joint application of three ministers and three elders from each of the regional synods, all of them serving currently as accredited delegates to the General Synod. Three week's notice of the session shall be given to the members of the synod, such notice to state the purpose of the session.*

It would be a daunting and expensive task to gather a special session of a national body. Special circumstances, however, may require the synod to meet in an extraordinary session. The order recognizes the extraordinary nature of such sessions by constructing imposing conditions for their call. Three ministers and three elders from each synod would, at the present time, mean that at least forty-eight delegates request a special session. And since *each* synod must provide six signatures, the need would encompass the entire variety of the church's life. Thus, no one theological or ecclesiastical commitment would be capable of engineering a special session.

> Sec. 3. *The presence of a majority of the minister delegates and a majority of the elder delegates is required to constitute*

a quorum at any meeting of the General Synod.

This section corresponds with similar prescriptions for lower assemblies on pp.76 and 114. See comments there.

> Sec. 4. *The General Synod shall celebrate the sacrament of the Lord's Supper during each session of the synod, unless the synod shall direct otherwise. The synod shall further devote a period of time on the first day to prayer and praise. Each morning meeting of the synod shall have its first half-hour devoted to prayer and praise to God.*

The *intent* of this section is clear. The General Synod is an assembly, and as such lives in obedience to its Lord. Indeed, as an expression of the church, it exists, theologically, as it is essentially constituted in Christ. Outside an ontological and ontic subsistence in Christ the synod does not exist. Liturgically, that oneness with Christ comes to full expression in the Lord's Supper. Thus, the Supper not only serves to remind the synod that its life is essentially in Christ, it actually constitutes that reality. Furthermore, we have observed how the order is shaped by Table and pulpit. The offices of the church receive their *raison d'etre* from the Lord's presence in Word and sacrament. Ministers and elders, then, are not permitted to presume their ministry of leadership apart from the fundamental marks of the church. This is as true for the officers of the General Synod as it is for officers in a local consistory.

But if the intention is clear, the execution is awkward, because this section has the General Synod, which is not a congregation and thus is not under the discipline of a board of elders, celebrating a sacrament. That is not odd simply because it transgresses an accepted rule of thumb. The Table shapes and forms particular communities, or communions, of those God calls to be a congregation. To have the General Synod celebrate the Lord's Supper is to suggest that the supper is somehow detachable from the church understood as constituted by a consistory.

This section also has General Synod meetings interspersed with what it calls "prayer and praise." One presumes that such means a sort of prayer service, although one misses in this wording the old Reformed practice of a sermon. Prayer and praise alone give voice to the believer, to the synod as it raises its voice to God. The sermon, on the other hand, presumes that God can and will speak to the synod, thus breaking through the kind of insistent subjectivity suggested by "prayer and praise."

Article 5. Officers of the General Synod

Sec. 1. *A president shall be elected from among the delegates to preside at the next session of the General Synod, and to undertake such other duties as may be assigned by the synod. It shall be the duty of the president to state and explain the business to be transacted, to enforce the rules of order, and, in general, to maintain the decorum and dignity belonging to the church of Jesus Christ. The president shall be a member of the General Synod until the close of the next annual session of synod.*

See the comments on presidency (p. 117). It might be added here that the president of the General Synod plays a greater role in the church than that adumbrated in this section. The synod's own rules of order provide for a presidential report. That report customarily includes a number of recommendations granted privilege to be presented to the synod. The president will also serve as moderator of the General Synod Council in the year immediately following the conclusion of her or his term as president. However, none of these duties, privileges, and responsibilities is of itself a part of the *order* of the church. The order keeps clear that the highest ruling power of the church remains an assembly, and the president's task is in service to the assembly itself. Indeed, service to the assembly is further emphasized by the requirement that the president be elected from among the delegates to the synod. Thus, the Reformed cannot understand the whole church to be gathered except in the body of the synod. Synod presidents are not elected from among the church at large.

> Sec. 2. *After the president has been elected, the synod shall elect a vice-president from among the delegates. The vice-president shall be a member of the General Synod until the close of the next annual session of the synod.*

It has become customary for the vice-president to become president upon the completion of his or her successor's term. In fact, that presumption has been written into the synod's rules of order. However, it is not a part of the order. It is *possible* because the vice-president is a member of the assembly.

> Sec. 3. *The General Synod shall have a general secretary whose duty shall be to present at each General Synod meeting a report articulating a vision for the church, including recommendations for the future; to keep faithful record of all the proceedings of the body, and to furnish official notices in writing to all persons directly affected by judicial decisions of the assembly. The general secretary shall also be responsible for forwarding to the denominational archives copies of minutes of the General Synod and subsidiary corporations, and shall undertake such other duties as may be assigned by the synod.*

Until 1968, the office of general secretary was designated as the stated clerk of the synod. Indeed, as this section displays, the general secretary's task includes duties assigned to stated clerks of the lower assemblies. However, the increasing "denominization" of the church, which requires an executive officer to coordinate the many boards, commissions, and agencies as well as a denominational staff, led the church to adopt a model in greater conformity with a corporate business.

In 1993, the phrase requiring the general secretary to present a report to the General Synod was added (interestingly, the general secretary's report is included in the order while the president's report is not.). A committee studying the restructure of the General Synod program agencies reasoned that the general secretary, as a continuing officer, was in a position to review the total life of the church within a longer historical context. This clause grants to the general secretary considerable power within a Reformed purview. However, his or her report contains recommendations only, and the assembly is under obligation to consider them only within its role as a gathering of offices of the church. The general secretary's report receives respectful hearing because he or she is granted the task of reviewing the life of the church. However, the recommendations bear no more particular weight than does the thought or reflection of an officer—minister or elder delegate—of the synod itself, as assembly.

Article 6. Transaction of Business

The General Synod shall be guided in its transaction of business by such rules of order as it shall adopt from time to time, and which are in accord with the Government of the Reformed Church in America. *The General Synod shall be incorporated.*

It is helpful and necessary to keep in mind the distinction between the provisions for the General Synod as provided by the *Government* (and which we are reviewing in this commentary) and the *Bylaws and Rules of Order* of the General Synod. The former are part of the church order proper; the latter are not. It is easy to assume that the synod's own structure, in agencies, commissions, and advisory committees, are part of the church order. They are not. They are a means by which the synod as assembly shapes its own life. The commissions, for example, are not autonomous bodies that act on behalf of the church, but are themselves creatures of the General

Synod. They act on behalf of the synod only as empowered by the synod itself. In fact, the rules for changing the *Bylaws and Rules of Order* differ from those for amending the *Book of Church Order*. Amendments to the synod's own rules are not ratified by the classes.

Article 7. Committees, Boards, and Agencies of the General Synod

> Sec. 1. *The General Synod Council is established by and responsible to the General Synod. Its responsibility is to implement decisions, policies, and programs of the General Synod through proper channels and agencies; and to support, strengthen, and correlate the work of the several boards, institutions, and agencies of the Reformed Church in America, thus seeking to increase the effectiveness of the mission and witness of the church.*

In 1993, the RCA combined the former General Program Council and the former General Synod Executive Committee into one body, the General Synod Council. The General Program Council itself had been a restructure of the old board system, whereby the various activities of the church were taken under one umbrella.[4] The General Synod Executive Committee was an executive body of the synod that functioned on behalf of the synod between sessions. The General Synod Council (GSC) took on both responsibilities, an executive task and a program task. A relatively large body, currently consisting of representatives from each of the classes as well as a number of at-large members, the GSC meets several times a year to execute the policies and actions of the General Synod. It is not itself an assembly of the church, and it is not qualified to establish policy except as empowered by the synod itself. It assists the synod, and thus the entire church, in its mission.

---

4. Hoff, Marvin, *Structures in Mission* (Grand Rapids: Eerdmans, 1985), pp. 148ff.

Sec. 2. *The custody of the funds, devises, bequests, and other property of the General Synod is exercised on behalf of the General Synod by its trustees, who are called the Board of Directors of the Corporation. The income or interest from funds shall be administered either by that board, or by such administrative agencies as the General Synod shall from time to time direct. Other boards and agencies of the church are not thereby precluded from receiving, exercising custody, or administering, under the general supervision of the General Synod, any funds, devises, bequests, and other property, which is given, devised, or bequeathed directly to them.*

As a legal corporation, the General Synod must have trustees who bear responsibility for its assets. The order conforms to this demand with its Board of Directors. However, the *BCO* melds the secular requirement with church order as it names the Board of Directors as an organic part of the General Synod as assembly. The board reports annually to the synod, and delegates are given access to the full range of financial reports and audits. As a matter of practice, the synod has directed the Board of Directors in its investment policy. For example, delegates have raised questions concerning investments in companies manufacturing tobacco or alcohol, or in companies engaged in policies that violate the church's deepest kingdom commitments. For example, the synods of the 1980s and 1990s directed the board to divest from companies that did business with South Africa and limited investment in certain companies whose primary business was the production of armaments.

Sec. 3. *The constitution or enabling document of every agency, board, and institution officially related to the General Synod of the Reformed Church in America, with its amendments, shall be approved by the General Synod.*

Sec. 4. *The members of all incorporated organizations, other than the colleges, shall be elected by the General Synod, or*

> by those organizations upon nomination by the General Synod.

> Sec. 5. *The governing boards of all institutions of higher learning in the United States which are officially related to the Reformed Church in America shall at all times include at least three members who are designated by the General Synod.*

Not only does the General Synod cause corporations to be formed (see Article 2, Section 11 above and comments there), but it must approve the constitution *and* amendments to its subsidiary bodies. In this way, such bodies maintain their organic connection to the assembly and consequently remain connected to the order of the church. Thus, the church continues to govern itself through its assemblies, and by the nature of assemblies, by the offices of the church.

The colleges are granted a special place in the order. They have become autonomous bodies that maintain their "official" connection with the church without being directly responsible to the synod. The General Synod plays no role in their governance, except to reserve for itself three positions on the governing boards of each institution.

Article 8. The Office of the General Synod Professor of Theology

The office of "doctor" or "professor" originated in Calvin's Geneva with the Draft Ecclesiastical Ordinances of 1541. It was the "second" (usually designated as the "fourth" office as an addition to the more usual three-fold office of minister, elder, and deacon in Reformed order) office in the "degree nearest to the minister and most closely joined with the government of the church." The "office proper to doctors is the instruction of the faithful in true doctrine, in order that the purity of the Gospel be not corrupted either by ignorance or by evil opinions."[5] The task included

5. Calvin, "Draft Ecclesiastical Ordinances," p. 62.

instruction of children and evidently was broad enough to cover the entire "liberal education."

The office of doctor was included in Dutch orders as early as Wesel (1568). It appears that the office also included instruction in liberal arts. However, by Dort (1619), the office of "Teachers or Professors of Theology" was described simply "to explain the holy scriptures, and vindicate the pure doctrines of the gospel against heresy and error" (XVIII).

The church order adopted by the General Assembly of the Reformed Church of New York and New Jersey in October, 1771, adopted the language of Dort verbatim. However, that order was established at the meeting which also adopted the Articles of Union.[6] That document clearly states that the American church is authorized to choose its own professors to teach theology. One must keep in mind the context of that decision. The American church desired its own professors in order that it could educate its own ministers. In large measure, the separation of the American from the Dutch church and the subsequent establishment of the American church turned on this question: the ecclesiastical capability of the American church to establish the professorate. The office of doctor, then, focused on the theological education of its ministers.

The Explanatory Articles of 1792 distinguish the office of teachers of theology from that of ministers of the Word by stating clearly that teachers are to be relieved of pastoral duties and thereby freed to "teach and defend the gospel" (Article XIX). However, the context of the article is crucial, for the Explanatory Articles continue at this point to discuss the professors' role in preparing candidates for ministry for classical examinations. The professorate had become a servant of the church in its preparation of educated ministers.

Professors continued to function in the instruction of the faithful. However, the locus had shifted from direct education of congregants to the education of ministers who themselves will be installed as

6. "Articles of Union," Article XXVIII, in Hugh Hastings, *Ecclesiastical Records of the State of New York* (Albany: J.B. Lyon, 1905), vol. vi, p. 4215.

"pastors and teachers" of congregations, and who will teach and preach the Word to the faithful.

This office holds a peculiar place within the order of the Reformed Church in America. The professor of theology alone, as an office, is responsible to the General Synod. The synod serves the church as it provides theological education for the church's ministers. The professor has historically been the agent through which the synod has executed that task. Until very recently, candidates for ministry received a "professorial certificate," thereby assuring the various classes that candidates had been taught the appropriate "interpretation of Scripture." Thus, the church as a whole has borne responsibility for the integrity of the gospel through one peculiar office.

Why is this an office in the first place, and why is it "most closely joined to the government of the church"? Recall that the offices were intended to be understood not in isolation, but as gathered for the leadership of the church under Christ. Furthermore, the offices gather within the presence of Christ at Table and in the preached Word. This is clearest as elders, deacons, and ministers gather in consistory, and as elders and ministers gather in classes and synods. How, then, do the professors of theology fit within this scheme? The most obvious answer is that the professors assist in this task as they educate ministers. Ministers cannot properly interpret Scripture unless they are educated in the languages, in exegetical skills, in theology, in church history (which is itself a history of the Word within and over and against the church), and in such practical disciplines that display the power and presence of Christ in the congregation and the world. So crucial is the education of ministers (and by extension elders and deacons) to the life of the church that it is of the essence of the church's life. That is, it isn't just "good" for the church, but the church cannot exist without the right proclamation of the Word (one of the marks of the church).

By separating the office of "doctor" from that of the minister of Word and sacrament, the church freed the teacher from the demands of pastoral ministry. Although the professor is the "degree nearest the minister" because both focus on the interpretation of scripture to the faithful, the practical demands of pastoral ministry do not allow ministers of Word and sacrament to pursue with appropriate time and rigor the interpretation of Scripture in its fullest sense. So the church sets aside its "doctors" to study not only the language, the setting, and the context of Scripture, but its theological import, its interpretive history, and the culture to which it addresses itself freshly each generation.

It is precisely because the Reformed have held Scripture in such high regard, and because they continue to trust its living treasure, that the church has retained this office. This "fourth" office not only teaches its ministers in their formation but reminds the church continually that Scripture is never exhausted in its interpretation—especially not when a pastor finishes her exegesis or a Bible study group completes its study.

Thus, the office has maintained a symbolic function that the RCA has been loath to cede. Almost in passing, a Committee on Ecclesiastical Office and Ministry in 1989 noted that "the Calvinist emphasis upon an educated clergy and laity [sic], as well as the centrality of the Word in Reformed theology, is reflected in the special place given to a teaching ministry in the Reformed tradition."[7] The role of catechesis has been central to the Reformed churches. Congregations are formed as they are educated in the knowledge of the faith. Although professors of theology, as a matter of fact, focus their educational ministry on ministers in formation, their very presence symbolizes the place of teaching within the church.

It must also be emphasized that with the professors as an office, the "doctors" remain doctors of the church, and not of the academy. The church will expect its professors to measure up to the demands of the various theological guilds. At the same time, the church confesses its faith on the foundation of the authority of Scripture. It expects its professors to assist the church in teaching

7. *MGS*, 1989, p. 211.

its understanding of Scripture. It also expects them to assist it in shaping its doctrinal life on behalf of the entire church, in its education of the faithful, and in witness to the world.

The professors live in unique relation to the General Synod and can offer unique assistance to the synod in its work. It remains an anomaly that the RCA refuses to have all of its professors present at its General Synod meetings. In any case, they provide a particular and special assistance to the synod's various commissions and committees in the shaping of the life of the church.

Recent RCA history betrays a certain ambivalence to the office. On the one hand, it has consistently refused to relinquish the office. A 1969 proposal to fold the office into that of the minister of Word and sacrament failed. On the other hand, the church has hesitated to grant the office much power. Attempts to increase representation from the office to the General Synod have also failed. Developments within the seminaries have replaced the "Professorial Certificate" with the "Certificate of Fitness for Ministry," a certification voted on by the entire faculty. The 1997 approval of the report of the "Committee on Standards for Preparation for the Professional Ministry..." further eviscerated the office of the professor. That action shifted much of the task of educating ministers to an amorphous groups of "teaching churches," and also shifted the establishment and certification of "standards" to a parallel agency of the General Synod.

> Sec. 1. *The office of professor of theology is to teach one or more branches of theology in a theological seminary; to administer the academic functions of a seminary, subject to the rules established by the General Synod and supervised through the board of trustees of an RCA seminary; and to exercise supervision over the students.*

The church order has clearly narrowed the office of professor to that of a teacher in one of the theological seminaries of the RCA

(Section 3 below). While professors are delegates to the General Synod and their advice there given weight, their advisory function is not explicitly described as pertaining to their office. In fact, the *BCO* has broadened the office somewhat to include administration of the seminaries and supervision of students. The office now serves the church almost solely as it pertains to theological education. Still, the office appears largely ceremonial since, as a matter of practice, a number of teachers at the seminaries are not members of the office, and the seminaries are usually administered by non-office holders.

> **Sec. 2.** *The professor of theology shall be a minister in good standing, sound in the faith, possessed of ability to teach, have the confidence of the churches, and shall have made recognized contributions to the church.*

This section further describes the office by positing five requirements that a candidate for this office must meet. That he or she is a minister is not immediately apparent. One can teach without having preached, although some would argue that only one who has been active as a minister can teach others to perform in the office. However, as a matter of order, the requirement that the professor be a minister places the office of professor "nearest" that of minister and emphasizes that the professor is not simply an academic. He or she is engaged most intimately in the ministry of the Word.

"Sound in faith" within a Reformed context denotes both that the professor teaches from within a Reformed confessional commitment (see the following section) and that she evidences a piety consistent with that taught and experienced within the Reformed tradition. Because they represent the church to its future ministers, the professors model a way of life and thought for those entrusted with the pulpit.

The professor is primarily a teacher. Thus, the office is not granted to ministers who represent a particular theological commitment, nor who have won particular academic honor.

> Sec. 3. *When a Reformed Church minister has completed three years as a full-time associate or full professor at one of the seminaries of the Reformed Church, the board of trustees of an RCA seminary may nominate that professor to the General Synod as candidate for the office of professor of theology. A professor of theology shall be elected by a majority vote of the members present.*

If Section 1 defined the professor and Section 2 described the office, this section outlines the means by which the church selects the candidate to this office. The church assures itself that the conditions set out in the previous section are met. First, by requiring that the candidate have attained a rank of associate professor or better and taught for at least three years, he or she will have demonstrated to a seminary his or her ability to teach. Second, the synod avoids the "unhappy consequences of partiality, haste, or undo influence in obtaining the office of such consequence" (Exp. Art., XXI) by requiring that a board of a seminary present the nomination. The boards themselves represent not only the interests of the seminaries, but the broader concerns of the church. Third, the synod assures the candidate's commitment to a Reformed confessional outlook by requiring him or her to subscribe to the *Form of Declaration for Professors of Theology.* Finally, the church assures itself of broad support by requiring the election by a majority vote of the synod. The nomination of a candidate should not presume on election.

> Sec. 4. *When an election of a professor of theology has been effected, the president of the General Synod shall authorize a service of installation for the newly elected professor. At the installation and before signing the* Form of Declaration for

> Professors of Theology, *the professor-elect shall present a letter of dismission to the General Synod from the classis of membership. Before entering upon the duties of the office, the professor of theology shall subscribe to the* Form of Declaration for Professors of Theology.

It has seemed odd to some that of the four offices of the church only the professor is not ordained, but rather installed into office. There have been occasional proposals to ordain to this office, but that effort has not succeeded. The *BCO* in fact treats the professor as a minister with a particular and special call. Perhaps this anomaly should be noted as a symptom of the RCA's continued ambivalence toward the fourth office.

Even in practice, however, the professor enjoys a peculiar place within the order. This minister alone is not under the discipline of a classis and must be dismissed to the General Synod. Only General Synod professors have their ecclesiastical identity subsist in the General Synod.

> Sec. 5. *A professor of theology shall be amenable in matters of doctrine solely to the General Synod, but the professor will be subject to the same policies and procedures of employment as the other professors of the seminaries established by the seminary boards, except that a professor of theology shall have the right of appeal to the General Synod against dismissal from a position at one of the seminaries.*

It was the intention of the church from the early years to provide funds for the support of its professors (Exp. Art., XXIV). Indeed, the General Synod paid the professors for many years. With the development of the seminaries as more autonomous institutions, the financial support of its teachers devolved upon the boards who acted on behalf of the synod. Further, internal academic procedures in the supervision of faculty further complicated the peculiar relation of the professor to the General Synod. The professor remains amenable to the synod in matters of doctrine but must conform to the particular policies of employment in the seminaries. One could suppose, for example, that a professor remains theologically acceptable to the General Synod but refuses to teach the number of courses required by the seminary. In such a case, the *BCO* escapes a confusion of authority by granting seminaries autonomy under prescribed conditions. However, the order also grants to the professor a right of appeal to the General Synod, thus preserving the character of the office as responsible to an assembly.

> Sec. 6. *A professor of theology shall not be the installed pastor or minister under contract of any congregation, but may preach and administer or assist in administering the sacraments in any church as a minister upon request of the pastor or consistory of that church.*

If the *BCO* betrays ambivalence toward the fourth office, it nonetheless honors its integrity as it prohibits the holder of the office from functioning as an installed pastor of a church. While one reason may be, as argued above, that the church acknowledges that the interpretation of Scripture in its fullest sense requires attention that active pastors cannot give, and thus the fourth office exists to assist pastors in their office, a further reason may be deduced from the order itself. For the professor to act as an installed pastor, she would need to enter into the consistory, gathered around Word and sacrament, and consequently would need to be under the discipline of a classis. However, the professor is peculiarly under the discipline of the General Synod. Nevertheless, since the professor is *also* a minister and thus a member of another office, he or she is permitted to function in that office, provided it happens at the invitation of the officers of a local congregation. Thus the integrity of all offices is maintained.

> Sec. 7. *A professor of theology shall continue in office until death, resignation, dismissal from the seminary, declaration*

by the General Synod as professor emeritus, or removal from that office by the General Synod.

Sec. 8. *When a professor of theology resigns the office elected to by the General Synod, or is no longer in full-time service at a Reformed Church seminary, the professor shall receive a certificate of dismission from the General Synod to a classis or other ecclesiastical body, unless declared a professor emeritus.*

Sec. 9. *Upon reaching the age of seventy years, a professor of theology shall elect to be declared professor emeritus, or to be dismissed to a classis or other ecclesiastical body.*

Sec. 10. *The professor of theology may be retired from office by the General Synod because of permanent disability.*

The order treats the fourth office differently from the other three. Elders and deacons retain office when not actively serving on the consistory. The order presumes that ministers continue to function while in office, but allow a minister to maintain the office while inactive. The professor leaves the office when she or he ceases to function as a teacher in one of the church's seminaries. The professor still retains an office to the extent that she or he cannot be removed from office except by discipline or dismissal from the seminary. That is, the General Synod cannot simply decide that a particular professor should no longer serve in that capacity. Removal by the synod would require a disciplinary action, with all the protections that adhere to a disciplinary procedure, an exception being granted in the case of a permanent disability suffered by a professor.

Upon ceasing to function in the office, the professor, now holding only the office of minister of Word and sacrament, needs to be placed within the appropriate ecclesiastical discipline. She or he is no longer amenable to the General Synod and must be received either by a classis—if within the RCA—or by another ecclesiastical body. The interesting exception is for professors who are declared emeritus by the General Synod. Apparently, they remain under the discipline of the General Synod. It is an odd situation, given that by Section 7 they are no longer professors of the General Synod by office!

The *BCO* does not allow a professor to continue in office beyond seventy years of age. Recalling, however, that it is an ecclesiastical office under discussion here, the order is silent as to whether a seminary may allow the person to continue teaching beyond the age of seventy.

> **Sec. 11.** *Removal from office shall occur if after due process and trial the professor is found to be unsound in faith or is guilty of such misconduct as is deemed a violation of the obligations entered into at the time of installation.*

This section moves the General Synod into a judicatory and introduces a disciplinary procedure (see the appropriate sections of the *Disciplinary Procedures*). Only two occasions for removal are foreseen here: unsoundness of doctrine and violation of "obligations entered into at the time of installation." Precisely what this last clause has as its referent is not clear. One may consider the declaration of the installee as formative of her or his obligation. It certainly requires that the professor remain within the discipline of the General Synod. One might also consider the obligations of employment at one of the seminaries. However, the *Disciplinary Procedures* will at least suggest that the professor is subject to the same grounds for discipline as any other member or officer of the church. This section simply and clearly articulates particular grounds for the removal of a professor from his or her office.

Rules and Amendments of the Government
of the Reformed Church in America
and Disciplinary Procedures

Sec. 1. *The General Synod shall have power to make all rules and regulations necessary to put into effect any and all articles of the* Government, *the* Disciplinary Procedures, *the* Formularies, *and the* Liturgy of the Reformed Church in America.

William Demarest remarks concerning this provision that a body of such rules once existed and had been printed together with old constitutions.[8] Such a body of rules is neither currently in common circulation, nor is there a general awareness that it even exists! In fact, one doubts that the General Synod of recent memory knows how it would go about providing such rules. The articles of the *Government* and the amendments to the *Discipline* or to the *Liturgy* or the *Formularies* are effected through the process outlined in the following section. Thus, there appears to be little for the General Synod to do to put the provisions of the *Constitution* into effect.

Demarest is correct, however, and its perusal is revelatory and in fact lends support to a recent proposal to revise the *BCO* by dividing it into sections provisionally entitled "Constitution" and "Canons." An 1876 version of the *Constitution*[9] includes a "Digest of the Laws of the General Synod." The digest covers twelve chapters: "Consistories," "Classes," "Synods," "Boards," "Educational Institutions," "Funds of the Church," "Church Government," "Doctrines and Morals," "Customs and Usages," "Correspondence with other Churches," "Religious Newspapers," and "Particularia."

A sampling of contents discloses, in a way that might be helpful for the contemporary church, how the rules were used. It also

8 Demarest, William H. S., Notes on the Constitution of the Reformed Church in America, (New Brunswick, 1928), p. 185.
9 *The Constitution of the Reformed Church in America* (New York: Board of Publication of the Reformed Church in America, 1876).

exhibits the authoritative attitude granted the General Synod in the life of the nineteenth-century church.

For example, the validity of Roman Catholic baptism was a matter at issue within the church. Under the heading, "Consistories," the General Synod declared that "the question of Roman Catholic baptism be left to the different consistories."[10] While the question itself might embarrass the late twentieth-century church, living as it does within an ecumenical context, it is interesting that under Reformed order the consistories did not of themselves have the power to decide the question; it was *granted* to them by the synod. Nor was this power granted within the order itself, but by the synod in the ordinary course of business, subsequently recorded. Thus the action of the General Synod acquired the status of ecclesiastical law.

A second example is clearer, especially as contrasted to provisions in the *BCO*. A recurring issue for a church in the context of American denominationalism has been the reception of ministers ordained by another ecclesiastical body. In the current *BCO*, the "Reception of Ministers and Licensed Candidates from Other Denominations" is taken up under Chapter 1, Part II, Article 12 as a responsibility of the classes. The "Digest" of 1876 addresses the matter: "No licentiate nor ordained minister, from any other ecclesiastical body, shall be received into any Classis until, either by documenting evidence or examination, they shall have become satisfied of his competent literary qualifications; nor until upon examination, in the presence of a deputatus, they shall become fully satisfied of his competent theological attainments, his piety, soundness in the faith and ability to teach, and shall have received his entire assent to the standards of our Church as to doctrine and discipline."[11] Again, the General Synod was capable to regulate the matter without recourse to amendment of the *Constitution* itself.

One further example illustrates the power of the General Synod never otherwise spelled out in the *Constitution* properly understood.

10. *Ibid.*, p. 8.
11. *Ibid.*, p. 11.

We commented under the "Responsibilities of the General Synod" . that that synod had claimed for itself the power to assess in order to "sustain the denominational program" (p. 233). The "Digest of the Laws" includes a provision for assessment: "*Resolved*, that the amount necessary to be raised in order to meet such deficiency as there may be in the revenues of Synod, be hereafter assessed directly by the General Synod upon the Classes, and that the Treasurer transmit to General Synod an estimate of the amount necessary to be raised, which document shall be placed in the hands of the Committee on the Board of Direction, who shall make the apportionment, and present the same to the Synod for adoption, which Synodical assessment shall be transmitted by the Stated Clerk to the several Classes."[12]

In 1994, in response to an overture from the Classis of the Greater Palisades, the General Synod instructed its Commission on Church Order to explore the division of the entire *Constitution* into two parts, "Constitution" and "Canons." The "Constitution" was to consist of "those items which are basic and truly constitutional and distinguish the very nature and character of the Reformed Church." The "Canons" were to include "items of an authority which are secondary, which interpret and apply the more basic principles of the *Constitution*, and which provide the regulations and procedures such as is already done with the *Bylaws of the General Synod*."[13] Little was to come of the initiative. However, the direction indicated offers a solution to two problems that afflict current practice and use of the *BCO*. The first is the degeneration of the *Government* into what too often looks like a procedural manual for the administration of the church. Such matters as how the church receives ministers from other denominations hardly appear constitutional in nature. At the same time, some such regulations are necessary for the good order of ecclesiastical life. The second problem has to do with the yearly process of amending of the *BCO*.

12. *Ibid.*, p. 85.
13. *MGS*, 1994, p. 248.

While the evolving nature of the church's life requires that the church be capable of reviewing its means of government, one might reasonably expect that what *constitutes* the church remain relatively stable.

A Reformed church should be capable of establishing its constitutional basis, which can be amended only after considered and patient reflection by the entire church, and at the same time constructing a set of rules that can be amended more easily to meet expected changes in circumstance. The Nederlandse Hervormde Kerk, for example, does precisely that in its church order with a relatively short (thirteen-page) constitution and a much longer set of "Ordinaties."

> Sec. 2. *Amendments to the* Government, *the* Disciplinary Procedures, *the* Formularies, *and the* Liturgy *and the* Directory for Worship *shall be made only upon adoption by the General Synod at a stated meeting, with recommendation to the classes for approval. At least two-thirds of the classes shall approve a proposed amendment in order to secure its adoption. If an amendment is approved by the classes, the General Synod, at its discretion, may pass a final declarative resolution on the amendment. When the declarative action has taken place, the amendment shall become effective.*

Amendments of the church's constituting document are of such importance that they cannot be taken hastily but require the approval of the entire church as represented by the various classes. In that way, the ministers and elders, as officers of the church, participate in the governance of the church. Likewise, the provision that the classes ratify proposed changes involves the church in its plurality of geography, demographics, and theological commitments. The threshold of a two-thirds vote of the classes also insures that the change be of sufficient merit that the entire church approves the proposal.

In addition, two general synods must vote on the proposed change. Two gatherings of officers from across the church review the proposed change. The second synod's vote is a "declarative resolution." Too often, that has been taken to be little more than a ratification of the broader church's wisdom as reflected by the vote of the classes. The declarative resolution should not, however, be viewed as a mere formality. The wording of this section makes clear that the second synod's action is taken "at its discretion," and that it "may" make its declarative action. Thus, the order allows for second thought on the part of the synod. The final vote still remains the responsibility of that assembly and ought not to be taken lightly.

This section on amendments betrays a curious omission. Recalling that the *Doctrinal Standards* are included in the *Constitution*, the *BCO* provides no procedure for amending those standards. It may, of course, be argued that the contemporary church cannot amend a historical document—for example, how could today's church change what was stated by the Synod of Dort? However, one still might ask how the church would, as it has proposed several times in recent years, *add* a doctrinal standard. How would the church go about confessing the faith in contemporary circumstances, especially when and if the church finds itself at that place where it is compelled to confess that faith?

6
Disciplinary and Judicial Procedures

Reformed churches are relatively distinct from other Christian communions in their ordered practice of Christian discipline. The Confession of Faith notes the third mark of the church as "Church discipline for the punishment of sin" (Art. 29). The church understands itself responsible both to God and to its members for the life of its officers, its assemblies, and its members. Indeed, Reformed churches have historically been characterized by the practice of discipline. One can read through the minutes of almost any Reformed assembly and discover a number of cases of ecclesiastical discipline.

It must be admitted, however, that discipline evokes images of an inquisitorial church meddling in its members' lives, often practicing a legalism that appears to be at odds with a gospel of grace. A culture steeped in radical individualism shudders at the notion of a church policing not only one's intimate activities but also one's thought and belief. Is that what a church is about: herding persons lockstep in thought and action? In fact, such reservations have taken hold in large sections of the church, with a consequent decline of the practice of discipline in Reformed churches.

However, if one reviews earlier church orders, it is clear that church officers exercised discipline with great caution, taking pains to avoid becoming a sort of "ecclesiastical police." To take one of the earliest orders in the Dutch tradition, that of the London church in 1554, the order is very cautious, directing that admonishments be given, so far as possible, quietly and privately—pastorally, one might say. When behavior threatened to become scandalous for the church, and thus to negate the very gospel that constitutes the church, the order required that a number of steps be taken. Before a person's name could be made known, the consistory was to meet with the person, not once but several times. When it became a matter for the entire congregation, the consistory did not publish the name of the sinner, at least in the first instance, but requested the prayers of the congregation for the sinner's repentance. The goal was not public "punishment" of the sinner, but repentance. Discipline was insistently pastoral.[1]

Cultures do not remain static, however. Recent concerns over ministerial misconduct, largely but not exclusively related to sexual practice, have wakened church bodies to the use of discipline within the church. However, the use of discipline in many cases appears to emphasize the very legalism that one hopes to avoid. In fact, church courts are sometimes used by victims to obtain satisfaction against injustice. Nor should we ignore the sense of moral satisfaction that the community feels as it "punishes the sinner." While that sort of communal catharsis is sub-Christian, it too often provides the motive for the use of discipline.

It is helpful to recall why discipline was judged so crucial as to be named as a mark of the true church. A Reformed understanding of the church is communal at its heart. The member, recall, becomes organically connected to the body of Christ in baptism, a member of Christ around the Table. Discipline, then, happens around the

---

1. See, for example, the London order of 1554. The order insists that no public notice be made of the disciplined until the consistory has made repeated attempts at pastoral correction. Micron, op. cit.

Lord's Table; the elder derives her or his task from the gathering at that central liturgical act of the church.

The member's full life is engaged at the Table. She is a member of the Communion as she leaves the Table to her life in family, vocation, community, and state. That Communion draws her into the congregation and thrusts her into the larger community of life. She is always under the Lordship of Christ. Her entire life reflects Christ's Lordship. Nor is her responsibility to Christ separate from this church. The offices of the church exercise Christ's Lordship in her life. Thus upon membership in the church she promises to "accept the spiritual guidance of the Church."[2] The church order of Dort makes it clear that discipline focuses on the Table. Article LVXXI states, "Such as obstinately reject the admonitions of the Consistory, or have committed a public, or otherwise gross offence, shall be suspended from the Lord's Supper."

The church exercises its responsibility pastorally. The elder's task of visitation is intended to aid the believer in her life's walk, opening to discussion of life in family, in work, in the demands and vicissitudes of life's way. The first task of discipline is not to probe to discover secret sins that the church can then bring to public knowledge to the shame of the sinner. It is to allow the Spirit to use the community as the Spirit sanctifies the lives of not only persons but the entire community.

Nonetheless, occasions present themselves when a more structured discipline is in order. Can the community gather with integrity around the Table when one of its members is engaged in practices that bring the church into disrepute? Or to put it more sharply, does the presence of one who commits scandalous sin so eviscerate the gospel of God's love that it causes others to doubt the gospel itself? To put it in the case of office, does the presence in the pulpit of a preacher who demonstrates by his life that he is unfaithful in marriage delegitimate the gospel he proclaims, the source of life and hope hungering souls gather to hear? Article LXXI of the Explanatory

2. "Reception into Communicant Membership, 1987," in *Liturgy and Confessions*, p. 2.

Articles puts it like this: "Ministers of the gospel must be an example to believers, and much of their success will usually depend upon their good character, and their holy walk and conversation. Their conduct must therefore be watched over with great attention, and their crimes punished with impartiality and severity." Or to set the matter in a slightly different context, does the church care enough about the sinner to bring him or her up short and call her to account in her responsibility to her Lord, and thus for her own sake?

The questions and reservations noted here indicate that the practice of discipline is difficult and dangerous and is to be embarked upon with care and caution. Assemblies that enter this path will need to pay very close attention to what they are about. Yet, such care expresses the church in its pastoral ministry, giving attention to its evangelical purpose.

The church order divides this chapter into three parts. The first part deals with the discipline of members and officers. It will detail the nature and the process of discipline. It focuses on how judicatories discipline persons. The second two parts deal with complaints and appeals. At issue will be the actions of assemblies or judicatories. While an appeal may concern the discipline of a person, it centers on the actions of a judicatory as such.

Part I. Discipline

Article 1. The Nature of Discipline

> Sec. 1. *Discipline is the exercise of the authority which the Lord Jesus Christ has given to the church to promote its purity, to benefit the offender, and to vindicate the honor of the Lord Jesus Christ.*

It will be crucial for an assembly or judicatory considering discipline to remember the purpose of discipline. Discipline can only be entered in humility. An assembly acts in the name of Jesus Christ, never to exonerate a particular moral suasion nor to further a peculiar notion of the nature of the church. It can never be used to "get at" others whom either an individual or an assembly find uncongenial. While the church exercises discipline on its authority, that authority is always derived, granted to the church by its Lord.

In Reformed order the church always exercises discipline through its judicatories or assemblies. An individual officer never exercises discipline on behalf of the church. While it may be the case that a minister or elder may privately admonish those in their care in the name of the gospel, that admonishment never becomes discipline except where conditions clearly set out in the order are met. Discipline always emerges from the community of the church. At the same time it is not the congregation as a whole that disciplines, but only those set aside to the office and so subject to Christ who exercise discipline. In this way, the individual is protected from the passions of the moment.

The order notes three purposes for discipline. The purposes stated here appeared for the first time in the 1833 church order (IV,I,1). First in order is the purity of the church. Does a minister preach a gospel, for example, that is so at odds with the church's understanding of the apostolic message that it calls that message into question? Or is a member's conduct of such scandalous nature that it destroys the church's ability to extend Christ's love to the world? Does the church care so little about its message that it turns a blind eye to the banker who pads his own profit through illegal activity, thus quietly condoning his action?

Second, the church exercises discipline for the benefit of the offender. While discipline will undoubtedly inflict some pain on the offender, that is not its purpose. Discipline is fundamentally pastoral in nature and is intended to receive the offender back into the fellowship of the church. The church doesn't undertake discipline simply to cast out the impure, but that the Spirit might use discipline as a means of sanctification.

Finally, in the pride of place, is the vindication of the honor of the Lord Jesus Christ. One might object, of course, that the *church* need do nothing to vindicate Christ's honor. God has done that through the resurrection and glorification of Christ. And yet, discipline recognizes that a member of Christ, one who is granted the peculiar honor of identification with Christ, has desecrated that honor. Can one who has denied Christ in life or belief be allowed to continue that identification? Can a person, for example, who denies that persons of a different race or creed are children of God continue to speak or live in the name of Christ? And must we not ask that question in Christ's name?

> Sec. 2. *The exercise of discipline may take the form of admonition, rebuke, suspension from the privileges of membership in the church or from office, or excommunication as the gravity of the offense in the opinion of the judicatory may warrant. Admonition and rebuke are pastoral in nature and are exercised by an assembly in the ordinary course of its proceedings. All further steps of discipline—suspension, deposition, and excommunication—are judicial in nature and require the formal presentation of charges to a judicatory.*

The order envisions that discipline will be exercised at various levels of intensity, according to the gravity of the offense. As discipline is considered, a judicatory must decide first whether it will admonish or rebuke, or instead shall enter into a judicial proceeding. In part, that decision may depend on whether a charge has been brought to the judicatory (see below). The committee described in Article 4, Section 4 below may resolve a charge brought to it through admonition and/or rebuke. If, however, the committee deems that the charge cannot be so resolved and the charge is of sufficient merit, the judicatory is bound to proceed to trial, thus moving to further stages described in this section. The level of discipline then deemed appropriate will be decided as described in Article 5, Section 13: "Imposition of Discipline."

The body must pay strict attention to the terms used in this section. When it admonishes or rebukes, it acts not as a judicatory but as an assembly. It does not function as a judicatory, and thus the provisions in Article 5, "Trying a Charge," do not strictly apply. The body acts by communicating with the offending party, calling him or her (or a lower assembly) to an amendment of ways. It attempts to resolve the matter as a body of believers calling its members to appropriate conduct and/or teaching. So far as circumstances permit, this level of discipline is to be preferred. However, an offense may be so egregious and the conduct or teaching so scandalous to the proclamation of the gospel that the stronger forms of discipline may be required.

It is crucial that an assembly have at its disposal a means to express discipline that does not require it to enter the judicial process. The offense may be clear but not, in the wisdom of the judicatory, so serious that the offender must be subjected to the more serious disciplinary measures of suspension, deposition, or excommunication. The assembly then may turn to an action of admonition or rebuke, which do not require the assembly to constitute itself as a judicatory.

However, an assembly needs to be very cautious lest it violate the purposes of discipline or fundamental standards of fairness. While it need not adhere strictly to the provisions of Article 5, it needs to adhere carefully to Article 2, on the nature of offenses. Otherwise, an assembly can easily fall into the admonition or rebuke of a person simply because he or she offends a general sense or ethos of the assembly. The assembly must proceed with great care before taking a public action that may have serious, even if unintended, consequences for the person who is admonished or rebuked. It is of course the case that all members and officers of a Reformed church live under discipline. Boards of elders, classes, and the General Synod may, and often do, engage in informal conversation with those under their care when inappropriate behavior becomes known. Many, if not most, matters of this sort are handled immediately and pastorally.

In any case, individuals who have been admonished or rebuked retain the right of redress. When it is the action of an assembly at issue, their recourse is through the means of *complaint*.

Article 2. Nature of Offenses

Sec. 1. *The only matters to be considered as offenses subject to accusation are those which can be shown to be such from the Holy Scriptures, or from the* Constitution of the Reformed Church in America.

It is crucial for an assembly or judicatory considering discipline to be clear about the distinction among *offense*, *accusation*, and *charge*. An accusation is not itself a charge. It alleges that a particular offense has occurred. Article 4 below describes how an accusation becomes a charge that must then be discharged by a judicatory. An accusation simply alleges that a member or officer has violated or offended the canon of behavior set by ecclesiastical law. Of itself it has no force until it has been discharged.

Before an assembly or a judicatory can even consider an accusation, it must determine that the offense meets the criteria of this section. To do so, the body must determine (and one would expect it to state clearly) precisely what in Holy Scripture supports the contention that the behavior in question is a violation. Older orders often included a list of the grosser sins. The Dort order, for example, states:

"The following are to be considered as the principal offences that deserve the punishment of suspension or removal from office, viz.: False Doctrine or Heresy, public schisms, open Blasphemy, Simony, faithless desertion of Office, or intruding upon that of another, Perjury, Adultery, Fornication, Theft, acts of Violence, Brawlings, habitual Drunkenness, and scandalous Traffic; in short, all such sins, and gross offenses which render the perpetrators infamous before the world, and which in a private member of the church would be considered as deserving excommunication" (LXXX).

Alternatively, the body may indicate how the *Constitution* has been violated (keeping in mind that the *Constitution* includes not only the *BCO*, but the *Standards of Unity* and the *Liturgy* as well). This provision prevents an assembly or a judicatory from allowing an accusation of an offense to be brought that offends only a commonly held value. A body might, for example, accuse a member of renting to a family of a different race when the congregation shares a segregationist mentality, obviously not legitimate grounds for discipline.

> Sec. 2. *Offenses which are known at most to a very few persons shall be dealt with first in a manner indicated by the Lord Jesus Christ in Matthew 18:15-17. If this procedure fails, the matter shall be presented to the judicatory to which the offender is amenable.*

The 1998 revision of the disciplinary procedures clarifies an old distinction between public and private offenses by eliminating the words "public" and "private."

The distinction of public and private was intended to further repentance as the goal of discipline and thus embody Jesus' injunction in Matthew 18. Nothing would be gained by making offenses public that had been repented. The Explanatory Articles may be taken as exemplary when it states in Article 69: "Nor shall any complaint of a private nature be noticed, unless the rules prescribed by the Lord Jesus, Matt. xviii, have been strictly followed." The old distinction has proven to be unworkable. By focusing on "public" and "private," judicatories were left wondering when a "private" offense crossed a boundary to become a "public" offense. The new wording simply states that some offenses by their very nature can be known by only a few persons. In their commission, they do not bring immediate disrepute upon the church.

Such offenses may be handled by the scriptural prescription that two or three meet with the offending party. It is then hoped that resolution may be brought to the matter. The offender may repent and resolve that the behavior cease. The judicatory must, however, be very careful in such proceedings that the wound not be "healed lightly." For example, an officer may have committed slander against another member of the church. If the offender professes a repentance that makes no reparation to the offended, the process can too easily be viewed as the judicatory sweeping the matter under the rug for the sake of the peace of the body.

However, once a matter has become public knowledge, the church must resolve the matter.

Sec. 3. *Notorious and scandalous offenses require immediate action by the judicatory.*

Some offenses may be known to many persons or they may be the subject of rumor. The order of 1833 articulated the concern of this section: "Public offences are those that require the cognizance of a church judicatory, as when they are so notorious and scandalous, that no private measures would obviate their injurious effects, or when, though originally known to one, or a few, the private measures taken have been ineffectual" (IV,III,1).

A church member who is charged with a criminal offense, for example, is known publicly. Or an officer who resorts to the pages of the public press to attack the doctrine of the Reformed church has acted in such a way as to place the church itself in question. In quite another instance, rumors may have spread through the community that a member or officer acts in such a way that is contrary to Scripture or the *Constitution*. Such matters cannot be left to rest either for the sake of the offender or for the church. The judicatory has no option but to act immediately. That does not mean that the judicatory enters into a disciplinary procedure. In the case of a rumor, for example, the judicatory, finding it to be groundless, may need to act simply to put the rumor to rest.

Article 3. Responsibilities for Discipline

The order delineates five categories subject to discipline and the bodies responsible for their discipline.

Sec. 1. Discipline of a Member

> *All members of a local church are under its care and are subject to its governance and discipline, as administered by the board of elders. The board of elders may suspend from the privileges of membership in the church a member who persistently rejects its admonitions or rebukes. If a member fails to show marks of repentance after suspension, the board of elders may, with permission of classis, proceed to excommunication. The board of elders shall publicly notify the congregation of its intention to excommunicate, and later, of its final action. The board may omit such public notification, if such omission will not impair the purposes of discipline and will best serve the spiritual welfare of the congregation. Such omission shall require a two-thirds vote of the board of elders.*

The judicatory responsible for the members of a congregation is its board of elders (see p. 88). The first step in discipline would ordinarily be admonition or rebuke as outlined in Article 1, Section 2 above. Persistent rejection of admonition or rebuke are occasion for "suspension from the privileges of membership." That next step in discipline would require the bringing of an accusation that will be judged to be a charge that in turn requires a trial before the board of elders. Suspension from the privileges of membership would include removing permission to gather at the Lord's Table. This is not yet excommunication, for that final action removes the person from the fellowship of the church. The board of elders suspend in expectation of receiving the member again at the Table. The discipline is entered in pastoral concern for the individual and for the congregation.

When this expectation has not been met, the board of elders may proceed to excommunication. This is a grave act, signaled as such in the order by the requirements placed on the board before it can take such action. It cannot happen in secret; there is no "star chamber" in the church order. Excommunication means that a person, cut off from the Table, can no longer enter full communion with the Christ who is her life and her hope. Thus, the board of elders must receive the permission of the classis. This is a matter on which the greater church must act in concert. Still, excommunication is discipline around the Table, and while it is sufficiently grave to draw in the greater church, it remains the responsibility of the elders as officers, as representatives of Christ, in the local congregation.

Likewise, in normal circumstances, the board also must notify the congregation of its intention to excommunicate. The decision by the board of elders does not by itself execute excommunication. The *Liturgy* includes an order for excommunication. The board only indicates its *intention* to excommunicate.

However, the order imagines instances when the board may find omission of public notification the wiser course. The board may reasonably expect, for example, that such notification will cause an uproar in the service of worship, thereby bringing further dishonor to the church. And if it can show that the purposes of discipline would nonetheless be served, it is wise to take alternative action. This is, however, an extraordinary tack, as indicated by the requirement for a super-majority vote by the board.

Sec. 2 Discipline of an Elder or Deacon

The board of elders shall have jurisdiction in the case of a charge against an elder or deacon. If the charge is proven, the elder or deacon may be suspended or deposed from office together with such other discipline as may be imposed in accordance with Section 1 of this article.

The previous section concerned members of a congregation, those who are gathered around the Table of the Lord. A Reformed order needs also concern itself with those who bear the offices of the church, and the BCO turns to the offices in this and the following sections, first handling the two offices of elder and deacon and dedicating separate sections to the minister and to the professor of theology.

Elders and deacons, as office-bearers, are responsible to the board of elders of the local consistory. An elder or deacon may, for example, cease to function in his or her office in which case she may be subject to the charge of desertion of office. Or a deacon, for example, may apparently slander another office-bearer. In such cases the person is acting within his or her responsibilities within the office to which she has been ordained. The board of elders is then to proceed on the matter as outlined in the article entitled "Procedure for Bringing a Charge." Upon disposition of a charge, should one eventuate, that board can suspend or depose the person from office. However, the charge may be of such gravity that the person's membership at the Lord's Table comes into question. Then the board of elders acts as outlined in the previous section of this article.

In a small board of elders, it may be difficult to execute this section. This is especially so if an accusation is lodged against an elder. The board then needs to constitute a small committee to investigate the charge. That committee may consist of only one person. It is an open question whether elders from the great consistory may be engaged to assist at this point. In any case, because such cases occur within a community of persons well-known to each other and often involve a consistory and congregation in often contentious interchage, these procedures will most likely be very difficult and thus requires great pastoral sensitivity and care.

Since it has become the practice in some consistories to ordain ministers who are not serving the congregation as elders or deacons, the question of the discipline of that minister raises special problems. A minister is amenable to the classis for discipline. That minister may be disciplined only by the classis. However, in his office as elder or deacon he remains under the jurisdiction of the board of elders as he functions in the office of elder or deacon. Thus, that board can suspend or depose him from the office of elder or deacon, but cannot discipline him in his office of minister of Word and Sacrament, nor in his membership at the Table.

Sec. 3. Discipline of a Minister of Word and Sacrament

a. Ministers are under the care of the classis are and subject to its government and discipline.

b. The consistory has the right to close the pulpit to a minister who has been accused of any notorious or scandalous offense which would render appearance in the pulpit inappropriate. Proceedings of the consistory in such a case are at its peril, but are undertaken to prevent scandal. This action is not to be considered a trial. The consistory must report its action to the classis immediately.

c. The classis shall have exclusive jurisdiction in the case of a charge against a minister. If the charge is proven, the minister may be suspended or deposed from office, suspended from the privileges of membership in the church, and/or excommunicated.

Ministers are subject to the discipline of the classis. Note the possible confusion between this section and the section in chapter 3, "The Classis" that prescribes that an installed minister shall be a member of the congregation she or he serves (p. 191). The minister is a member of the congregation only in a limited sense. She or he is not subject to the board of elders, and thus is not a member of the congregation in the full sense. By designating that the classis alone has disciplinary authority over the minister, the order protects the *congregation* for the free preaching of a Word that at times convicts, and thus offends. Nonetheless, the order also provides the possibility for a *consistory* (not board of elders) to close the pulpit on occasion. Circumstances may demand that the minister not be allowed to stand in the place that speaks God's Word, as doing so might occasion offense against that very Word! This is an extraordinary step, and is taken at "peril." Such action is not, in itself, discipline and makes no disposition toward an accusation. Article LXXII of the Explanatory Articles states that such an action "...is only intended, that in certain public and notorious offences, which would render the appearance of a Minister in the pulpit in such a situation, highly offensive; it shall be the duty of the Consistory, in order to prevent scandal, to shut the door against such criminal, and refer him to be tried by the Classis, as soon as possible. The proceedings of the Consistory in such cases...is not to be considered as a trial, but only a prudent interference, and binding over the person accused, to the judgment of his peers."

The action must *immediately* be reported to the classis, which, one presumes, will take immediate steps to initiate the appropriate steps toward discipline.

The order provides two cautions to consistories contemplating such action. First, an accusation must have been brought against the minister. The consistory may not close the pulpit on mere rumor or simply at its own discretion. The consistory, or one of its elders or deacons, may of course bring the accusation. However, it may do so only under the conditions that, first, the offense is "notorious or scandalous," and, second, that it meet the provisions outlined in Article 2, Section 1 above.

Second, the consistory takes this action at its "peril." What does that mean? The consistory makes itself vulnerable to being charged itself. If the minister could show, for example, that the consistory acted out of malice or that its action was baseless, she or he (or the classis) might in turn accuse the consistory of breaking its vows to work for things that make for "purity and peace" within Christ's body.

This section further outlines the kinds of discipline that apply to a minister. Upon proving a charge, the classis will impose discipline as outlined in Section 13 below. That may include suspension: the minister cannot function in the office for a period of time; deposition: the minister is removed from office; suspension of privileges of church membership: as accords with the first article of this section; or excommunication.

Sec. 4. Discipline of a General Synod Professor of Theology

Professors of theology are under the care of the General Synod and are subject to its government and discipline. The General Synod shall have jurisdiction in the case of a charge against a professor of theology. If the charge is proven, the professor of theology may be suspended or deposed from the Office of General Synod Professor of Theology or the Office of Minister of Word and sacrament or both, suspended from the privileges of membership in the church, and/or excommunicated.

As a separate office, the professor of theology is exclusively under the discipline of the General Synod (see p. 252). The peculiarity in this case is that the professor is under the synod's discipline not only in terms of his or her office as professor but, because she also is a minister of Word and sacrament, the synod has disposition of her continued function in that office as well.

Sec. 5. Discipline of a Consistory

Consistories are under the care of the classis and are subject to its government and discipline. A classis has the authority, after trial, to suspend a consistory accused of unfaithfulness to duty, or of disobedience to the classis, or of violation of the Constitution of the Reformed Church in America or the laws and regulations of the church. If a consistory is suspended, all of its members shall be disqualified for re-election until the classis has removed the disqualification. The classis shall fulfill the responsibilities of the consistory (including those of the boards of elders and deacons) so suspended until a new consistory has been legally constituted.

The previous sections have described the possible removal from office of an individual; this section allows that a consistory may be removed from office—as a body. A local consistory is responsible to its classis. The order is clear that this responsibility does not extend to the wisdom of all of the consistory's actions but is exercised within the conditions set forth in this section. The classis could not overrule a consistory's decision to ask an organist to resign, for example; it could, however, intervene on an accusation that in doing so the consistory violated the *Constitution*.

The classis must clearly distinguish discipline of a consistory from the action of supersession, described on pp. 136-39. The classis acts in chapter 1 as an assembly. The action described here is discipline; it thus requires that an offense have been committed and a trial occurred.

Discipline of a consistory will have the same *effect* as supersession in so far as the classis will be required to act (most likely through its appointed agents) as the consistory of the local congregation. However, the classis will act to constitute a new consistory through election, ordination (if necessary), and installation.

Article 4. Procedure for Bringing a Charge

The 1998 revision of the *Disciplinary Procedures* most significantly altered the older order in the process of charge, trial, and disposition of a charge. The change intended to remove what was widely held to occasion injustice in the old system. The old order prescribed that a judicatory first determine that a charge had merit and then proceed to try the charge. That system allowed the body both to initiate the charge and subsequently to try it. Thus the judicatory acted as both "prosecutor" and "jury" (as well as "judge"). The body would most likely have already determined the truth before it went to a trial intended to discover the truth! The revision requires a smaller body within the judicatory to ascertain whether an accusation can become a charge, without allowing that smaller group to participate in the determination of fact.

The revision also clarifies how an accusation becomes a charge, how that charge moves through a judicatory, and how the judicatory can dispose of a charge, including the possibility of resolving the charge short of a trial.

> Sec. 1. *A charge is a written accusation of an offense filed with the clerk of the responsible judicatory specifying the name of the accused, the nature of the alleged offense, and the time, place, and attendant circumstances of the alleged offense. (For the form of the charge, see Appendix No. 11). The clerk of the judicatory shall provide a copy of the charge to the accused within three days of its receipt.*

An accusation becomes a charge when it takes the shape described in this section. It must be written, must name the offense alleged, and further must describe the attendant circumstances. In this way, the accused is protected against general allegations and is able to prepare a defense. The charge must be presented to the responsible judicatory, thus assuring that the proper body within the church handles what are often sensitive and explosive matters that bear on a person's life and reputation. The order protects members and officers from sweeping allegations that easily taint persons and destroy the life of the church.

> Sec. 2. *A charge may be brought by an individual who is subject to the jurisdiction of the responsible judicatory. If the charge is brought by an individual, it must be signed by and made in the name of the individual who must come forward openly to support the charge(s) throughout the proceedings.*

This, along with the following section, prescribes who is authorized to bring a charge. An individual may bring a charge under two conditions. First, she or he must be subject to the jurisdiction of the responsible judicatory. The meaning of this requirement formed the (partial) substance of an appeal to the General Synod of 1993. Two women accused a minister of sexual misconduct. One of the women was not a member of the Reformed Church in America; the other was an RCA member, but a member of a different classis. The accused claimed that neither had standing to pursue a charge. The opinion of the General Synod's Judicial Business Commission is worth quoting at length:

> The commission believes there are two [policy] considerations [in such cases], one rooted in civil jurisprudence and one in church polity. From civil jurisprudence, the commission draws the concept that judgments should have a substantial degree of finality. When a person under the jurisdiction of a church files an accusation with the church, she necessarily agrees to be bound by the authority of the church dealing with her charge. Once the accuser has filed her charge with the classis, she submits to the authority of the classis to determine the truth or falsity of the charges, and to discipline of the accused if required. She acknowledges that the dispute will be resolved by the church using the process prescribed by the church, and not by some other means. In short, once the ultimate decision is reached within the church structure, the matter is concluded.
>
> The second consideration, drawn from church polity law, is that the church's judicial process must require those involved to be accountable to the church. Persons should not be permitted to file frivolous accusations without any risk. It is important that the classis have the ability to discipline the accuser in the event the charges are found to be frivolous or malicious. For this reason, one should not be able to submit oneself to the jurisdiction of the classis lightly.

...If the *BCO* were read to preclude an RCA member from voluntarily submitting himself or herself to a judicatory's jurisdiction, an accusation could be filed only where and when the accuser and accused were already subject to the same classis. This would require the real party in interest to find a surrogate or nominee within the classis to file the charge. This could well have a chilling effect on potential accusers, and exalts form over substance.[3]

The synod ruled that the non-RCA member was not qualified to bring the charge; the RCA member was so qualified. This might appear to disqualify a board of elders, for example, from considering a matter in which a member has committed an offense against one outside the church. However, the following section provides the means by which such a charge can be brought.

The second condition the individual must fulfill to be able to bring the charge is his or her willingness to stand publicly to bring the charge. This requirement precludes "secret" charges being brought that thus prevent the accused from the fair possibility of defense. It further prevents individuals from bringing frivolous charges or prosecuting with malicious intent.

Sec. 3. *A committee designated by the responsible judicatory may also bring a charge.*

Offenses described above in Article 2, Section 3, as notorious and scandalous would most likely be handled in this manner. The judicatory, through a committee, would investigate such offenses and determine whether a charge should be brought. However, the judicatory may face certain cases in which an individual is not capable of bringing a charge. He or she may be under age, not under the jurisdiction of the responsible judicatory, lacking in appropriate mental capacity, or in an extreme case, dead. It is then incumbent

3. *MGS*, 1993, p. 80.

on the judicatory through a committee to determine whether an accusation deserves to become a charge.

It is to be noted that the *Disciplinary Procedures* have introduced a "committee" at this point. The order does not prescribe the identity of this committee. Some bodies may have a "judicial" or other committee in place to handle such matters. However, the judicatory may appoint a committee at its discretion. One can envision smaller boards of elders that would appoint a committee of one. The intent of the order is that a smaller group within the larger body perform this task, thus freeing the larger body to determine fact should the matter come to trial.

Sec. 4. *If filed by an individual, the charge shall be referred to a committee appointed by the judicatory to determine whether there is sufficient merit to the charge to warrant further consideration. If the charge is filed by the committee designated by the judicatory, that same committee shall continue its proceedings to determine whether there is sufficient merit to the charge to warrant further consideration. In either case, in making this determination, the committee:*

a. *May interview the accuser, the accused, or any witnesses.*

b. *Shall consider the number and credibility of the witnesses and the length of time between the occurrence of the alleged offense and the date when allegations were made. If the alleged offense occurred more than two years prior to the date of the charge, the charge shall be dismissed by the committee except when the committee concludes that circumstances prevented the accusation from being brought earlier.*

c. *Shall determine whether efforts to resolve the matter short of trial would be appropriate. Such efforts may include mediation, admission by the accused that the charge is true and acceptance of appropriate sanctions, or any other disposition to which the committee and the accused may*

> *agree. Any demission, suspension, deposition, or*
> *excommunication must be approved by the appropriate*
> *judicatory.*

The mere filing of a charge does not of itself indicate that a trial must go forward. The judicatory through its designated committee must make a first determination on the merit of the charge. The charge may be disqualified at this point if the committee appointed finds it to be baseless, thus preventing unnecessary pain or even scandal to the accused or to the church. This section outlines how a committee may make the appropriate determination. Older Reformed orders intended that care be taken to ascertain the veracity of an accusation. Specification began to appear in the 1833 order:

> To constitute a general rumour, or fama clamosa, it is necessary—
> 1st. That it specify some particular sin, or sins.
> 2d. That it should have obtained general circulation.
> 3d. That it not be transcient.
> 4th. That it be accompanied with strong public presumption of its truth

The committee may, but need not, interview the accuser, the accused, or any witnesses. However, one presumes that a committee would ordinarily do so to determine the quality of witnesses as well as to ascertain an initial impression as to the veracity of the accuser—and the accused, and thus to fulfill the conditions set out in the subsection b.

The earlier form of the *Disciplinary Procedures* required the testimony of more than one witness for a charge to be of merit. Thus the order prevented the spectacle of one person bringing a malicious allegation. This requirement proved to be unworkable in cases of, most especially, sexual misconduct, where the nature of the case was often its extremely private nature. However, the committee must still consider the number of witnesses. In the case of sexual misconduct, a witness might be a party informed within a proximate time to substantiate the alleged behavior. Likewise, the committee will judge the credibility of such witnesses.

The order also includes a "statute of limitations." Ordinarily, the judicatory cannot be caught in a maelstrom of old history. The limit of two years offers sufficient time to bring an accusation. Still, the order also acknowledges that circumstance may prevent the bringing of an accusation. Recent experience has shown that recipients of sexual abuse often are not psychologically capable of acknowledging the offense against their persons for a number of years. In such cases, the order allows the two-year limitation to be waived. However, the burden then is on the accuser or the committee to show the waiver to be valid. If that cannot be shown, the committee is required to dismiss the charge.

Subsection c makes clear that the matter need not go to trial, even if a charge warrants further consideration. In determining the appropriateness of resolution, the committee will need to judge the criteria against which such appropriateness can be measured. It would be advisable to refer to the purpose of discipline stated in Article 1, Section 1, above in order to give serious attention to the question of justice on behalf of the accuser, the accused, and any other party—not least of which includes the church. Such criteria may change from case to case, and each case can only be judged in its particulars.

The order explicitly envisages two means to resolution without trial. One is mediation. The accused may admit to the alleged behavior, and the matter may be brought to conclusion as the accuser and accused engage in a process that leads to reconciliation. If the offense is such that the committee does not judge that further discipline is helpful or necessary, that *may* be the end of the matter. The committee may, however, judge that while personal reconciliation is appropriate, the offense is of such seriousness that, for example, the accused should not be allowed to continue in a church office.

That leads to a second resolution. The accused may admit to the offense. Since the purpose of a trial is to determine whether the offense was in fact committed, the trial is now unnecessary. The committee may then propose a disposition to which the accused agrees. However, since it is the judicatory that disciplines, such disposition must be approved by the judicatory. Reformed order demands that actions of such magnitude occur through the gathering of the offices in appropriate judicatory.

> Sec. 5. *The committee shall conduct its work in a confidential manner in order to protect the reputations of all persons involved and to preserve the impartiality of the judicatory if the charge moves forward.*

This "confidentiality" section was added in the 1998 revision in recognition of the highly charged nature of accusations within the church. Rumor alone can ruin lives and destroy churches. The church needs a means to investigate allegations in such a way that they can be fully handled without doing extraneous damage in the mere process of investigation. This section further protects members and officers from the damage done by malicious or ignorant allegation.

At the same time, it is crucial to protect the integrity of the next step in discipline, the trial. If members of the parent body begin to pick up (usually partial) information in the investigative stage, they begin to discuss and consequently to form provisional conclusions. The entire process thus becomes tainted, and all parties lose confidence in the fairness of the proceedings—and the church likewise exposes itself to ridicule and scandal.

> Sec. 6. *If the charge is not otherwise resolved, and the committee determines there is sufficient merit in the charge, the judicatory shall proceed to trial. If there is not sufficient merit, the committee shall dismiss the charge. This dismissal shall be the final resolution of the charge by the judicatory.*

Sec. 7. The action of the committee shall be reported to the judicatory.

If the provisions outlined in Section 4c above are not enacted, the committee has two avenues open. If the committee judges that the charge has sufficient substance and that the offense has likely occurred, the judicatory has no option but to proceed to trial. It would then move to the procedures outlined in the subsequent article. If the committee judges that there is not sufficient merit in the charge, the matter ends with dismissal by the committee. This provision prevents the judicatory from having to rehear all the evidence, weigh the number and credibility of the witnesses, and the like. Were this not the case, little would have been gained by the formation of the committee.

Nevertheless, the judicatory is charged with discipline. The order must allow the judicatory to engage in the discipline. The order presumes that a committee can act in the stead of the judicatory, and indeed in this case provides just such a procedure. The judicatory remains informed of the actions of the committee by means of report. That report need not be detailed, especially in cases where a charge is found to be without merit. To report the name of the accused and attendant circumstances in a report may do as much damage as a trial itself. Therefore, a committee may report only that a charge had been brought and dismissed. On the other hand, a disposition outlined in Section 4c may need to be reported for the approval of the full judicatory (suspension, demission, etc. are in any case public outcomes to the procedure).

Article 5. Trying a Charge

A judicatory that has reached this point has entered the trial phase of discipline. The purpose of a trial is the determination of fact: can the charge be supported with sufficient evidence to convince the judicatory that the offense did in fact occur as detailed in the charge? The order foresees that one party will move the charge forward through a process of presenting evidence. The accused holds the privilege of defending him or herself. The judicatory itself will receive, evaluate, and make final judgment.

Church bodies are not ordinarily in the business of conducting trials. Most judicatories venture into *terra incognita* at this point. It is thus advisable that the parties, with representatives of the judicatory, review together the provisions of this article. The order is silent on a number of details, allowing the parties to work them out together. When will the trial be held? How long is it expected to last? Judicatories do not have unlimited time, so trials cannot be conducted in the open-ended manner of civic courts. Who will rule on the admissibility of evidence? How will the credentials of the delegates be authorized? How will the outcome be reported, and to whom? The order does not require such pretrial discussions, but they appear advisable to assist the fairness of the trial. Judicatories are to be encouraged to keep a record of pretrial agreements in order that an appellate body may review the fairness of the proceedings if necessary.

> *Sec. 1. The clerk of the judicatory shall issue a citation (for the form of the citation to an accused person or consistory, see Appendix, No. 12) signed by the president and clerk, requesting the accused to appear before the judicatory at a specified time and place. The citation and a copy of the charge shall be provided to the accused.*

> *Sec. 2. The accused shall file a written reply to the charge with the clerk within twenty days of the receipt of the citation and a copy of the charge. If the accused acknowledges guilt or fails to file a reply to the charge, the judicatory shall impose the appropriate discipline.*

The provision of the charge to the accused fairly offers him or her the information necessary to reply to the charge. The accused is, within the Reformed understanding of the church, responsible to the judicatory. He must provide a response. Just so, he places himself before the judicatory. He may plead innocence and offer supporting argument or evidence, if relevant. He may acknowledge guilt. As in Article 4, Section 4c, the judicatory then moves directly to disposition. However, if he does *not* reply, the judicatory also moves to disposition. This provision in the order prevents a "no plea" from bringing the procedure to a halt. According to the order, silence is received as an acknowledgement of guilt.

> Sec. 3. *The judicatory shall try the charge within thirty days of the filing of the reply, unless the trial is postponed to a later date by consent of the parties and the judicatory involved.*

Fairness demands trial with reasonable dispatch and avoids the harm done when matters boil over, usually outside the bounds of the judicatory itself. Circumstances may, of course, prevent a trial from being held within the limits of thirty days. In that case, if all parties and the judicatory are in agreement, the trial may be postponed, although the order assumes that the delay will be of a reasonably short duration.

> Sec. 4. *The judicatory may try the charge, even though the accused is not present, if it is satisfied that proper notice was provided.*

> Sec. 5. *The clerk of the judicatory shall issue citations to persons who are requested to appear as witnesses for or against the accused and, at the same time, shall provide a list of the witnesses to all parties. Persons who have not received a witness citation may be permitted to testify at the trial, if the presiding officer concludes that to allow the testimony is not fundamentally unfair.*

Fairness to all parties requires that all know the identity of the witnesses in order to prepare a defense or to respond to the evidence brought. The order recognizes that "surprise" witnesses unfairly prejudice the process. This is especially true in the church; the aim is not to "win" a case, but to arrive at the truth fairly. Still, non-cited witnesses *may* testify. However, it is incumbent upon the presiding officer to determine whether such testimony is fair to all parties. In that case, however, the judicatory must recognize that it is vulnerable to appeal on just this point. It may need to argue that fundamental fairness was not violated in a specific instance.

> Sec. 6. *Neither the accuser, accused, counsel for any party, witnesses, clerk of the judicatory, members of the committee of the judicatory as described in Article 4, nor any person with a conflict of interest shall participate in the deliberation or the decision of the judicatory at any stage of the trial.*

A number of the persons denoted in this section will be members of the judicatory, and others may be. In ordinary circumstance they possess the right to engage in deliberation and vote by virtue of their membership in the body. In this instance, the order waives that right for understandable reasons. In the case of accuser, accused, counsel witnesses, and members of the committee, their very participation in the procedure thus far has most likely already determined their judgment on the facts at issue. To allow them to engage in deliberation may unfairly tilt the decision of the body. Their participation thus far has already granted them considerable power within the judicatory. The clerk also has had considerable participation in the case and likewise may have formed a prejudgment. By restraining the clerk from participation in the deliberation, the order allows him or her to perform the necessary function of assisting the judicatory through the appropriate steps of the procedure. By adding this provision, the order prevents the judicatory from acting as both accuser and judge of the matter, thus protecting the basic fairness of the trial procedure. This waiver of right to deliberation, however, does not extend to the imposition of discipline outlined in Section 13 below.

Sec. 7. *Unless the accused refuses or fails to appear after proper notice, witnesses shall be examined in the presence of the accused. The accused shall be permitted to cross-examine adverse witnesses. No affidavits shall be admitted.*

The order prohibits determination of guilt where the accused is prevented from being present. The church does not judge "behind closed doors." The process is open to the extent that an accused person can engage those who bring or support charges against her or him. This prevents the possibility of collusion against a person who is unpopular with members of the judicatory. There is to be no "kangaroo court" in the church. The accused is permitted to cross-examine witnesses. In actual practice, the counsel for the accused generally will examine witnesses in the name of the accused. However, it is expected that the accused will be present in such cases.

A commentary added to the *Disciplinary Procedures* notes that "in the presence of" may involve such things as screens, video testimony, and the like. This may be most advisable when, for example, a witness is a child who testifies to sexual misconduct. The judicatory must be careful to protect the weaker party at the same time as it acknowledges and protects the right of the accused.

The prohibition of affidavits may appear puzzling. Affidavits appear to offer supporting evidence. However, it is in the nature of a trial that the body who must decide the case judges the veracity of witnesses not only by the content of their testimony, but also by ascertaining how the witnesses present themselves. That is not possible with affidavits. Furthermore, an affidavit does not provide an occasion for cross-examination. Even if affidavits are presented as collateral to testimony, they may prejudice the judicatory in a particular direction. Therefore, the judicatory is limited to the presentation of the witnesses.

Sec. 8. *The judicatory may, at its discretion, appoint a committee to take testimony of a party or witness at a location other than*

> *that of the place of hearing, upon the request of any party. Ten day's notice shall be given to all parties of the appointment and membership of the committee and the time and place of its meeting. The parties shall examine the witness(es) and shall have the right of cross-examination.*

Circumstances may not allow crucial witnesses to be present. For example, age and physical ability may prevent a witness's presence. Or the witness may be a child, for whom presence before a large and imposing body may not be desirable. In such cases, the judicatory may, under the conditions of this section, provide for the taking of testimony on behalf of the entire body.

> **Sec. 9.** *A verbatim record of the trial, including the judgment, shall be preserved and entered into the records of the judicatory. Parties to the case shall be given reasonable access to the record.*

The verbatim record is necessary if the judgment is appealed. Access to the events of the trial provides, in part, a basis on which the appellate body can make its decision. The verbatim record might include a transcript produced by a recorder. With new electronic technologies, however, the judicatory can provide the record through other means.

This section does not require the body to incorporate the verbatim record into the *minutes* of the body. It must simply be preserved so that reasonable access can be granted to the parties. Only so can the parties be expected to prepare argument and response in the event of appeal.

> **Sec. 10.** *Parties and the judicatory may be represented by counsel of their own choosing, provided that such counsel is a minister, elder, or confessing member of the Reformed Church in America. Counsel shall not be compensated for their time or efforts but may be reimbursed for expenses.*

A trial is a disciplinary proceeding within the church.

It presumes to take place within the ambience and under the norms of a body that is, in its essence, theological. Such a claim supposes that all parties operate with a shared understanding of the norms of its life and behavior. Counsel outside the church cannot be expected to live and to function within that context. Nor are such counsel responsible to, and thus under the discipline of, Christ as expressed through the Reformed Church in America.

The prohibition of compensation may seem onerous, especially when a case requires a great deal of time and preparation. It does, however, ensure that the quality of counsel is not a function of any party's ability to pay, thus preventing at the least the appearance of doling out judgment to the highest bidder.

The judicatory may retain counsel. That counsel's task is not to advocate for either party but to assist the judicatory as it finds its way through an area that is usually foreign to its operation. Counsel for the judicatory can indicate hidden shoals, anticipate difficulties in the trial, and assist the body as it works toward a fair procedure.

Sec. 11 Procedural Rules

a. The judicatory shall establish such administrative rules for the trial as it deems appropriate to ensure that the trial will be conducted in a fair and impartial manner.

As suggested above, the rules established by the judicatory may well be developed in agreement with the parties, thus ensuring mutual agreement on the procedure. By engaging all parties at this stage, the judicatory avoids appeal on the grounds that the rules of procedure have been violated.

b. No member or groups of the Reformed Church in America, nor any person connected with the case, shall circulate, or cause to be circulated, any written or printed arguments or briefs upon any charges before the final disposition of same, including appeals, if any.

This rule helps avoid a case being decided outside its proper venue. The judicatory alone is to decide the case on the basis of the evidence and arguments presented in the trial itself. This rule further prevents a case from becoming a cause within the greater church, violating the appropriate process for judgment (and consequently the integrity of the church order) and disturbing the purity and peace of the church. Violation of this rule may cause the judgment to be negated on appeal. Or, in the case of the accused, may make him or her vulnerable to further discipline.

One notes, however, that this rule does not require that a party may not discuss a case at all with others in the church. That would be to place an intolerable burden on any one party. The rule carefully denotes *written* arguments or briefs, the very documents that are to be placed before the proper judicatory. The judicatory must, in some cases, judge whether arguments that have found their way into the public violate this rule by attempting to lobby for the desired outcome with additional, outside pressure.

> c. The required quorum for a judicatory conducting a trial shall be the same as is required for a regular or stated session of that assembly.

> d. The accuser shall be responsible for moving forward with the evidence.

This rule places the onus on the one who brings the charge before the judicatory. At this point the judicatory is not of itself investigating the truth. The case must be put before it. Nor can the accused attempt to "prove" something, for he or she would be attempting to show a negative, that something *didn't* happen. Practically, the accuser must place the evidence before the body through the witness of those who will establish the case. This doesn't mean that the judicatory and the accused will not have questions. Nor does it mean that the accused may not present witnesses. This rule simply means that the accuser must take the initiative in showing that the alleged behavior did in fact take place.

e. The charge(s) must be proven with a high degree of probability.

Prior to the introduction of this rule in 1998, the church order had no standard of proof. Many judicatories assumed that a trial was analogous with a criminal trial, and that the charges must be proven "beyond a reasonable doubt." Other judicatories functioned with a much lower standard, that of "preponderance of evidence," in which the body judged that the alleged behavior more likely occurred than not. Such a diversity of assumptions made for confusion. The standard that was accepted resides in the middle, between "beyond a reasonable doubt" and "preponderance of evidence." *How* a body will judge a "high degree of probability" is, of course, a relatively subjective matter. It is, however, a standard borrowed from civil jurisprudence, where it is used to define "clear and convincing evidence."

f. Receipt of evidence shall not be controlled by formal rules of evidence. However, the presiding officer may exclude any evidence if the officer determines that to admit such evidence would be fundamentally unfair.

Civil jurisprudence possesses detailed rules of evidence. Ecclesiastical bodies, however, cannot boast a history of rules of evidence. Nor can church courts be expected to be expert in such matters. To introduce them would more than likely catch a judicatory in a tangle of argument that would most likely consist of half-truth and ignorance. Still, a trial demands fairness. The order leaves the decision of the fairness of evidence in the authority of the presiding officer. That officer may consult with the counsel for the judicatory; however the decision remains his or hers alone.

> *g. The only persons who may attend the trial are the parties, their counsel, the members of the judicatory, and such other persons as the judicatory deems appropriate.*

This rule may appear to hide the church's business behind closed doors. However, this is a proceeding within a church. Its purpose is not a public inquiry into truth, but a discipline the intent of which is pastoral and the goal of which is the honor of the church. The decision and imposition of discipline will be made known to the church. By nature a trial evokes curiosity, perhaps even a morbid taste for scandal. To open a trial to all comers would turn it into a circus for the curious and would, in fact, impose a sort of discipline in ruined reputations and the like.

The order is careful that the parties themselves be present. It also allows the judicatory to judge whether there are others who may be present. This may be most necessary with regard to the counsel for the judicatory, who need not be a member of the judicatory.

> *h. Only members of the judicatory shall be present for the deliberation on the evidence. However, the counsel for the judicatory, if any, may be present.*

One might note that this rule does not exclude those indicated in Article 5, Section 6, above from being present. For example, the clerk may need to be present to record the decision. However, they cannot participate in the deliberation itself.

Section 12. Decision

> *a. The vote on whether the charge(s) has been proven shall be by written ballot. A simple majority of those present and voting shall be required to reach a decision.*

A written ballot assures that those who vote hold credentials as members of the judicatory and further guarantees the integrity of the decision (no one is counting hands). The standard of a simple majority honors the fact that this body acts as a judicatory within a Reformed polity. The *body* makes the decision, not simply a certain number of officers within the body.

> b. *The judicatory shall record its decision, stating the reasons therefor. A copy shall be provided to the parties.*

The outcome of a trial is a written decision. The judicatory shall state what it has decided. Its reasons may be quite brief: the body judges that the evidence has supported the charge. However, it is possible that a charge may have been brought with a number of accusations. In that case, the judicatory will have had to judge each "count" separately. The judicatory may judge, for example, that certain of the incidents do not fit the criteria of Article 2, Section 1, above. Or it may deem that the one bringing the charge does not meet the standard set in Article 4, Section 2, above. In any case, the judicatory must give all parties access to the decision and the reasons that support it.

Sec. 13. Imposition of Discipline

> a. *The judicatory shall impose such discipline as is appropriate for the offense and as is consistent with the Holy Scriptures and the* Constitution *of the Reformed Church in America.*

The decision reached in trial does not complete the discipline. It simply has determined the fact(s). The judicatory then moves to a new stage in discipline, that of the imposition of appropriate sanctions. This is a separate stage and a new deliberation. The order presents a very limited array of options from which a judicatory may choose (Article 1, Section 2, above). As crucial as the resolution of the trial may be, the decision on discipline itself is of equal weight. Will this person be allowed to continue in office? Shall she be restrained from the Lord's Table? Is an admonition or rebuke sufficient in the matter at hand? These are decisions of moment not only for the accused, but for the church itself.

A judicatory may be tempted to consider suspension for a definite period of time. That would be a mistake. Article 6, below, makes clear that the lifting of a suspension is contingent upon the expression of repentance by the one disciplined. Repentance cannot be predetermined; it can only await the peculiar dynamics of God's work with the disciplined.

> b. *The judicatory shall record its actions, stating the reasons therefor. A copy shall be provided to the parties.*

The reasons for imposing suspension, for example, rather than deposition may be more difficult for the judicatory than the determination of fact at the trial. However, careful attention is crucial; in the case of office holders, we decide in the context of ordination. The matter of who leads the church, who stands in the stead of Christ in the leadership of the church, is at issue. Recalling that we are functioning within a Reformed order, the judicatory does not simply decide on the professional competence or the "career" of persons.

A further reason to articulate carefully the reasons for discipline offers itself in Article 6, below. When the judicatory anticipates restoration and/or reinstatement, it will refer to its own reasons for the discipline it chose.

> Sec. 14. *The recorded decision and the disciplinary action shall be made available upon request to other assemblies within the Reformed Church in America and other appropriate ecclesiastical bodies. In addition, the judicatory, at its discretion, may distribute the recorded decision and disciplinary action to assemblies within the Reformed Church in America.*

The provision outlined in this section avoids the possibility of a suspended or excommunicated member seeking the Lord's Table in another church where the outcome of discipline is not known. Such an outcome would defeat the purpose of discipline, and thus be of harm to the person him or herself. More likely, perhaps, would be the possibility of a suspended minister moving to another area of the country and beginning to practice ministry anew in the Reformed Church or another denomination. This section requires that the judicatory supply its decision and disciplinary action to appropriate ecclesiastical bodies.

It further allows the judicatory to distribute the decision and disciplinary action to assemblies within the Reformed Church in America. The judicatory may have discovered, for example, that the accused has harmed persons within a congregation in a set of behaviors that it either suspects or fears may have been part of a larger pattern. The judicatory communicates with other assemblies out of pastoral concern for others who may have been harmed by the accused. It also cares for other church bodies, congregations or classes that have themselves been harmed. This section provides an ordered way for the judicatory to pay ecclesiastical attention to the wider implications of the actions of the disciplined.

Judicatories will need to pay particular attention to civil law in those sections of the country that may require reporting of certain violations. A state may mandate, for example, that members of certain classes of persons who engage in acts against minors, or in sexual misconduct, be reported. The recipient of such reports may vary from state to state, and it is incumbent upon the judicatory to be cognizant of such reporting procedures, on penalty of civil law.

Article 6. Restoration and Reinstatement

If discipline was not completed with the conclusion of a trial that determined guilt, neither is it completed with the imposition of discipline. The goal of discipline is not punishment but restoration and reinstatement. Discipline is an action of the body of Christ. It intends to draw the offender back into the fold, to witness to forgiveness and reconciliation. The step into this most wondrous, but also most difficult area, may be the most difficult step of all. And, in some cases, it may not happen.

> Sec. 1. *A member who has been suspended or excommunicated may be restored to the privileges of membership in the church upon repentance expressed before the judicatory which suspended or excommunicated the member. If public notice of the judgment of excommunication had been given, due public notice of reinstatement shall also be given the congregation.*

The restitution of a member to the Table happens through the act of repentance. This was always the intention of discipline—not punishment or casting the offender as a moral untouchable, but repentance. It was signaled in the old orders. Again, Dort may be taken as exemplary, when in Article LXXII, it describes how the penitent can be restored to the life of the congregation, around the Lord's Table. It signals that at issue is not a moral transgression per se, but a theological reality. Christ, through the instrument of the church, has brought the person to discipline to call him or her back to himself. That interchange is completed when the person turns anew and opens himself or herself to the wonder of grace that awaits. Thus, the penitent does not simply acknowledge a wrongdoing and apologize. She acknowledges herself as a sinner, standing with the company of sinners that gather in the church, opening herself to the forgiveness mediated through gospel. Because this is a theological interchange, one expects the church to maintain a responsibility toward the disciplined. A judicatory is well-advised to establish pastoral contact to assist the disciplined in finding the way to repentance. This will require theological and pastoral sensitivity to the dynamics involved in repentance. Depending on the nature of the case, the judicatory may include statements of repentance toward particular persons, provided this is done appropriately and in the presence of the judicatory.

The presence of the judicatory may in some cases appear daunting, however, perhaps even impossible. The judicatory can fulfill this requirement by delegating the task to a smaller body who stands in the stead of the judicatory. The goal is not to wring humiliation from the penitent but to provide a glad avenue by which the penitent can come before God through God's representatives.

The *Liturgy* presents an interesting question at this point. The provision of this section seems to place the expression of repentance only before the judicatory. The *Liturgy*, however, includes an order for "Readmission of the Penitent" that assumes the restoration to take place before the congregation. To celebrate such a service would acknowledge that discipline entails a break with the body of Christ and that restoration is to the full community. However, the introductory note to the 1968 *Liturgy* includes this comment: "General Synod in 1960 exempted this order from revision because its public use was considered to be of doubtful spiritual value. Discipline is the responsibility of the elders; but if any consistory decides to make it public, this Order may be used."[4]

Apparently, then, the "spiritual value" of such a liturgical restoration is at the judgment of a board of elders. It may be helpful to recall that in any instance a judicatory may find it advisable to design some sort of liturgical acknowledgment of the significance of the joyful step now being taken.

> Sec. 2. *A person who has been suspended or deposed from office may be restored to office upon repentance and renewal of vows before the judicatory which suspended or deposed that person, provided that the judicatory is satisfied that the honor of the office will not be impaired and that the welfare of the church will be served by such a restoration, and provided*

---

4. Vander Lugt, Gerrit T., ed., *Liturgy of the Reformed Church in America together with The Psalter* (New York: The Board of Education, 1968), p. vii.

> *that the restoration is approved by a two-thirds vote of those*
> *present at the meeting of the judicatory. Restoration after*
> *deposition shall include reordination to office.*

Restoration to office is different from reinstatement of membership. In the latter case, one's identity within Christ's body is at stake. It has to do with a person's fellowship in Christ. Office, on the other hand, has to do with ministry within the church. Shall this person be authorized to preach or to join in decisions made in Christ's name? Not all members are ordained. Nor does ordination signal a higher status. The classis, sitting as an assembly, decides whether candidates for ministry are qualified for office. Now, as a judicatory, it may ask similar questions concerning one requesting reinstatement.

Thus, while repentance is a necessary condition for reinstatement, it is not sufficient. The judicatory must judge whether reinstatement is in the best interest of the ministry of the church.

Part II. Complaints

Parts II and III of chapter 2 of the church order do not concern discipline per se. They provide recourse to actions and judgments of ecclesiastical assemblies and judicatories. As such, they articulate an important principle of Reformed order. Just as members subsist always in an organic relation around the Table, so, too, assemblies and judicatories are not autonomous bodies within the church. They live and work within a responsible matrix. That does not mean that they do not enjoy relative autonomy. The further Reformed principle that each assembly is authorized to act—as gathered offices under the authority of Christ—limits the range of responsibility. The order carefully delimits those matters that can be complained or appealed.

Reformed orders have consistently granted to members and officers recourse from the original assembly or judicatory through the privilege of complaint or appeal. This was so already in the order of Wesel (chapter 8, paragraph 11). Complaints and appeals became a separate article in the church order in 1874.

Because clarity is crucial in distinguishing between complaint and appeal and because that distinction had been difficult for assemblies and judicatories to maintain, the 1998 revision of the judicial procedures separated complaint and appeal into separate parts. A good deal of what this commentary has to say about complaints will apply *mutatis mutandis* to the third part on appeals. Commentary there will be limited to those portions that are relevant to appeals.

Article 1. Nature of Complaints

Sec. 1. *A complaint is a written statement alleging that an action or a decision of an assembly or officer of the church has violated or failed to comply with the* Constitution *of the Reformed Church in America or other laws and regulations of the church.*

A complaint has to do with an action or decision of an *assembly* or an officer. This is to be distinguished from an appeal which is described in Part III, Article 1, below. The complaint gives those authorized in the following section access to redress. At issue is the action of an assembly as it functions in its governance of ecclesiastical life.

This section limits the subject of complaint, however. Those authorized cannot complain a decision or action simply because they disagree with a decision. A church member may, for example, consider a consistory's decision to alter its order or style of worship highly distasteful, but the consistory is fully within its responsibilities to take such action provided it coheres and is consistent with the *Constitution*. It is the responsibility of a complainant to show that the decision or action fails to comply with the *Constitution* (remembering that the *Constitution* includes the *Standards* and the *Liturgy* as well as the *BCO*). In this instance, a complainant would be on firm ground if she argued that the consistory had decided to use an order for the Lord's Supper not authorized by the Reformed Church in America.

> Sec. 2. *A complaint may be filed only with the judiciary that has immediate superintendence of the assembly or officer.*

By this section, a church member would complain the action of an elder or a deacon to the board of elders, of the minister to the classis. A consistory's action would be complained to the classis, the action of a classis to the regional synod of which it is a member, and that of a regional synod to the General Synod. In this manner, the integrity of a Reformed order is maintained.

> Sec. 3. *A complaint may be filed only by:*
>
> a. *One or more confessing members in good and regular standing against the consistory or board of elders having superintendence over them.*
>
> b. *One or more members of an assembly against that assembly of which they are members.*
>
> c. *An assembly against that assembly having immediate superintendence over it.*

Upon receipt of a complaint, a judiciary will need to pay particular attention to this section. Among the first matters to be decided will be whether the complainant is authorized to bring the complaint. It may happen that someone who is not a member of a local congregation desires to bring a complaint against a consistory. Because that person is not under the discipline of the local board of elders, he is not authorized to bring the complaint. Likewise, a minister or elder may judge the action of a classis of which he is not a member to be out of order. By this section, he has no standing to bring the complaint. Nor can a classis in New Jersey, for example, bring a complaint against a classis in California—or a neighboring classis in New Jersey, for that matter. This section inoculates the church against the confusion that easily could be brought about by free-ranging and self-appointed critics.

That does not mean that a judicatory need necessarily ignore complaints brought by those who are not authorized. It may judge the subject of the complaint of sufficient concern to intervene pastorally with the lower body. This must be done carefully, however, and it does not bear the weight of judicial action.

> Sec. 4. *Neither notice of intent to complain nor the complaint itself shall have the effect of suspending the action against which the complaint is made, unless within thirty days one-third of the members of the assembly complained against who were present when the action was taken file a request for such suspension until a decision is made in the higher judicatory.*

Were it possible for a complaint to suspend an action of the assembly, one or more persons could effectively bring the governance of the church to a halt or create very difficult pastoral situations. What would happen in a local congregation, for example, if a complaint were made against the firing of an organist and that action were suspended. The church would have to continue with the organist in place, at odds with the congregation's constituted leadership. On the other hand, the order allows the assembly to judge that the action be put on hold if it deems that course to be wisest.

Article 2. Process for Complaints

> Sec. 1. *Written notice of intent to complain shall be filed with an officer or with the clerk of the assembly or judicatory which took the action in question. This filing shall be completed not later than twenty days after having received official notification*

> of the action taken. In default of this requirement, the case
> shall not be heard.

Notice of intent is not of itself a complaint. It simply signals to the appropriate assembly that the complainant(s) will bring a complaint. This notice need not be long. It does not outline the grounds of the complaint, but it should include the action or decision that is being complained. One notes carefully that *this* notice is directed to the assembly complained against, while the complaint itself will be addressed to the supervising judicatory.

The time limit on the notice protects an assembly from having all its actions open to review for an indefinite period. Both the right to redress and the integrity of the assembly's actions are protected.

> Sec. 2. *The complaint and the reasons therefor shall be filed
> with the clerk of the higher judicatory within twenty days after
> the filing of notice of intent. In default of this requirement, the
> complaint shall be considered to be dismissed and the clerk
> of the higher judicatory shall notify the parties involved.*

> Sec. 3. *Within this same period the clerk of the lower assembly
> shall file with the clerk of the higher judicatory the original
> record of all the proceedings pertaining to the complaint,
> including the notice of intent and any other documents
> bearing on the complaint. These constitute the record of the
> case. The clerk of the higher judicatory shall forward upon
> receipt to each of the parties a copy of the record of the case
> and all documents subsequently submitted in the case to the
> higher judicatory.*

The complaint together with the record constitute the written documentation that will appear before the higher judicatory. It is the task of the clerks of the relevant bodies to execute this task through reception of the complaint and submission of the appropriate documentation. The documentation from the assembly complained against will include at least the minutes of any meeting(s) at which the action at issue occurred. It may also include official correspondence, reports from committees, minutes of committees meetings, or any official written material that bears upon the complaint. This record, along with any arguments brought to the judicatory, will be the basis for the judgment of the judicatory.

It is a matter of simple fairness that all parties be granted full access to the record in order that the complainant can prepare his arguments and the assembly can prepare its response.

> Sec. 4. *The clerk of the higher judicatory shall, upon receiving the record, promptly notify its judicial business committee, call a meeting of the committee at a suitable time and place, and give notice of such meeting to all the parties involved. The committee shall determine whether the case and its attendant papers are in order. The committee shall promptly advise the several parties if it finds any irregularities. A period of not more than twenty days shall be allowed to correct such irregularities. The committee may request further written response or arguments to be submitted within the same twenty days. If less than thirty days remain before the next regular session of the judicatory to which the committee is to report and the committee determines that it is unable to prepare an acceptable report, it shall immediately record this determination and the reasons therefor with the clerk of such judicatory and request permission to delay its report until the next session. The clerk shall promptly confer with the officers of the judicatory who shall promptly rule upon the request.*

This long section details a crucial stage in the consideration of a complaint. The clerk of the higher judicatory would have ascertained, as per the previous section, that the proper documents have been submitted. He or she then initiates the process not only by notifying the appropriate committee of the judicatory, but by calling a meeting of that committee. It is important that the clerks maintain a clear record of this stage in the process, as their actions may become part of the record if the complaint is appealed to a higher judicatory. While the parties must be notified, they need not be present at this meeting. The committee then takes as its first task the determination that the complainant is authorized to complain in accordance with Article 1, Section 3, above; that intent to complain has been filed within the appropriate time; and that the committee has the appropriate documentation before it. Interestingly, and crucially, the committee is not allowed to "throw it out on a technicality." It must allow the parties to correct any "irregularities." Some irregularities may not be correctable. For example, the complainant may not be authorized to bring the complaint, or the deadlines have not been met. However, the complainant may need to provide evidence that the action at issue was a violation of the *Constitution* or other "laws or regulations of the church." Or the assembly may not have produced the needed documentation.

In addition, the committee may judge that either party needs to bring further argument before the matter can go forward. Thus the order grants considerable access to the parties.

The committee is not itself the judicatory but assists the judicatory in its appropriate task. It will prepare a report that recommends an action to the full body. In the normal course of events, that report would be offered at either the next meeting of the judicatory, or at a special meeting. However, complaints registered less than a month before the next *regular* session of the body may not offer sufficient time for proper deliberation. In that case, the order provides a means by which the matter can be delayed until the next session of the body (sitting in either regular or special session).

Sec. 5. *If the case is in proper order, the committee shall then consider its merits. It shall consider the record of the case and such additional arguments as have been submitted. It shall also hear the parties together with such counsel as may be requested by the parties. Counsel shall meet the qualifications set forth in Chapter 2, Part I, Article 5, Section 10. This hearing shall be conducted in a fair and impartial manner with all parties present. If the complainant in person or by counsel fails to appear, the committee may declare the case to be defaulted.*

Prior to this stage in the process the committee is *not* to deliberate on the merits of the complaint. The complaint is not before the body before it is deemed valid. This prevents not only a rush to judgment, it also prevents the supervising body from becoming involved in unnecessary debate or any discussion that could be construed by any party to be a "ruling" on a case. Were that to happen, a party could continue to disturb the peace of the church by claiming that while the body did not accept the complaint, they were "really on my (or their) side."

The committee deliberates by reviewing the record, by considering the arguments offered, and by hearing the parties who are given opportunity to argue their case before the committee. The committee may be well advised to establish rules for the hearing prior to the gathering, such as time limits for arguments, order of appearance, presence of the parties, and similar matters.

The order is clear that all parties shall be heard together. That is, the parties are present during the presentations of all before the committee. This prevents the accusation that either party was given preferential treatment by the committee.

The failure of a complainant to appear either in person or through counsel allows the committee to declare the complaint to be defaulted, in which case the matter ends there. However, the committee need not make that determination and may deem it wise to allow the complaint to proceed.

> Sec. 6. *The committee shall report in writing its findings and recommendations to its parent judicatory by a date determined by the parent judicatory prior to the next stated meeting or a special meeting and shall furnish a copy of its report to each of the parties. After receiving the report of the committee the judicatory may request to hear the original parties in the case with their counsel. The recommendation(s) of the committee may be adopted, rejected, amended, or referred back to the*

> committee. The judicatory may confirm or reverse, in whole
> or in part, the action of the lower assembly, or remand the
> matter to it with instructions.

The committee concludes its work with a written report that will include its findings and its recommendation(s). The judicatory is the parent body and thus must make the final determination. The committee's report becomes the basis for the judicatory's decision. While the committee is required to submit its report to the parties, that does not automatically grant the parties opportunity for further argument. Otherwise, the committee would become a party in the case. The judicatory, however, may (but need not) agree to hear the original parties. The oral arguments then offered to the judicatory would become part of its deliberation.

The committee can recommend confirmation or reversal of the action of the lower assembly in whole or in part. This is a remarkable power within Reformed order, for it grants a higher judicatory the ability to reverse the action of a lower body. However, the committee may also recommend remanding the case back to the original assembly with instructions. Instructions may include such matters as how the lower body is to deliberate afresh and so act in conformity with the *Constitution* or the laws and rules of the church. In such cases, the lower body may come to the same decision, but this time in accordance with how the church understands itself to be governed.

The judicatory must act on the recommendations of the committee either through acceptance, rejection, amendment, or referral back to the committee. However, the order appears to open the way for the judicatory to reject the recommendation(s) of the committee and then act on its own. That would be proper within Reformed order. However, caution is advised lest the emotion of the moment carry the day.

> **Sec. 7.** Persons who have voted on the matter in a lower
> assembly or who have a conflict of interest shall not vote

upon the case in a higher judicatory.

This section disallows those who have taken part in a decision in the original assembly a "second bite" in the case. However, this section clearly notes that those who have *voted* be disallowed. Members of the original assembly who are members of the judicatory, but who have not voted, are allowed to vote. It is often difficult to determine whether or not someone has already cast a vote. For this reason, it is thus often the practice of members of the original assembly who anticipate a complaint to register in the minutes that they have refrained from voting on the matter.

> Sec. 8. *The judicatory shall record its decision, stating the reasons therefor.*

The decision with its reasons communicate to the parties the "why" of the decision, thus assisting the church as it governs itself in the future. The reasons also allow for fairness in the process. Furthermore, the reasons will provide a basis for appeal, if any.

> Sec. 9. *When a complaint is filed, the complainant has the burden of moving forward and proving by a preponderance of the evidence that the respondent has violated or failed to comply with the* Constitution *of the Reformed Church in America or other laws and regulations of the church.*

On the "burden of moving forward" see the comment on Part I, Article 5, Section 11d, above.

The level of proof required for a complaint differs from that required in a trial under Part I. A "preponderance of the evidence" is a lower standard than a "high degree of probability." "Preponderance" means that the judicatory judges that it is more likely than not that a violation has occurred.

> Sec. 10. *No member or groups of the Reformed Church in America, nor any person connected with the matter, shall*

*circulate, or cause to be circulated, any written or printed
arguments or briefs upon any complaints before the final
disposition of same, including appeals, if any.*

See comments on Part I, Article 5, Section 11b, above.

Sec. 11. *No complaint can be taken against any action or
decision of the General Synod.*

Since there is no body to which the General Synod is accountable,
no complaint can be made against it. Disputes within the church
must stop somewhere, lest the church be caught in endless dispute
and division. The order grants to the offices gathered at General
Synod the final determination on all matters.

Part III. Appeals

Article 1. Nature of an Appeal

Sec. 1. *An appeal is the transfer to a higher judicatory of a
complaint, a charge, or an appeal on which judgment has
been rendered in a lower judicatory. The right of appeal
belongs to either of the original parties in a case. That right
may be exercised when a party considers itself to be aggrieved
or injured by a judgment of a judicatory.*

Appeals are of two sorts. A *complaint* that has been disposed by a
lower judicatory can be reviewed by the judicatory that has
superintendence over the lower body. At issue in an appeal is not
the substance of the complaint, but such matters as are adumbrated
in the following section. That is, the higher body does not re-hear
the substance of the case but reviews the action of the lower body
in accordance with the grounds set forth in the appeal itself.

A disciplinary procedure (under Part I of Chapter 2) can also
become the subject of appeal. Again, the higher judicatory acts as

an appellate body. However, the right to appeal, according to this section, belongs to the "original parties." The parties to a disciplinary procedure would include the person disciplined and the person (or body) bringing the charge. A member of the lower judicatory does not have the right to bring an appeal simply by virtue of her membership in the judicatory.

The same restriction adheres to any instance in which a complaint is transferred to a higher body. In those cases, however, the parties will include the lower judicatory and the person or persons bringing the original complaint.

> Sec. 2. *The grounds of appeal include: irregularity in the proceedings of the lower judicatory; refusal of reasonable indulgence to a party on trial; receiving improper, or declining to receive proper, evidence; rendering a decision before all the testimony is taken; bias or prejudice in the case; and manifest injustice in the judgment.*

This section makes clear that the appellate body does not retry a case. It does not, as it cannot, evaluate the credibility of witnesses as they appeared before the lower body. The appellate process exists to protect the church from injustice within its proceedings. It is possible that a lower body may be so caught up in the particulars of a case as to exhibit inappropriate bias against a party. And it is possible for a lower body to err in its procedures so egregiously as to make fair judgment impossible.

It is the appellant's burden to show how the lower body erred in one or more of the ways stated in this section (see Article 2, Section 9, below). It is not incumbent upon the higher judicatory to discover through investigation whether or how the lower judicatory failed in its procedures.

It is sometimes argued that the appellate body is only to be concerned with *procedural* matters, determining whether the lower body followed the prescriptions of the *BCO*. However, grounds for appeal make it clear that a judicatory may have followed all the "rules" and still have erred in, for example, showing bias or prejudice. Or the appellant could show on the record that the lower body exhibited manifest injustice. For example, the charge may have alleged that an officer stole church funds, while the record shows no testimony to support the charge, and the body finds the officer guilty nonetheless. Such a decision would represent manifest injustice and would be subject to appeal.

> Sec. 3. *Notice of intent to appeal suspends the judgment of the lower judicatory until the appeal is finally decided. But when the judgment which is appealed from results in suspension, deposition from office, or excommunication, the person against whom the judgment has been pronounced shall be required to refrain from the sacrament of the Lord's Supper and from the exercise of office until the appeal is finally decided, unless exception is made in the judgment of the lower judicatory.*

In contradistinction from a complaint, appeal *does* suspend the judgment of the lower judicatory. However, this provision is less permissive than it first appears. Since in matters of suspension or deposition from office and excommunication, the accused is restrained from either performance of office and/or participation at the Lord's Table, a large exception has been made. Likewise, since the complaint itself does not suspend an action of an assembly, that too is allowed if the lower assembly refused to sustain the complaint. If, however, the lower body has found merit in the complaint, the assembly subject to the complaint is restrained from its original decision or action.

> Sec. 4. *The regional synod shall be the final court of appeal for all cases originally heard by a board of elders. However, the General Synod may hear such an appeal if one delegate to the regional synod from each of the classes in that regional synod, with the exception of the classis from whose action*

the appeal is taken, shall give written notice to the clerk of the regional synod within thirty days of its adjournment that there is just cause for appealing a case to the General Synod.

In general, an appeal can move "two levels up" from its original court. Thus, a matter originally heard before a classis may be appealed to the regional synod, and subsequently to the General Synod. However, a judicial matter heard before a board of elders will in most cases be concluded at a regional synod. It is possible, but quite difficult, to appeal such a judgment. The provision in the order makes it clear that this would occur only in those cases in which a clear violation of ecclesiastical justice had occurred.

Article 2. Process for Appeals

Sec. 1. *Written notice of intent to appeal shall be filed with an officer or with the clerk of the judiciary which took the action in question. This filing shall be completed not later than twenty days after having received official notification of the action taken. In default of this requirement, the appeal shall not be heard.*

Sec. 2. *The appeal and the reasons therefor shall be filed with the clerk of the higher judiciary within twenty days after the filing of notice of intent. In default of this requirement, the appeal shall be considered to be dismissed and the clerk of the higher judiciary shall notify the parties involved.*

Sec. 3. *Within this same period the clerk of the lower judiciary shall file with the clerk of the higher judiciary the original record of all the proceedings of the case, including the notice of intent, the evidence, the arguments, and any other documents bearing on the case. These constitute the record of the case. The clerk of the higher judiciary shall forward upon receipt to each of the parties a copy of the record of the case and all documents subsequently submitted in the case to the higher judicatory. The higher judicatory shall not admit or consider as evidence anything not found in this record without consent of the parties.*

The final sentence of this section differs from the corresponding section on complaints. The difference highlights the appellate nature of the proceeding. The higher judicatory will make its determination on the basis of the record, along with arguments made on the basis of that record. Parties are not allowed to introduce new evidence unless all parties agree. An appeal is not a second chance to try the case.

Sec. 4. *The clerk of the higher judicatory shall, upon receiving the record of the case, promptly notify its judicial business committee, call a meeting of the committee at a suitable time and place, and give notice of such meeting to all the parties involved. The committee shall determine whether the case and its attendant papers are in order. The committee shall promptly advise the several parties if it finds any irregularities. A period of not more than twenty days shall be allowed to correct such irregularities. The committee may request further written response or arguments. If less than thirty days remain before the next regular session of the judicatory to which the committee is to report and the committee determines that it is unable to prepare an acceptable report, it shall immediately record this determination and the reasons therefor with the clerk of such judicatory and request permission to delay its report until the next session. The clerk shall promptly confer with the officers of the judicatory, who shall promptly rule upon the request.*

Sec. 5. *If the case is in proper order, the committee shall then consider its merits. It shall consider the record of the case and such additional arguments as may have been submitted. It shall also hear the original parties, together with such counsel as may be requested by the parties. Counsel shall meet the qualifications set forth in Chapter 2, Part I, Article 5, Section 10. This hearing shall be conducted in a fair and impartial manner. Either party may elect not to appear in person or by counsel at the hearing.*

One notes a difference from the corresponding section on complaints. There, if a party does not appear, the judicatory may declare the case defaulted. In an appeal, no prejudice is laid against a party if it chooses not to appear at the hearing. In fact, it remains incumbent upon the committee of the higher judicatory to consider the merits of the case. In such a case, the committee will have before it the written record, along with attending arguments. These provide the basis for its decision.

Sec. 6. *The committee shall report in writing its findings and recommendations to its parent judicatory by a date determined by the parent judicatory prior to the next stated meeting or a special meeting and shall furnish a copy of its report to each of the parties. After receiving the report of the committee, the judicatory may request to hear the original parties in the case with their counsel. The recommendation(s) of the committee may be adopted, rejected, amended, or referred back to the committee. The judicatory may confirm or reverse, in whole or in part, the decision of the lower judicatory or assembly, or remand the case to it with instruction.*

Sec. 7. *Persons who have voted on the matter in a lower judicatory or assembly, or who have a conflict of interest, shall not vote upon the appeal in a higher judicatory.*

Sec. 8. *The judicatory shall record its decision, stating the reasons therefor.*

Sec. 9. *When an appeal is filed, the appellant shall have the responsibility to establish that the lower judicatory erred in its decision.*

> Sec. 10. *The judiciary hearing the appeal shall give deference to the decision of the lower judicatory, particularly in the matter of credibility of witnesses, and shall uphold the decision of the lower judicatory if it is supported by substantial evidence in the record when the record is viewed as a whole.*

The order prejudices an appeal toward the lower judicatory. In doing so, it follows Reformed order's commitment that the greater body intervene in the life of the lesser body only in matters clearly adumbrated by the church order. In fact, evidence that a lower body has erred does not of itself nullify its action. That evidence must be judged to be "substantial" as the case is reviewed in its entirety. On appeal, the burden is thus placed upon the appellant to produce and argue for this "substantial evidence."

> Sec. 11. *No member or groups of the Reformed Church in America, nor any person connected with the case, shall circulate, or cause to be circulated, any written or printed arguments or briefs upon any appeals before the final disposition of same.*

> Sec. 12. *No appeal can be taken from any decision of the General Synod.*

Index

317

Index